KATHMANDU

INSIGHT *City* GUIDES

Produced and Edited by Lisa Choegyal

APA
PUBLICATIONS

KATHMANDU

ABOUT THIS BOOK

Welcome to *Cityguide: Kathmandu Valley!* This book is a culmination of many years' work by many people who love this mountainous land, having traveled and lived in it. Conceived by **Hans Höfer** as one of the first *Insight Guides* at the same time as Bali, before even the establishment of Apa Publications, this book is a reincarnation of the much heralded *Insight Guide: Nepal*. Now updated, expanded and refined, it gives you the very best of the cultural melting pot of the Kathmandu Valley.

Lisa Van Gruisen Cheogyal, a director of Tiger Tops Mountain Travel and of the Tiger Mountain group in Kathmandu, produced and edited **Cityguide** *Kathmandu Valley*. Resident in Kathmandu since the mid-1970s, British-born Cheogyal is one of Apa's best correspondents.

Rallying her distinguished team of experts, she was able to adapt much from the original manuscript by writer **Marcel Barang** and Austrian professor **Carl Pruscha**. Cheogyal contributed the "Land of Festivals", revised the entire "Places" travel section of the Cityguide and created "Exploring the Valley" and "Beyond the Valley".

The Right Staff

Cheogyal relied heavily on the know-ledge of **Desmond Doig**, remembered with great affection and much missed as Kathmandu's top expatriate writer and artist. He assembled the book's section on history, arts and hippies. Besides stringing for internationally renowned publications such as *The Statesman*, *National Geographic*, *Life* and *Time*, he founded India's popular youth magazine, *JS*. He authored five books, his photographs were syndicated and his paintings exhibited. Doig also designed two of Kathmandu's leading hotels before his demise in October 1985 in Nepal.

Elizabeth Hawley, a journalist and historian, widely regarded as a one-woman Himalayan mountaineering institute with details of every Nepal expedition filed in her computer, is also the Executive Officer of Sir Edmund Hillary's Himalayan Trust. Hawley contributed the piece on contemporary Nepalese history.

Dr Harka Gurung, who wrote on geography, is one of Nepal's leading scholars and authors. Educated at the University of Edinburgh, with a doctorate in geography, Gurung was Nepal's first Minister of Tourism (1977-1978) and has since held portfolios for Industry, Commerce, Education, Transport and Public Works. A consultant with *New Era*, Gurung is a prolific writer and has published several books and over 100 articles for various magazines and journals.

Kunda Dixit, whose contribution to this book include the section on "Nepal Today" and on the Newar people of the Valley in "Daily Life", is a leading Nepali journalist greatly concerned with the country's development and environmental dilemmas. Having run a news agency in Sri Lanka, Dixit is currently based in Manila, filing news stories and writing.

Rev Father John Locke, a Jesuit priest who has made a lifelong study of Hindu and Buddhist religions in the Valley, contributed the section on religion, "A Unique Vision of the Divine." He has lived nearly 30 years in Nepal and has published several authoritative books on religion and history.

Cheogyal

Doig

Gurung

The "Beyond the Valley" section was derived from **Al Read's** contribution on trekking, river rafting and climbing. As former Managing Director of Mountain Travel Nepal and a distinguished pioneer of adventure travel in Nepal, his experience in this field is unrivalled.

John Sanday is the British architect who restored the Hanuman Dhoka Palace and lived for years in Nepal under the auspices of UNESCO, coordinating their Programme for the Conservation of the Cultural Heritage of the Kathmandu Valley, publishing several books and starting his own consultancy company. Now based in Los Angeles, he is architectural adviser to the Paul Getty Trust. He advised generally on architectural aspects of the temples and palaces and contributed much of the material on "Walks Around the Valley".

Picture Perfect

Most of the photographs were taken by **Hans Höfer** on his many visits to Nepal over the last twenty years, and some by **Walter Andreae**, an early associate. As *Insight Guide Nepal* was first taking shape, Höfer encountered the New York-based photographer **Bill Wassman** and was overwhelmed by the stunning depth and beauty of Wassman's Nepal photography, first showcased in many of this book's spreads. A graduate of Indiana University, Wassman has traveled and photographed extensively throughout Europe, North Africa and Asia since the early 1960s. Since the first publication of this book, his distinctive style of photography has become extremely well known, though by his own admission seldom so well produced.

Additional photography was selected from work by **Kalyan Singh**, a young Indian photographer, and **Alain Evrard**, based in Hong Kong. The brilliant photograph of the Royal Bengal tiger was taken in the wild by **Charles McDougal**, the Director of Wildlife for Tiger Tops, using an automatic pressure plate. The watercolors are by **Dr. H.A. Oldfield**, surgeon to the British Residency in Kathmandu from 1850-1863, and the drawings are by **Gustav LeBon** who visited in the late 19th century.

Special thanks must certainly go to **His Majesty's Government of Nepal** who contributed Himalaya-sized assistance, especially the **Ministry and Department of Tourism** and **Royal Nepal Airlines**. Of special help were **A.V. Jim Edwards**, Executive Chairman of the Tiger Mountain Group and **Manorama Mathai Moss**, novelist and expert on the complexities of the Hindu pantheon and Nepal festivals.

A tip of the topi and a cheery *Namaste* to all who helped in one way or another to make this book a reality.

—Apa Publications

Dixit

Bista

Wassman

CONTENTS

History & Heritage

Shrines of the Gods

Dwellings of Man

Features

Maps

TRAVEL TIPS

Nestled in the cradle of the highest mountains on earth, it is not surprising that Nepal has come to be known as the kingdom where deities mingle with mortals.

Here are the Himalaya, the "Abode of the Gods." Here, too, is Mount Everest, the world's greatest peak, known as Sagarmatha (Mother of the Universe) by Nepalese. Sherpa artists picture the peak as the goddess Chomolungma (Mother Goddess) riding a snow lion through clouds of many hues.

Ancient sages sought the highest climes for meditative seclusion, amongst gods who bestowed love or sudden anger on a worshipful people.

Here are Gauri Shankar, home of Shiva and his consort, Parvati; Ganesh Himal, named for the elephant-headed god, Ganesh; and Annapurna, the goddess of plenty. The devotion of ages past remains among Nepalis today: whether Hindu, Buddhist or animist, the people of Nepal live close to their gods.

Truth, no less colorful than fiction, has made Nepal one of the world's most incredible countries, a geographical wonder, an ethnological conundrum.

A Land of Diversity: No one taking a daytime flight into Nepal can fail to marvel at the land below. There are the flat, checkered plains of the lowland Terai, the Siwalik (Churia) Hills swathed in hardwood jungles, the ochre-red farmlands of the Inner Terai, the plunging flanks of the Mahabharat range, the deep gorges of turbulent Himalayan rivers, and layer upon layer of foothills blued by distance. Beyond, the Himalayas soar to unbelievable heights along the northern horizon.

This is the home of 19 million Nepalis. These people, their languages and their customs, are as diverse as the terrain. From mountain to mountain, valley to valley, plateau to plain, ethnic groups vary as much as the climate.

Squeezed between the vastness of China to the north and India to the south, east and west, Nepal is the world's most precipitous staircase to the frozen heights of "the Roof of the World."

Within a single day, one can fly closely past Everest and its neighboring summits, pause in the emerald valley of Kathmandu, then descend to the plains and ride elephants through tropical jungle and view wild tigers.

Nepal is the world's only Hindu kingdom. King Prithvi Narayan Shah of tiny Gorkha, who unified a country of feuding states and principalities in the late 18th Century, described his kingdom as "a root between two stones." The Gurkha king may not have appreciated the full truth of his words. He knew from his expansionist forays the almost unending size of his gigantic neighbors, China and India; but it takes a study of today's maps to realize the precarious position of Nepal, a rectangle 800 kilometers (497 miles) long and from 90 to 220 kilometers (56 to 137 miles) wide, bent to follow the curve of the central Himalayas, a country the size of Austria and Switzerland combined.

Such a land, precariously strategic and beset by the disadvantage of being land-locked, is truly a slender root between two vast boulders, not stones. This fact is cause for as many political headaches among his descendants as it was for King Prithvi Narayan Shah himself.

But for the narrow strip of Terai plain along its southern boundary, and temperate valleys spread across its middle, the country is everywhere mountainous. Indeed, it is eternally frozen along its high northern border with Chinese Tibet, an impassable barrier penetrated by high passes through which armies, waves of settlers and traders have made their way over the centuries.

Nepalese Geography: This stupendous mountain pedestal causes more than a quarter of Nepal's land area to be over 3,000 meters (9,843 feet) in altitude. It also includes eight peaks higher than 8,000 meters (26,250 feet): Everest, Kanchenjunga, Lhotse, Makalu, Cho Oyu, Dhaulagiri, Manaslu and Annapurna. Mountain relief is asymmetrical, with rock strata inclined to the north, leaving steep south faces. Deep river gorges incise across the range to fall rapidly to the lower valleys. The steep slopes prevent the formation of large glaciers; a snowline varying between 5,000 and 6,000

Preceding pages: Ganesh, the elephant god; King and Queen at 1975 coronation ceremonies; Bodhnath's all-seeing eyes; the Red Machhendra's penetrating stare; time-weathered faces. Left, peaks tower above the Valley mists.

meters (16,400 to 19,700 feet) also limits glaciation.

Below the Himalayas, running in a similar west-northwest to east-southeast direction, are two parallel ranges. Ninety kilometers (56 miles) south of the great range, the Mahabharat Range rises to elevations between 1,500 and 2,700 meters (4,900 and 8,900 feet). Broad tropical valleys are encased in the range's complicated folds, but only three narrow river gorges slice through it.

Immediately south are the Siwalik Hills, also known as the Churia, which rise abruptly from the Terai plain to heights of 750 to 1,500 meters (2,450 to 4,900 feet). The dry, immature soils support only a sparse population.

In the northwest of the country a fourth, trans-Himalayan range defines the boundary between Nepal and Tibet. Peaks of 6,000 to 7,000 meters (19,700 to 23,000 feet) lie about 35 kilometers (22 miles) north of the main Himalayas; their relief is less rugged, with wind-eroded landforms predominant.

Each of these mountain ranges is separated from the next by lowlands or valley systems. On the south is the Terai extension of India's vast Ganges plain. Twenty-five to 40 kilometers (15 to 25 miles) broad within the Nepalese border, the Terai's gentle topography is in sharp contrast to the rugged relief of the rest of the country.

At a slightly higher elevation, but with similar vegetation, lie the *dun* or Inner Terai valleys between the Siwalik and Mahabharat Hills. Until recently, this region was an impenetrable, malaria-infested jungle; today, with much of its indigenous wildlife endangered, it has become Nepal's most populous region. Almost all of the modern industry is in the Terai and Inner Terai, and the flat lands are ideal for growing rice and other grains.

Summers are hot in the Terai and the *dun*, with temperatures often exceeding 38°C (100°F). Winters are considerably cooler, with temperatures down to 10°C (50°F). Rainfall comes primarily in the June-to-September monsoon season, heaviest in the east. The strong, straight sal tree, compared by some to the mahogany for its durability, and the *kapok*, or silk cotton tree, are frequently seen in Terai forests.

Between the Mahabharat and the main Himalaya lies a broad complex of hills and valleys. This *pahar* zone has been heavily

eroded by rivers and streams. Here is the traditional heartland of the Nepalese people, and here is located the Kathmandu Valley.

Nepal's capital is a city of about 500,000, at once medieval and modern. Despite its 1,331-meter (4,368-foot) elevation and the snowy summits looming at its northern horizon, Kathmandu has a mild climate. Summer maximums are about 30°C (86°F) and mean winter temperatures about 10°C (50°F). Winters are sometimes frosty, but are dry and snowless, while summer monsoons bring heavy rain. The moderate climate permits three harvests a year and small plantings in between. Oaks and alders are oft-seen trees, and rhododendron and jacaranda are beautiful when in bloom. Visitors often are surprised to learn that Kathmandu's latitude – about 27°40' North – is the same as that of Florida and Kuwait, and slightly south of New Delhi.

Beyond Kathmandu, high in the mountains, thunderstorms are frequent and winter frosts limit agriculture. Nevertheless, potatoes are grown to 4,000 meters (13,100 feet), and barley even higher. The mountain population finds sanctuary in isolated valleys, where juniper and birch share the terrain with sub-alpine grasses.

There is a distinctly alpine climate in the highlands above 4,000 meters. Summers are short, winters severe and dry, with high snowfall, low temperatures and strong winds. In western Nepal and north of the Himalayas, there are elevated *bhot* valleys reminiscent of Tibet, with broad, open profiles and arid climate – particularly where the Himalayan rainshadow blocks out the monsoon rains.

People of Nepal: It is much more pleasant in Kathmandu. The Valley is a veritable crucible in which, over the centuries, many races, religions, languages and customs have been molded into a handsome, artistic people. Kathmandu's Newars are a striking example of the ethnic evolution of Nepal.

Most chronicles mention an original Valley people and an original mountain people. But no one knows where they came from. Over thousands of years, migrants from north, south, east and west settled in what is now Nepal.

Saints, like the immortal Guru Padma Sambhava, walked the length of the Himalayas to Tibet from distant Swat in today's northernmost Pakistan. The guru spread the teachings of Tantric Buddhism as he journeyed, an example of how one man, let alone a migrating

Left, the eyes of Swayambhunath.

people, could influence the lands he visited. Another was the *sadhu* Ne Muni, who may have given his name to Nepal.

It was not uncommon for warring Himalayan kingdoms or principalities to invite an Indian or Tibetan prince to lead them in battle and accept a vacant throne. Such foreign royalty, with its inevitable entourage of soldiers and retainers, remained to settle and intermarry, leaving its own peculiar mark on the population of its adopted land.

Tibetan influence is seen in the story of the beautiful Buddhist goddess Tara. In historical reality a Nepalese princess of the 7th Century who married into Tibet and took as her dowry the Buddhist region, "Green Tara" has long

since been deified. It is romantically believed that the powerful King Tsrong-tsong Gompo invaded Nepal to woo and wed this legendary beauty. More likely, he took her as part of the tribute he extracted from a subject people.

Land of Diverse People: The King's far-reaching conquests left a residue of Tibetans all over the northern region. These include the Tamangs, a gentle artistic people whose name suggests they were once Tibetan cavalry or the grooms of Tibetan invaders. Sherpas migrated from the far north-eastern Tibetan province of Kham. The people of Mustang are unadulterated Tibetans.

Meanwhile, people of Tibeto-Burmese stock and Indo-Aryan languages spread throughout the hills, valleys and plateaus of central Nepal. The south was overrun by a bewildering variety of Indian peoples.

A review of Himalayan history uncovers even more confusing facts. There are distant connections with Alexander the Great's Greeks, whose invasion of India left a legacy in the western mountains. People of Polynesian blood may have visited the far eastern Naga Hills. Neither of these groups may have reached Nepal – but then again, they might have.

Legends, more forthright than history, traditionally told the Nepalese people all they needed to know about their origins, attributing unknown beginnings to great heroes or gods. But in the sudden explosion of modern education, legends don't carry the same meaning they once did.

In the last two centuries, a measure of popular mobility – brought about by population pressure and, more recently, by political unification and development of communications – has started to alter age-old patterns.

Still, the sense of belonging to one nation may not have spread to all the diverse peoples of this land. To this day, it is not uncommon to have hill people refer to Kathmandu as "Nepal" – even though they all recognize King Birendra Bir Bikram Shah Dev with great reverence and affection.

Two Major Religions: No fewer than 36 languages and dialects are spoken in Nepal. Similar diversity is observed in rites and religions, with wide variations between one ethnic group and its immediate neighbor. The prevailing pattern is of Hinduism in the south and Buddhism in the north; but animist rites and shamanistic practices, known as jhankrism, has survived in a highly integrated form.

Both major religions coexist in most of the country. It is only in the heart of the land, in the Kathmandu Valley, that they merge, so that Hindu and Buddhist share the same festivals and the same places of worship. This unique blend of religions has created a homogeneous and sophisticated culture and civilization.

But if Kathmandu has long been considered to be Nepal, Nepal is not only Kathmandu. Think of the capital as a marvel of a microcosm, a flawless emerald in a filigree setting.

Left, the colorfully clad Royal Calvary. **Right**, crossed *khukris* atop a ceremonial mace precede a parading Nepalese soldier.

In the distant dawn of unrecorded time, so legend tells us, the Valley of Kathmandu was a turquoise lake. Upon this lake rested a wondrous lotus flower, from which emanated a blue light of awesome magnificence. This was a manifestation of Swayambhu or Adhi-Buddha, the primordial Buddha. So beautiful was the lake, so sacred the flame, that the devout came from many lands to live in caves along its shore, to worship and meditate.

From a mountain retreat in China came the patriarch Manjushri. Wishing to worship the flame more closely, he sliced the restraining Valley wall with his flaming sword of wisdom, draining the water and allowing the lotus to settle to the Valley floor. There Manjushri built a shrine that was to grow into the great stupa of Swayambhunath. He also founded a city of perishable wood and clay called Manjupatan, reaching from Swayambhunath to Pashupatinath, and bestowed upon one of his followers the kingship of the Valley.

Another version of this legend has the Hindu deity Krishna hurling a thunderbolt at the Valley wall to release the lake's waters. Flaming sword or thunderbolt, there is to this day a gorge at Chobar as narrow as a blade. Below it, enshrined in a temple, is a stone shaped vaguely like Ganesh, the elephant-headed god; some believe it is Krishna's thunderbolt.

Both legends are as acceptable to modern science as legends can be. Geologists have confirmed that the Kathmandu Valley was indeed under water at one time. Krishna is said to have peopled the Valley with Gopalas, or cowherds, who built a city and established the legendary Gopal dynasty. The Gopalas were later absorbed by the Ahirs, one of several successive waves of Tibeto-Burman migrants. These people probably came from today's north Bengal, sweeping across the hills and valleys of northeast India from Burma and beyond.

The Kirati Culture: The coming of the Kiratis in about the 8th or 7th Century B.C. is nearer recorded history. These apparently fierce tribal people may have been the Kiriaths of Old Testament Babylon. They invaded from the east, established a kingdom in Kathmandu, and left a legacy of outstanding kings in the rich fabric of early Nepal. Yalambar was the first and best remembered Kirati king. Legend credits him with meeting Indra, the lord of heaven, who strayed into the Valley in human guise. He had the dubious honor of being slain in the epic battle of the *Mahabharata*, in which gods and mortals fought alongside each other.

There were 28 Kirati kings. In the reign of the seventh, Gautama Buddha and his beloved disciple Ananda are believed to have visited

the Valley. There are stories of how the Buddha dwelt awhile in Patan, where he elevated the blacksmith caste to goldsmiths and bestowed upon them the name of his own clan, Sakya.

By then, the Kiratis had developed their culture to a point where the 4th Century B.C. chronicler Kautilya describes them as exporting 20 different grades of woolen blankets, carpets, treated skins and hides. They were largely sheep breeders and shifting cultivators; irrigation was unknown to them.

Two centuries later, the great Indian emperor Ashoka, who embraced Buddhism and set to converting everyone in his huge empire to the new religion, visited Lumbini – the

Preceding pages, floating on air. **Left and above**, the patriarch Manjushri depicted on a *thangka* and in bronze.

Buddha's birthplace – and raised an engraved column. He is said to have also visited the Kathmandu Valley, where he erected stupas at the four cardinal points of Patan, and may have enlarged upon the stupas of Swayambhunath and Bodhnath. His daughter, Charumati, married a local prince, Devapala. They founded the cities of Chabahil and Deopatan close by the holy shrines of Pashupatinath and Bodhnath. A stupa and monastery in modern Chabahil are said to date back to Charumati. When the Kirati dynasty came to an end, so did its crafts and architecture. But though the Kirati people vanished from the Valley, they remained in the mountainous east, where they are considered to be forebears of the Rai and Limbu people.

The Licchavis and Thakuris: The last Kirati ruler of the Kathmandu Valley, Gastee, succumbed to Licchavi invasion from India in about 300 A.D. The Licchavis were possibly Deopatan, not far from Pashupatinath, was so fabulous it has passed into legend.

Amsuvarman married his sister to an Indian prince and his daughter Bhrikuti, perhaps as a token of vassalage, to Tibet's powerful King Tsrong-tsong Gompo. Bhrikuti is believed to have taken as part of her dowry the begging bowl of the Buddha and other artifacts of Buddhism. She is now a legendary figure, best known as the Green Tara of Tibetan Buddhism, subject of countless *thangkas* and images. Tsrong-tsong Gompo's second wife, a Chinese princess, became known as the White Tara. She took with her to Tibet an image of the Buddha and her unshakable faith. Together, the princesses converted the king and Tibet.

Chinese travelers who visited Nepal after Amsuvarman's reign were awed by his legacy. The palace, said Yuan Chwang, was seven stories tall and ornamented with gems and

Rajputs from today's Bihar and Uttar Pradesh. They brought with them the first golden age of Nepalese arts, and introduced the division of society through the Hindu caste structure.

The Licchavis gave Nepal its first great historical figure, Manadeva I, in the 5th Century. An inscription in stone at Changu Narayan, dated 464 A.D., confirms him to be a king of considerable talents, responsible for conquests in the east and west. While Licchavi sculptors created masterpieces in stone, King Manadeva's politicians and widespread armies consolidated the kingdom. His successor, Manadeva II, had a tremendous mother fixation known through royal inscriptions: Mom's virtues were extolled almost more than those of her son. When Manadeva II rode to battle, his mother either accompanied him or sent a close confidant.

In 602, the first Thakuri dynasty began with the ascent of Amsuvarman. He inherited the throne upon the death of his father-in-law, the Licchavi king Vasudeva. Amsuvarman himself was not a Licchavi. He may have been a Gupta from northern India. His palace in pearls. Golden fountains shaped like dragons gushed clear water. The king sat upon a lion throne, wearing golden earrings, jade, pearls, crystal, coral and amber. Officials and courtiers sat on the ground to the king's right and left, and hundreds of armed soldiers kept guard.

The people of the Valley, wrote this Chinese pilgrim, bathed several times a day. They wore a single garment, and pierced and enlarged their earlobes as a form of beauty. They loved theatrical performances and the music of trumpet and drum. Traders exchanged copper coins with a portrait on one side and the figure of a horse on the other. There were copper utensils, houses of carved and painted wood, and "sculpture to make one marvel."

The 'Dark Ages': There were two more Thakuri dynasties after the one founded by Amsuvarman. The Thakuris of Nuwakot, a settlement to the northwest, imposed their might

Above, a portion of an ancient Licchavi inscription at Changu Narayan. **Right**, an image of the fabled Green Tara of Swayambhunath.

in 1043, and a second Rajput dynasty assumed command of the Kathmandu Valley in 1082.

Despite turmoil and strife in the Valley and the thrust of more than one foreign invasion, trade and commerce flourished and settlements grew all along the trade routes. The capital was forever expanding, and numerous monuments to the glory of various gods were erected.

Two kings of this long, rather obscure period, generally known as Nepal's "Dark Ages," deserved to be remembered. Gunakamadeva, a 10th Century ruler, is generally credited with founding Kantipur, today's Kathmandu (although some scholars place Kantipur's origin in the 12th Century). This king is also said to have inaugurated the three great festivals of

Indrajatra, Krishnajayanti and the Machhendranath Jatra. Legend says a god came to the Valley in disguise to watch one of these festivals. He was recognized by powerful Tantrics who bound him with a spell until he promised them a boon: a celestial tree. From this tree's wood was constructed a large building, known as the Kasthamandap or "House of Wood." It gave its name to Gunakamadeva's new city.

In 1200, King Arideva assumed the title of Malla and in so doing founded a new, highly accomplished dynasty. It is said the king was wrestling when told of the birth of his son. Immediately he bestowed the title "Malla," meaning "wrestler," upon the infant. Nearer

the truth, perhaps, is that intermarriage, court intrigue and power struggles swept the Mallas to the throne.

The Early Mallas: The early Malla period is often thought of as a stable age of peace and plenty, when art flourished and traders brought riches and recognition to the Kathmandu Valley. But hardly had the Malla rule begun when a terrible earthquake struck the Valley cities and killed thousands of people. Then invaders from the northwest plundered the weakened Valley, setting fire to villages and towns. Patan was laid waste in 1311.

The most important figure of ensuing years was the Raja Harisimha or Hari Singh. He came to the Valley between 1325 and 1330 from Tirhut, a kingdom in the foothills south of Kathmandu. Some believe he was a conqueror who vanquished the cities of Bhaktapur and Patan and ascended the throne of Kathmandu, bringing with him South Indian retainers known as Nayars – from whom the Newars may have gotten their name. Others maintain he came as a refugee, expelled from his kingdom by the Muslim invader Ghiyas-uddin-Tuglaq, to live in Bhaktapur but not to rule there. Whichever version is correct, King Hari Singh made a lasting and valuable contribution to Nepal's religion. He brought with him the royal goddess Taleju Bhawani, and this South Indian deity remains to this day the royal goddess of Nepal.

The early Malla monarchs held absolute power by divine right: they were considered to be incarnations of Vishnu, as are the present Shah rulers. Although the Mallas were Hindu Shaivites following strict Brahmin rituals, they were tolerant of Buddhism, which was widespread at the court and among the people – especially in its Tantric form, the cult of Vajrayana. A feudal administrative structure was imposed, dominated by an aristocratic elite whose powers at times overshadowed those of the sovereign. Below them, Brahmans and Chhetris monopolized all offices of profit around the palace. Next on the social ladder were the traders or farmers, divided into occupational castes.

Patterns of Settlement: To protect themselves from invaders and bandits, and to preserve the limited arable land, villagers clustered together in compact settlements on upland terraces and along the main trade routes. Houses were built of brick and tile and streets were paved with bricks. In some cases, protective walls were erected around the villages. The caste system ensured a tightly knit social fabric and easy domination by the rulers. It was during this early period that hill people from the west began to settle on mountain slopes surrounding the Valley. Unlike the lower hill dwellers, they lived in scattered hamlets of thatched mud houses, clearing the forests and building terraces to grow maize and millet.

An era of progress was followed by a period of great instability that split the Valley, pitting king against king, royal princes against parents, and feudal lords and aristocratic families against their monarchs. Into this confusion swept the conquering Muslim hordes of Shams-ud-din Ilyas of Bengal. These armies destroyed temples and religious foundations, desecrated

doms, 46 in all, ruled by Hindu princes or chieftains who had fled the Muslim invaders. It was from one of these, the mountain-perched kingdom of Gorkha, that the present Shah dynasty emerged four centuries later.

Rise and Fall of a Dynasty: By this time, the Valley not only had been divided among the three principal cities; it had been fragmented so that feudal lords controlled new fiefdoms about the Valley. Rivalry between the three cities grew so severe that walls were erected. The cities were built in concentric patterns around the king's palaces, with the higher castes in the immediate vicinity of their rulers and the lower castes on the periphery. Each city developed independently in keen compe-

images, shattered Pashupatinath, and greatly damaged the stupa of Swayambhunath. People and their priests were put to the sword. "The whole of Nepal was ravaged by fire," said a chronicler of the times.

The passing of the Muslim storm from India – short-lived in the Kathmandu Valley – had swept away most of the Brahmin empire. Waves of refugees from northern India forced their way into the mountains of Nepal. Here they established small Rajput fiefdoms and king-

tition with its neighbors. The rulers led lives of amazing affluence, luxury and indolence.

Then in 1372, King Jayasthiti Malla took Patan and established the third Malla dynasty. Ten years later, he moved his capital to Bhaktapur. A new and durable age began. Civil strife was quelled and the Valley unified. The caste system was reinforced into 64 divisions, recognizing both the social differentiation and the occupations of the people. Though storms continued to sweep the Malla scene, by the 15th Century a wonderful age of art and culture had blossomed. Newari was introduced as the court language and everywhere, in all three cities and many of the small towns, a renaissance flour-

Left, a carving of Vishnu Vikrantha dating to Licchavi times, found at Changu Narayan. **Right**, the medieval-looking Kasthamandap.

ished. Most of the great buildings, the fine woodcarving and powerful sculpture belong to this period. A prime patron was King Yaksha Malla (1428-1482), who also expanded his territory as far as the Ganges River in the south, the border of Tibet in the north, the Kali Gandaki in the west, and Sikkim in the east.

Upon his death, the kingdom was divided between his three sons and his daughter. The ensuing small kingdoms, though related, were soon warring among themselves. Conflict continued for almost 200 years. A good deal of the land available for cultivation in the Valley had been cleared by this time, and irrigation had become sophisticated. In the 17th Century, maize and other cash crops like chilies, sugar

Gorkha kingdom was subjugating minor principalities and growing in strength. Finally, King Prithvi Narayan Shah summoned his forces to invade the Kathmandu Valley. How alluring the lush Valley and the rich cities must have appeared to the mountain king. Little wonder he was obsessed with the conquest of the Valley. In 1768, after 10 years of preparation, siege and attack, Kathmandu fell to Gorkha on the day of the festival of Indra and the Virgin Goddess. The Malla age was at an end.

Prithvi Narayan Shah was the ninth king of the Shah dynasty of tiny Gorkha, about halfway between Kathmandu and Pokhara. His ancestors were believed to have been Rajput princes originally from Udaipur (Rajasthan).

cane, ginger and tumeric were introduced, greatly enhancing trade. The Valley provided passage for goods between its northern and southern neighbors; it also produced goods for export: unrefined sugar and mustard-seed oil for China and Tibet, metal ware and religious instruments for India and Tibet. Cottage industries had developed with the introduction of sugar and mustard-oil presses, as well as the use of spinning wheels and looms for textiles, demand for which was growing. All exchanges were done in Nepalese currency.

The Birth of 'Modern' Nepal: But the political rivalries among the divided kingdoms led to the Mallas' demise. In western Nepal, the

Fleeing the persecutions of Muslim invaders, they had first settled in the Kali Gandaki river basin, and conquered Lamjung and Gorkha in the mid-16th Century.

The new Shah rulers, transferring their seat of power to Kathmandu after its conquest, undertook to expand and consolidate their territory. But in 1790, their troops met Chinese resistance while marching to Tibet, then a vassal of China. In the clashes that followed, the Gorkha rulers sought the help of the British East India Company, whose traders and troops were then busy instituting British rule in India. A British envoy arrived in Kathmandu in 1792. He was too late: 70,000 Chinese troops had invaded Nepal, and the Tibetan war ended in defeat for the Gorkhas. The Nepalese signed a treaty pledging them to desist from attacks on Tibet, and agreed to send a tribute every five years to the Chinese emperor in Peking. This practice was discontinued only in 1912.

The British emissary, Col. William Kirkpatrick, was not the first white foreigner to have entered the Valley. In the 1730s, the Malla kings had allowed the establishment of an Italian mission of Capuchins. But the padres were expelled by Prithvi Narayan Shah, who charged that foreign priests supported their religion first with trade and later with guns.

A 'Treaty of Friendship': At the turn of the 19th Century, Nepal signed a commercial treaty

with the British. But England was becoming increasingly concerned with Nepal's territorial expansion: by 1810, the kingdom extended from Kashmir to Sikkim and doubled its size. Frontier disputes with the British in the Terai led to a full-scale war of almost two years.

The 1816 "Treaty of Friendship" that ended it was most unfavorable for Nepal. The Gorkhas' expansionist ambitions were checked in all directions. The eastern and western borders

Left, a 1793 view of the Kathmandu Valley. Above, a 1795 depiction of Gorkha King Prithvi Narayan Shah surveying the Valley prior to his conquest.

were fixed in their present locations; Sikkim became a British protectorate; most of the rich Terai was taken away from Nepal; and a British resident was established in Kathmandu. The Nepalese were so resentful of his presence that he was settled on land they considered lethally malarious and infested by spirits. In fact, the resident found it to be a very healthy location.

The treaty also provided equal opportunities for Nepali and Indian traders to establish commercial enterprises in each other's countries, paving the way for the expansion of Indian business interests in the kingdom. Nepalese trade with Tibet was not immediately affected, but Kathmandu's monopoly was taken away when Britain opened a new trade route to Tibet at the beginning of the 20th Century. This 1816 treaty was abrogated only in 1923.

After the so-called "honorable defeat" of 1816, the Nepalese rulers, distrustful of all foreigners, closed their borders, not to be reopened until 1951. The British resident and his successors were the only aliens within Nepal's frontiers for well over a century. The Nepalese retained full control of the country, with emphasis on military preparation, and kept "a standing army of brave soldiers always ready for war or plunder," according to one British account. Between 1819 and 1837, the strength of the Nepalese army jumped from 12,000 to 19,000 men, with twice as many men in reserve.

There was one more aftermath of the 1816 conflict. The gallantry of the Gorkha soldiers had so impressed the British that they inducted them into the British India army. Since then – through two world wars and dozens of lesser conflicts, including the 1982 Falklands crises – the Gurkhas have earned fame as outstanding soldiers for the British and Indians.

The Fashionable Renas: In 1846, after a period of bloody palace intrigues, a young, shrewd and opportunistic Kathmandu army general named Jung Bahadur Rana had himself designated prime minister and later "Maharajah," with powers superior than the nominal sovereign. He made the office hereditary, establishing a line of succession that would pass first to his brothers, then to their sons, and in so doing inaugurated the century-long Rana oligarchy.

Political enemies were assassinated or persecuted, and the power structure was reorganized to the sole benefit of Jung Bahadur Rana himself, his immediate circle of relatives and friends, and his successors. The Shah kings were kept under strict vigil in their own palace

and were no longer permitted to exercise authority. As soon as he had firmly established his rule, Jung Bahadur Rana took the highly unorthodox step of traveling – at a leisurely pace and in full royal regalia – to England and France in 1850. Upon his return, no doubt duly impressed by what he had seen, he launched an architectural vogue of neo-classical palaces. Moreover, he proved his progressive inclinations by abolishing the practices of suttee, immolation of widows on their husbands' funeral pyres, and restricting the application of capital punishment. Ladies of the court were forced into crinolines and bustles, amazingly contrived from saris of added length, and wore ringlets, kiss curls and heavy make-up. Men wore fanciful European attire and uniforms. A later prime minister abolished slavery and reformed the forced labor system introduced by the first Shah rulers, easing the lot of agricultural workers. Another prime minister built a school, a college and a dispensary in Kathmandu. Another started a newspaper, and one dared to emancipate women by starting a college for them. All these institutions remain today.

In spite of these advances, the most valid criticism that can be leveled against the wealthy Ranas is that during their 104-year-reign, they simply did not do enough for the country. If Kathmandu, the seat of their excesses, could feel neglected, it can be imagined how deprived people were in the rest of the country. The huge palaces the Ranas built, the grandiose but spurious lives they lived, contrasted sharply with the austere houses of Kathmandu, the mud huts of village Nepal, and the lifestyle of the common man. Agricultural methods improved little during the Rana period. Irrigation, in fact, receded in later years. Land was unequally distributed to Rana friends and relatives. In fact, although the king retained rights of property to all land, his holdings were allocated to feudal military overlords acting as local representatives of the central government.

Major changes began taking place during the years followed World War Two:

• The union of India, freed of British rule in 1947, swallowed 500 autonomous principalities and a few kingdoms. Indian Prime Minister Jawaharlal Nehru wrote that Nepal also was an integral part of India.

• China's revolutionary labors resulted in its independence in 1949. A year later, the new People's Republic of China annexed Tibet. Thousands of Tibetan refugees fled to Nepal; settling in the Kathmandu Valley, some remained in the Buddhist border areas of the north.

• Within the kingdom, tensions were growing. A "liberal" Rana prime minister proposed a new constitution offering a measure of people's participation through an administrative system known as *panchayat*. Democratic in character, this would have involved a council of village elders, or *panchas*, solving problems locally, with leaders elected to a national *panchayat*. But this reformist was soon replaced by a hard-liner who saw the solution in increased

isolation and authoritarianism, a concept not shared by people fired by the ideal of freedom.

With the support of the Indian Congress Party, opponents of the Rana rule – including some prominent Ranas – joined the Nepali Congress Party under the leadership of B.P. Koirala. The rightful sovereign of Nepal, King Tribhuvan, still powerless in his palace, was heralded as the embodiment of the democratic aspirations of his people. In November 1950, the king, on the pretense of taking his family on a shooting picnic, escaped to the Indian embassy in Kathmandu, and from there fled to India. In Delhi, he was welcomed by Nehru as Nepal's reigning monarch. In King Tribhuvan's absence, the Ranas chose his four-year-old grandson, Prince Gyanendra – who had been left behind by the royal hunting party to allay suspicion – to replace him. The child was proclaimed and crowned.

At this point, Koirala and his backers stepped in, with India's blessings if not her weapons, and called for the overthrow of the Rana tyrants. The "freedom fighters" liberated most of the Nepalese Terai, set up a provisional government in Birganj, and engaged Rana troops in battle. But the action was not decisive, and eventually India presided over a compromise agreement between the rival parties.

On February 15, 1951, King Tribhuvan returned from his self-imposed exile with gar-

that provided for a parliamentary system of government. The first general elections in Nepal's history were held over several weeks in February and March 1959. It was widely assumed that none would gain a clear majority, and that King Mahendra would thus be able to manipulate the political scene as actively as in previous years. But the Nepali Congress Party, whose members described themselves as social democrats, surprisingly won a substantial majority of seats in the new parliament.

Koirala, the party head, was a charismatic figure with a large personal following – and strong convictions about how the government should be run. As prime minister, his views frequently clashed with those of King Mahen-

lands of flowers around his neck, and began a new rule with a cabinet that was half Rana aristocrats, half Congress Party commoners. A few months later, the Rana prime minister was forced to step down. He went to live in India, thus ending more than a century of extravagant, despotic rule by the Ranas.

Upheaval and Panchayat: King Tribhuvan opened Nepal's doors to the world, establishing diplomatic relations with many lands. But his 1951 promise to establish a truly democratic government did not achieve immediate fruition. In fact, it wasn't until four years after the King's 1955 death that his son, King Mahendra, finally promulgated a constitution

dra. The Shah ruler did not want himself relegated to a ceremonial role. So at noon on December 15, 1960, he took actions to assure that would not occur.

Declaring that politicians had led the nation to the brink of chaos, and that foreign political concepts did not suit his Himalayan kingdom, King Mahendra suddenly sent army officers to arrest the cabinet. He followed his action with the announcement that he himself had taken over direct rule. Political parties and their activities were banned, parliament was dismissed, and a 21-month experiment with democracy ended abruptly.

Two years later, King Mahendra announced

a new national constitution establishing a system of indirect government. Local five-man *panchayats* chose representatives to district *panchayats*, which in turn sent delegates to a national *panchayat*, a legislative body with few real powers. The prime minister and his cabinet were chosen by and were responsible to the King. Political parties remained outlawed, and freedom of speech, press and assembly were greatly curtailed.

King Mahendra died in January 1972 and was succeeded by his son, the youthful King Birendra. The new king affirmed his belief that a political system truly suitable to Nepalese conditions had been well established. His government, he said, would turn its efforts towards

The following morning, King Birendra told his people on Radio Nepal that a nationwide referendum would be held to determine whether the citizens of Nepal wished to continue the existing system of government, under which party politics were forbidden, or to replace it with a multi-party system. The King's announcement immediately brought peace to the troubled land. It was followed by a royal proclamation granting considerable freedom of expression and assembly. At the same time, former Prime Minister Koirala, who had been either jailed or in self-exile since 1960, was free to campaign for restoration of party politics.

Koirala lost the May 1980 referendum to a vote of 55 percent in favour of the existing

improving the standard of living of his people.

By the spring of 1979, popular discontent with insensitive and corrupt officials, arbitrary tax assessors, steeply rising prices, and inadequate supplies of basic necessities, reached a climax. This frustration erupted in public demonstrations. Widespread violence broke out in Kathmandu on April 23, for the first time in living memory.

Left, a royal hunt in south Nepal. **Above**, a rare photo showing (at far right) Rana Prime Minister Juddha Shamsher Jung Bahadur Rana (1932-45) with King Tribhuvan. Third from right is Crown Prince Mahendra (King from 1955 to 1972).

system. But by then, the King had declared that whichever side won the plebiscite, the national legislature would be directly chosen by the electorate. The prime minister would in turn be elected by that legislature, and his cabinet would be responsible to it. The national constitution was amended by the King to put these changes into effect, and a year later, in May 1981, the first general elections were held under the partyless system.

Democratic change came to Nepal on 8th April 1990 with the announcement by King Birendra, following widespread demonstrations and riots, that the legal ban on all political parties was lifted.

Century after century, Nepalis have carved a precarious living from the steep slopes of the Himalaya and their foothills. Generation after generation has farmed the terraced fields that wrinkle the hillside of a country where only 10 percent of the land is arable. But if the past has been threatening, the future overwhelms the Nepalis with Himalayan odds. Population is increasing at a rate of 2.6 percent per year, and land productivity has fallen. Massive deforestation has caused landslides, and the whole mountain ecology has been thrown off balance. There seems to be little hope for the poor Nepali farmer clinging to the thin skin of topsoil on which his life depends.

Land Reforms: In the last three decades, various governments have tried to tackle the problem in different ways. In 1955, in an attempt to give the lower classes greater opportunity, the system of *zamindari* (absentee landlords) was abolished and a comprehensive land-reform plan was announced. The plan didn't become effective until 1964, when a ceiling on land ownership was established (allowing farmers up to 17 hectares in the Terai, 4.11 in the hills and 2.67 in the Kathmandu Valley). Prior to these reforms, 450 families owned all the farmland in the kingdom. The tiller, surviving on the edge of poverty with neither incentive nor capital to improve his lot or his crop, was laden with debts, inherited and contracted. The Land Reforms Program abolished sub-tenancies, fixed rent at 50 percent of produce, and took measures to liquidate peasants' debts and secure compulsory savings from the farmers.

After seven years, however, not even half of this target had been met. The reform had actually institutionalized inequalities between landowners and tillers. Redistribution did take place, but landowners used convenient loopholes to beat regulations by transferring property deeds to family members. Money lenders still supply 79 percent of farmers' credit, despite the recent activity of several development banks.

In July 1976, after the failure of the land reforms had been tacitly accepted, the government gave the go-ahead to organize embryo cooperatives, known as *sajha*, under the aegis of local village leaders. These have been slow in finding a solution to problems.

Success Stories: There are bright spots in Nepal's development struggle. About 3,000 kilometers (1,864 miles) of viable motor roads have been built, and 40 airstrips have been constructed in remote parts of the country otherwise accessible only by weeks of trekking.

Four power stations, generating 80 megawatts of electricity, are in operation, and this is only the tip of an iceberg: Nepal's hydroelectric generation capacity is 70,000 megawatts, probably the highest per capita potential in the world. The most recent addition to the national grid is the Kulekhani Project, which stores monsoon runoff in a valley near Kathmandu and can generate up to 60 megawatts of peak-hour power. Partly because of this project, electricity became available in Kathmandu 24 hours in 1982. The biggest development effort has probably gone into education. Long-time trekkers often comment on the number of village schools that have sprung up in the past 20 years – a trend obvious because new schools often are located on exposed ridges that previously had been ideal camping places. Official figures show the literacy rate nearing 20 percent, or about three million persons; 25 years ago, there were no more than a few thousand students from privileged families.

Food: The Best Medicine: But Nepal is still beset with many problems, chief of which is rural poverty. Hunger, premature death and inadequate housing are rampant. There are only three doctors in Nepal for every 100,000 people, and only one per 100,000 outside of the Kathmandu Valley. One child out of five dies in the first few weeks of life, and 35 out of 1,000 die between one and four years of age. Contributing to this tragic statistic are malnutrition and poor sanitation. One report says that the only medicine most Nepali children need is a well-balanced diet. This would cure most fatal complications of dysentery and pneumonia.

In the central hills and the mountains, farmers produce barely enough to feed their families for six or seven months of the year. When the off-season arrives, they must seek temporary employment or migrate to the Terai or

Preceding pages: American diplomats pose with the court, circa 1950; a face on the streets of Kathmandu. **Left,** umbrellas protect against the monsoon rain and sun.

India for work. The Terai has often been called Nepal's grain basket because of the surplus food it produces, but even this surplus has been steadily declining in the face of migration from the hills and from India. Demographic pressure, fragmentation of the land, and falling productivity may soon force the Terai to deal with the same problems currently facing the people of the mountains.

Nine percent of Nepal's population has emigrated to India for permanent work. Nevertheless, population is increasing at an alarming rate. Despite a family planning program financed mainly with foreign aid, there are 270,000 extra mouths to feed in Nepal every year. The annual rate of population increase in

Maintaining the Peace: Sandwiched between two colossal neighbors, Nepal is constantly trying to keep both India and China happy. King Birendra's proposal to turn Nepal into an internationally recognized "Zone of Peace" has been endorsed by 108 countries, including China. India has rejected the proposal, emphasizing the "kinship of countries on this side of the Himalaya." Nepal, however, is not confined to the southern slopes of the Himalaya. Its territory stretches over the mountains into the trans-Himalayan region, and Nepalis insist they are as much a part of Central Asia as the South Asian subcontinent.

China is taking an active part in the development of this Himalayan kingdom, mobilizing

the mountains is 1.8 percent, the hills 2.6 percent, and the Terai a whopping 4.2 percent. Some pockets of the Terai even show 6 percent annual growth. If present trends continue, the Terai population will double in less than 10 years, with disastrous results. Although grain production is increasing in volume, the population is climbing even faster.

Few if any of Nepal's mineral resources can be exploited industrially. Industry is confined mainly to the Terai belt, with a few factories and workshops in the Kathmandu Valley. Jute represents 90 percent of all exports, most of which are absorbed by India and do not earn hard currency.

tens of thousands of Nepali workers to build and maintain important segment of all-weather roads. Strategic considerations have prompted India and various other foreign powers to offer additional aid; as a result, parts of Nepal never before accessible have been linked by roads.

Nepal's geographical juxtaposition between India and China may be its best guarantee of survival as a Himalayan buffer state. Neither country would tolerate political encroachment by the other in Nepal, but the Indian subcontinent has always been politically volatile, and Nepal cannot afford to relax its vigilance.

Dependence on India is almost complete. Eighty percent of Nepal's trade is with her southern neighbor. The Indian market also has a mighty hold on the tourism industry, Nepal's biggest foreign exchange earner. Indeed, India is in a position to call the shots in the economic sphere. With no other access to the sea, Nepal must trade with India.

This overriding dependence often disturbs Nepalis, creating uneasy feelings of potential political intervention by India. Certainly, Indian pressure could bring Nepalese industry to a standstill, should a crisis arise. This fear has sometimes led to fierce anti-Indian demonstrations in Kathmandu and in some towns of the Terai. Trade relations have been adjusted several times, taking into account transit facilities in Indian ports for goods bound for Nepal.

international banking, but U.S. influence is still perceptible. Direct Soviet aid, once notable, has dwindled to nothing. Through barter deals with India, the U.S.S.R. supplies most of Nepal's crude oil needs. Nepal's government still relies heavily on foreign aid and expertise in its development programs. By international standards, this aid – while steadily increasing – is still negligible. But aid is a mixed blessing. The heavy reliance on foreign funds is criticized in influential circles by Nepalis who feel a loss of sovereignty. King Birendra himself has stressed the importance of self-reliance. But economic necessity may dictate otherwise.

After a tremendous increase in tourism through the 1960s and 1970s, arrivals have

Goodwill and detente now appear to be the order of the day, thanks in part to a certain rapprochement between India and China.

Foreign Aid: A Mixed Blessing: If the rivalry between the two "big brothers" has been put to good use by Kathmandu, other foreign powers and international institutions have also contributed to Nepal's development efforts. American aid in recent years has largely been confined to

<u>Left</u>, Singha Durbar was built in 1911 as the home of the ruling Rana prime ministers. Today it houses various government offices. <u>Above</u>, King Birendra in ceremonial dress graces the 100 rupee note.

leveled off at about 160,000 visitors per year. For the first time since 1955, the total number of visitors actually declined in 1981. Tourism, despite the growth in trekking, remains confined largely to the Kathmandu Valley.

Fortunately, so do the after-effects and cultural fallout. The fragile, somewhat artificial wealth carried by tourism has brought an overdose of westernization to Kathmandu's traditionally conservative social structure. The society has become generally service-oriented. Antique thefts and hard-drug usage, while hardly rampant, are a fact of life. And the almighty rupee has found a niche in the pantheon of gods.

There are few places so designed for festivals as Nepal. Here in the shadow of the mountain gods, celebrations are so frequent that they often overlap each other. There are more than 50 such occasions a year, with as many as 120 days set aside to celebrate. Thousands of gods and goddesses, demons and ogres, restless spirits and the family dead must be appeased and remembered. The various seasons must be honored, and there are appropriate rites for the blessing of seeds to be planted and of crops newly harvested. As the lunar calendar dictates, the gaiety of processions and the sombre symbolism of incense find their way into the people's lives. Some of Nepal's festivals are ancient indeed, having their origins in animism or legend. Others are more recent, the direct result of a monarch's command. The majority are tied to one or both of the two great religions of the land, Hinduism and Buddhism. Devotees of one religion take part in the others' festivals, adapting some of the rites of the other faith to their own festivals. Collective fun, a sense of accomplishment, and communion with the gods are of the essence.

The New Year: The official Nepalese New Year begins in mid April. With the arrival of **Magh Sankranti**, Nepalis rejoice at the passing of the unholy month of **Poush** which begins in mid December, and is so ill-omened that most religious ceremonies are forbidden, no weddings take place and no new enterprise is undertaken. With Magh Sankranti, however, the threat of misfortune is past.

One of the few holidays which does not follow the old lunar calendar, it marks the movement of the winter sun towards the northern hemisphere, bringing the promise of warmth. Often, Magh Sankranti is the coldest day of the year, yet devotees will be seen at holy bathing spots, the confluences of rivers, as this is one of the most important days for ritual bathing.

Auspicious foods will be consumed: sweet potato, sesame seed, spinach and *khichadi* (rice cooked with lentils). Married daughters come home and the mother blesses everyone with a drop of mustard oil on the head and a few drops in the ears, for a long and happy life.

Basant Panchami is the festival of spring

Preceding pages, New Year procession at Thimi; a timid boy with the terrifying Bhairav. *Left*, a Newar ceremony.

and also of Saraswati, goddess of learning, who visits the Valley on her birthday in February. On her birthday, children are introduced to the alphabet and it is auspicious to get married. Basantapur and Hanuman Dhoka are the venues to witness the season's inauguration, in the King's presence, with gun salutes and elaborate ceremonies. Saraswati shrines are inundated with fruit and flowers to break her fast.

On the full moon of **Falgun** in February, the shrines at Pashupatinath and the sacred Bagmati are worth a visit. At midday the bells ring out, drums throb and cymbals clash to announce the ceremony of **Maha Snan**, the holy bath given to Lord Shiva. He is washed in cows' milk, bathed with yoghurt, honey, sugar and ghee (clarified butter), then dressed anew. When night falls an enormous bonfire is lit around which the faithful keep vigil. Sankhu is the usual venue.

One of the most beautiful festivals is **Losar**, celebrated on the Tibetan New Year, usually in February, below the towering gold spire of the great stupa of Bodhnath. It is worth participating in this joyous event. The white dome of the stupa is newly painted and anointed with bucketfuls of yellow marigold juice. The air is fragrant with juniper incense burnt to bless the newly-hung strings of prayer flags to dispel the evil spirits of this world. Everyone wears their best clothes and finest jewelry. Processions of colorfully-clad *lamas*, carrying banners and a portrait of the Dalai Lama under a ceremonial silk umbrella, make their way through throngs of Tibetan people converged from distant mountains for the event. There is one wonderful moment when everyone present, tourists and Tibetans alike, flings a fistful of *tsampa* (barley flour) into the air to the chant of "Sho, sho." As evening falls, the surrounding monasteries blaze with votive oil lamps and there is often celebrations of Tibetan dancing.

Shivaratri: In all temples dedicated to Shiva, the Hindu god of destruction and rebirth, his birthday is celebrated, usually in March, at the great festival of Shivaratri. This is the most important festival of the year at Pashupatinath, where thousands of pilgrims from all over the subcontinent converge to make reverent offerings and take ritual baths, many having walked all the way from India. Prayers are also offered to Shiva in his form as Lord Pashupati, the protector of animals and special guardian of the Kathmandu Valley. Tousled Indian *sadhus* contort themselves into unbelievable forms on the *ghats* by the river. They mingle with ascetics and pilgrims, all presenting a weird and colorful spectacle as they keep votive oil lamps burning all night and sing and beat drums until dawn.

The rowdy festival of color, **Holi**, calls for wearing one's oldest clothes, for during the eight days of Holi you may well be doused with colored water. Its origins are obscure, though, falling in March it probably represents a springtime or fertility celebration. Holi is marked in the Kathmandu Durbar Square with the raising of a 25-foot high *chir* or bamboo pole. On a gun salute, flute and drums echo around the square and red powder is sprinkled on the pole and on outstretched hands. The pole is

burned on the eighth day, which precedes the full moon. Dedicated to Krishna and Vishnu, the festival is a variation of the annual water festivals held elsewhere in Asia.

Ghorajatra, the horse festival celebrated with horse races and gymnastics on the Tundikhel in March and April, is also the occasion for celebrating the Newari festival of **Pasa Chare**. After these horsemanship displays, the demon Gurumpa is carried to the Tundikhel in a midnight procession.

The separate festivals of **Chaitra Dasain** and **Seto Machhendranath** or **Rath** occur simultaneously towards the end of March. Ritual offerings are made to Durga at midday on Chaitra Dasain, exactly six months before an equivalent day during the festival of Dasain.

The Seto Machhendra image is taken from its shrine near Asan Tole and is placed in a towering chariot. Hundreds of young boys tow the vehicle, which stands on wheels six feet (1.8 meters) in diameter, through the streets of Kathmandu in the early evening hours for four days. The chariot's size dwarfs the buildings it passes. Each night, it stops at specific places; residents of the locality tend to the image. On the final day the Machhendra is transported back to his temple on a small palanquin.

The place to be for the week-long **Bisket**, one of the most exciting festivals of the Valley, is Bhaktapur. Ceremonies start around dusk in the Taumadhi Tole in front of the Nyatapola Temple. A large four wheeled chariot containing the deities Bhairav and Bhadrakali becomes the prize of a mammoth tug-of-war between the eastern and western halves of the town. The winning side is entitled to play host to the divinities for the next seven days. The deities are paraded through Bhaktapur and down a steep, twisting lane to the banks of the Hanumante River, where an enormous pole is raised – and the next day felled to signify the beginning of the Nepalese New Year in April.

Bisket (a corruption of the words *bi*, snake, and *syako*, slaughter) commemorates the death of two serpent demons. Legend tells of an insatiable princess of Bhaktapur who demanded a new lover each night, for every morning her prior night's lover was found dead in her bedroom. With the number of eligible men dwindling, a cunning royal prince offered himself to the lady. After a torrid night of love, the princess fell asleep and the prince kept watch. Soon two venomous serpents emerged from the sleeping lady's nostrils. The prince drew his sword and severed their heads. The following morning, the city rejoiced to find the prince alive and the princess in love. This festival is the result of their joy. The pole erected is symbolic *lingum*, or phallus; two banners hung from it represent the snakes.

Two miles west of Bhaktapur the village of Thimi celebrates the New Year with a spectacular gathering at the temple of Bal Kumari, known as the **Bal Kumari Jatra**. Her *chirag*, unique with its four combined torches, must stay alight or disaster will follow. Amid torch-lit processions, celebrants sprinkle one another with vermilion powder in honor of the goddess, a consort of Bhairav.

Matatirtha Snan is highlighted by ritual baths at Matatirtha, near Thankot, for persons whose mothers have died during the past year. Living mothers are also honored.

Buddha Jayanti, the birthday of Lord Buddha, is celebrated by pilgrimages to Buddhist shrines. Bodhnath and Swayambhunath are the places to be on this occasion which usually falls in May.

Kumar, the handsome warrior son of Shiva, rides the sky on a peacock to celebrate his birthday in June, **Sithinakha**. Rice planting begins on this day and wells are cleaned as their snake inhabitants are supposedly away tending to their own rituals. Newars engage in stone throwing contests. Go to Jaisedewal south of the Kathmandu Durbar Square which will be thronged with people.

Tulsi Bijropan is one of the most important *Ekadasis*, the eleventh day of each lunar fortnight, which total 24 in a year, when no animal of children erecting arches of leafy branches and asking for money. They will tell you this is for the demon's funeral procession and the feast for his many wives that he left penniless.

Patan sees one of its biggest annual festivals in the summer, **Rato Machhendranath Jatra**. This chariot festival begins in Pulchok where the chariot is built. The Rato (or red) Machhendra, considered by some to be the same god as the Seto (or white) Machhendra of Kathmandu, is the god of compassion and of the harvests and is equally venerated by Hindus and Buddhists. The chariot wends its way through the streets of Patan for about a month. Because of its immense size, members of the Nepalese army are called upon to assist in pulling. The festival, also known as the **Bhoto**

can be slaughtered and no rice eaten. This is primarily a feminine ritual entailing fasting and purification. The *tulsi* plant, a close cousin to our herb, basil, sacred to Hindus, is planted in a special place in the home and worshipped.

The 14th night of the dark lunar fortnight, traditionally the last day for rice planting, is the Night of the Devil, **Ghanta Karna**. This dreaded demon, sworn enemy of Vishnu, hated him so much that he wore *ghantas* (bells) over his ears so as never to hear his name. He was finally outwitted by a frog. Look out for groups

Left, Newar priests. **Above**, drummers are an integral part of most festivals: where there is religion, there is often music.

Jatra, culminates at Jawalkhel, the exact month fixed by astrologers, when a sacred bejewelled waistcoat or *bhoto*, supposedly belonging to the serpent king, is displayed in the presence of the Royal Family. The festival is designed to ensure a successful monsoon rainfall. Machhendra is the patron of the Kathmandu Valley.

The Rato Machhendra deity is shared by Patan with the neighboring village of Bungamati, and spends three months of every year there. Once every 12 years this mighty chariot must be pulled all the way from Patan to Bungamati, a distance of about six kilometers (four miles) over a dirt road that is hilly rocky. It is a major undertaking, and progress is slow, punctuated with ritual, prayers and offerings.

The birth of Krishna, beloved infant, ideal of manhood and most adored deity is celebrated at **Krishna Jayanti** by worshippers carrying lavishly decorated idols in procession on the eve of his birth. Throngs of women literally cover the Krishna Mandir temple in Patan Durbar Square, keeping vigil until the midnight hour of his birth. Lit by flickering oil lamps, they make offerings of the sacred *tulsi* and sway as they chant the many names of him who came as an infant and grew on this earth to fulfil his destiny.

During **Srawan** (July-August), every Brahmin and Chhetri wears a yellow sacred thread or *munja* around their wrists, right for men and left for women. They will be worn from this day, the Shiva festival of **Janai Purnima** or **Raksha Bandhan**, for three months when, no longer yellow, they are removed and tied to the tail of a cow during Lakshmi Puja. When death comes, the cow will be ready and waiting to pull the soul across the great divide. Ceremonies are held at the Kumbeshwar Temple at Patan as well as the Gosainkund Lake in the mountains north of Kathmandu.

Snake gods are widely worshipped in Nepal as controllers of rainfall, earthquakes and the guardians of treasure. At **Nag Panchami**, pictures of the snake gods are displayed over front doors which are first ritually cleansed. Milk, honey and rice are set out for the *nags* (snakes) and prayers said, at Pashupatinath, to propitiate them and prevent their angry underground writhing.

The epic love of a king and queen is remembered in **Gaijatra**, the festival of cows held in and around the Durbar squares of Kathmandu, Patan and Bhaktapur during **Bhadra** (August-September). An eight-day festival, it honors those who have died during the past year. Legend tells of a queen who was inconsolable after the death of her most dearly loved son. The king ordered every family which had lost a member during the past year to drive cows through the streets, so the queen could see she was not alone in her suffering. When this failed to console her, the king offered a reward to anyone who could make her laugh. As fantastic costumes and satire blossomed in the streets, the queen finally smiled. Thereafter, the king ordered an annual festival. Bereaved families still parade their decorated cow, both bovine and human, and dances and music accompany the frolicking of children disguised as cows.

Eight Days For Indra: The most spectacular of all Valley festivals is the eight-day **Indrajatra**, celebrated usually in September and best seen

Dragging the Bisket chariot through Bhaktapur.

from the Hanuman Dhoka. Legend holds that Indra, the lord of heaven and god of rain, once came to steal flowers from a garden in the Valley. Unrecognized, he was caught and kept captive as a common thief, while his mount – the sacred elephant – searched the streets of Kathmandu for days and nights, looking for its master. In time, Indra's distraught mother descended from heaven to reveal her son's and her own identity. She granted two boons, taking with her to heaven the souls of all those who had died in the past year, and promising heavy dew and morning mists to ripen the autumn and winter harvests. This was the cause for great rejoicing and feasting among the people of the Valley, who proclaimed a festival.

Today the festival begins with the torchlight dance of Indra's elephant, now a clothed and human-legged beast, who prances through the streets. On the first day of the festival, which is the twelfth day of the waxing moon, Indra's flag is raised at Hanuman Dhoka. The flagpole is made from a 50-foot pine tree, selected by a priest, sanctified by animal sacrifice and dragged in solemn procession from Bhaktapur by the men of Thimi. At the Tundikhel, the people of Kathmandu take over the task and festivities begin when the pole reaches Hanuman Dhoka, where masked dancers stage a colorful display of classical dancing.

On the third day, the *Kumari,* or Living Goddess, is paid homage by the entire Valley, including the King – himself regarded as an incarnation of the god Vishnu. The *Kumari* is seen to exemplify the harmony of Hinduism and Buddhism in Nepal. Chosen from the Newar Buddhist Sakya clan of goldsmiths, she represents the royal Hindu goddess, Taleju Bhawani, and is selected for 32 mystic virtues and a horoscope which exactly complements that of the King. On this day, she emerges from her nearby home painted like a hummingbird, and is carried through the streets in a special chariot, accompanied by her attendants, Ganesh and Bhairav, represented by two young boys.

Along with Indra and the *Kumari,* the god Bhairav is honored during this festival. Innumerable masks of Bhairav are exhibited everywhere, including a gold mask exposed to the public only on this one annual occasion. At certain times of the day, *chang* or beer pours forth from its mouth through a spout; local revellers cheerfully battle for a drink. In the beer is a fish, and he who gets it is particularly blessed.

Gokarna Aunshi or Fathers Day is highlighted by ritual bathing in the Bagmati River in August/September at the fine Mahadev temple at Gokarna for those whose fathers have died during the past year. Living fathers are presented with flowers and sweets.

Teej is a colorful three-day festival for women only who must walk to Pashupatinath to take a ceremonial bath in the Bagmati in honor of their husbands – to become a widow is the very worst thing that can befall a Hindu woman. Married women wear scarlet and gold wedding *saris* and jewels, and the unmarried young sexinging and dancing in their brightest clothes to pray to Shiva and his consort, Parvati. The fast ends on the fifth night of the waxing moon, usually early September.

The Festival of Dasain: The festival of Dasain, also known as **Durga Puja** is held throughout Nepal. Normal life comes to a standstill. As its name implies, it is 10 days of intense, sacrificial and joyous worship in late September, celebrating fertility and the victory of good over evil, represented by the goddess Durga Bhawani and the gods who battle demons. Every house becomes a shrine in which the goddess is asked to take up residence, and every person is expected to take ritual dawn baths at special sacred *ghats*.

On the first day of **Ghatasthapana**, the goddess is besought to bless with her presence a vessel of holy water which is specially placed in a purified place to receive her. At an auspicious moment determined by astrologers, her spirit alights on the rim of the vessel for "only as long as a mustard seed can stand upright on a cow's horn". The blessed water is worshipped throughout the festival.

On the fifth day, there are kite competitions. On the seventh day, known as **Phulpati**, offerings of flowers and leaves are made to Durga. A *phulpati* or votive offering of flowers and leaves, carried by runners from the distant town of Gorkha, the ancestral home of the Shah kings, is received by the King as a royal salute booms out over the land. The eight day or **Mastami**, is Armed Forces Day and there are military parades at the Tundhikhel parade ground and a procession from Hanuman Dhoka to Trichandra College, in front of the clock tower. Orthodox Hindus fast all day in preparation for **Kal Ratri**, the Black Night, when the animal sacrifices commence in earnest.

Animal sacrifices continue throughout the ninth day. They are especially notable around the Taleju Chowk in Kathmandu Durbar Square and Hanuman Dhoka. Every household and institution offers buffaloes, goats and chickens to the demanding goddess Durga, who favors entire black, male animals. During this time all vehicles, including all Royal Nepal Airlines fleet, and all tools used throughout the year will be daubed with blood for protection. Images, shrines and temples throughout the Valley are bathed in blood. The final day of Dasain, known as **Vijaya Dashami** (Day of Victory), sees the opening of the Royal Palace. Even the most poverty-stricken subject may line up to receive a *tika* from the hands of the King or Queen.

The Festival of Lights: Tihar, also known as the Festival of Lights, is held in late October over a five-day period. On the first day, crows – the "messengers of death" sent by Yama, the lord of the underworld, are fed rice from the rooftops. On the second day, dogs – who guide souls across the river of the dead – are honored with garlands of flowers, special food and *tikas*. Cows are similarly honored on the third day, **Lakshmi Puja**. Lakshmi, the celebrated goddess of wealth and prosperity, is believed to visit every home which has been suitably lit and decorated to attract her. Oil lamps, candles and colored lights adorn balconies and windows to welcome her, in this prettiest of all festivals.

The fourth day, **Mha Puja**, worship of one's own body, coincides with the Newari New Year and there is much feasting and gambling. On the fifth day, **Bhai Tika**, sisters must pay homage to their brothers, blessing them with a *tika* and pampering them with food and sweets.

The most auspicious fortnight of **Haribodhini Ekadasi** ends a long summer of uneasiness for men and gods when Vishnu is welcomed back from his annual four-month rest far below the earth. During this long vacation from earthly responsibility he sleeps dreamlessly on the coiled body of a gigantic snake, as represented by the huge sculpture at Buddhanilkantha. This is where festivities culminate after hundreds of fasting devotees have concluded the long pilgrimage to his four peripheral temples of Changu Narayan, Bisankhu Narayan, Sekh Narayan and Ichangu Narayan, each 10 miles or more apart. Many will walk the entire distance, following ancient tradition, while others cling to overcrowded trucks and buses for as far as they will go. Singing and chanting, each shrine must be circumambulated. Fasting for 24 hours is vital for he who fails to observe this *Ekadasi* may be reincarnated as a rooster.

The Newari festival of **Yomari Purnima** is celebrated with a fair or *mela* at Panauti in December. The people make a special cake out of rice flour called *yomari* and a *puja* is offered to the family paddy store.

The Machhendra chariot in Patan.

Every day before dawn, when sacred cows and stray dogs roam aimlessly in empty streets and when farmers are hurrying to market with their loads of vegetables or chickens, devotees of Nepal's religious cults wake up their gods in sacred temples. As the misty rays of dawn begin to stream through the doorways, men, women and children set out for Hindu and Buddhist temples, carrying ritual offerings – *puja* – for the multiple gods of their pantheons.

They carry small metal, usually copper, plates piled with grains of rice, red powder and tiny yellow flower petals to scatter on the deities' images. Afterward, they mix the offerings with clay, and apply a small amount of the mixture to their own foreheads, between the eyes: this is *tika*, a symbol of the presence of the divine.

Puja such as this is made at any and all times in Nepal, for any occasion or celebration. It is a cornerstone of Nepali religion, inherited from the most ancient of ancestors. Offerings renew communion with the deities most important to each individual's particular problem, caste or inclination.

Some of the devout have a special sequence of offerings, carefully arranged in a partitioned copper tray; they go from god to god for the best part of the morning. Others arrive with a couple of cups of yoghurt or *ghee*, and perhaps a few coins for the priests. Still other people may stay near their homes, contenting their deities by throwing rice, powder and petals on a particular rock or tree.

Ritual sacrifice is Nepali religion's other "cornerstone." Whether for a wedding or initiation rite, a seasonal festival for a deity, or a blessing for the construction of a house, sacrifices are carried out with utter simplicity or with utmost pomp and ceremony, from the Himalayas to the Terai. The sacrifice of a chicken, goat or buffalo, always a male animal, is not only a way of slaying a beast in the presence of the divine. It also gives an "unfortunate brother" a release from his imprisonment as an animal, and the opportunity for rebirth as a man.

At the time of Nepal's biggest feast, the Dasain festival of early autumn, some 10,000 animals, mainly goats, are sacrificed in the

space of a few days. More commonly, there are biweekly sacrifices of chickens and goats at the Dakshinkali Temple – to the fascination of tourists crowding outside the sacrificial pits. In other lesser known temples and courtyards, such sacrifices are a normal Friday and Saturday occurrence.

In Nepal, obedience to the gods' laws and placation through ritual are a part of every person's daily routine. Each individual partakes in the divine in his personal way. For the common folk, this often involves a matter-of-fact repetition of gestures. But it is part of an

all-pervading perception of religiosity, enhanced by a strong sense of human dignity.

Religious Mainstreams: The two main spiritual currents underlying the religious practices of Nepal are Hinduism and Buddhism. It is often hard to distinguish the two, especially since they are interwoven with the exotica of Tantrism on a background of animistic cults retained from the distant past. The result is a proliferation of cults, deities and celebrations in variations unknown elsewhere on earth. With such diverse beliefs, religious tolerance is of the essence. In fact, proselytism is forbidden by law – with a lengthy jail term awaiting offending parties, converter and convert.

The bulk of Kathmandu's Newars can be

Preceding pages: Swayambhunath penetrates the morning clouds; meditating at Budhanilkantha. **Left**, sacrifice of a goat near Sankhu's Bajra Jogini. **Right**, a Hindu devotee applies *tika*.

called Buddhist, in the sense that their family priests are Tantric Buddhist priests rather than Hindu Brahmans. Such classification, however, has never prevented a villager from worshipping Tantric Hindu gods who are the village's patron deities.

By becoming a follower of the Buddha, one does not cease to be a Hindu. Buddhists, in fact, regard the Hindu trinity of Brahma, Shiva and Vishnu as *avatars* of the Primordial Buddha, and give the triad important places in the Buddhist cosmogony. Hindus likewise regard the Gautama Buddha as an incarnation of Vishnu. It has been said that, if one asks a Newar whether he is Hindu or Buddhist, the answer will be, "Yes." The question is meaningless, implying an exclusive choice which is

foreign to the religious experience of Nepal's people.

The political leaders of the Kathmandu Valley have always been Hindus, but most of them have consistently and equally supported development of their peoples' other faiths.

The 7th Century King Narendradev, for instance, received Chinese Buddhist travelers with utmost respect, and took them to visit all the Buddhist temples and monasteries in his realm. Chinese journals describe the king as a devout Buddhist who wore an emblem of the Buddha on his belt. But inscriptions left behind from Narendradev's reign insist that he regarded Shiva as his principal god.

Beginning with the time of King Jayasthiti Malla in the 14th Century, growing pressure was put on Nepal's population to conform to the social structure of Hindu society. Even the Malla family deity, the goddess Taleju, was an import from south India. This trend was strengthened when the present Shah dynasty acceded to the throne over 200 years ago, adopting as its patron deity a deified Shaivite yogi, Gorakhnath.

The Rana prime ministers increased the caste differences in their century of power, enhancing the wealth and power of the ruling class. At the same time, innovation in religious arts was discouraged, with material wealth shifting to earthly "lords." Architects turned to building palaces rather than temples, and little was left for beautification of the religious heritage. The current government, however, realizes the importance of religion and has been promoting this cultural legacy.

The Hindu Heritage: Nepal's religions actually had their origins with the first Aryan invaders, who settled in the north of India about 1700 B.C. They recorded the *Vedas*, a collection of over 1,000 hymns defining a polytheistic religion. Out of this grew the caste-conscious Brahminism, linking all men to the god-creator Brahma. The Brahmans, or priest class, were said to have come from Brahma's mouth; the Chhetris, or warrior caste, from his arms; the Vaisyas, artisans and traders, from his thighs; and the Sudras, or serfs, from his feet. This same general caste classification persists today.

As Brahminism evolved into modern Hinduism, people of the subcontinent began to feel increasingly that existence and reality were subjects too vast to be encompassed within a single set of beliefs. The Hindu religion of today, therefore, comprises many different metaphysical systems and viewpoints, some of them mutually contradictory. The individual opts for whichever belief or practice suits him and his particular inclinations the best.

Hinduism has no formal creed, no universal governing organization. Brahmin priests serve as spiritual advisers to upper-caste families, but the only real authority is the ancient Vedic texts. Most important is that the individual comply with his family and social group.

Different sects have developed a particular affinity with one or another deity – especially with Brahma "the creator," Vishnu "the preserver" and Shiva "the destroyer." Most Nepali Hindus regard Brahma's role as being essentially completed. Having created the world, he can now sit back astride his swan and keep out of everyday affairs. Both Vishnu and Shiva are very important in Nepal, however.

Vishnu, whose duty it is to assure the preservation of life and of the world, is traditionally considered to have visited earth as 10 different *avatars*, or incarnations. Nepalese art pictures him as a fish, a tortoise, a boar, a lion, a dwarf, and as various men – among them Narayan, the embodiment of universal love and knowledge; Rama, a prince; Krishna, a cowherd and charioteer; and Gautama Buddha, who corrupted the demons. The King of Nepal also is regarded as an *avatar* of Vishnu.

The stories of Rama and Krishna are particularly important to Hindus. Rama is the hero of the *Ramayana*, perhaps Asia's greatest epic tale. The ideal man, Rama is brave, noble and virtuous. His beautiful wife Sita (whose legendary home of Janakpur in the eastern Terai is a

harata epic, particularly in that portion known as the *Bhagavad-Gita*. In this important story, Krishna appears as a charioteer for the warrior Arjuna, who meets an opposing army manned by his friends and relatives. Arjuna is reluctant to strike until convinced by Krishna that he must be true to his own role in life; he goes on to battle and exterminates the opposition.

Nepalis love the many tales of Krishna's pranks and antics as a cowherd. It is said he once appeared to the *gopis*, the cowherd girls, in as many embodiments as there were women, and made love to each of them in the way she liked best.

But for all the devotion paid to Vishnu and his avators, it is Shiva who gets the most attention in Nepal. Those who worship Shiva

site of pilgrimage for Hindus) is the perfect wife, loyal and devoted. On a forest foray, Sita is captured by the demon Rawana, who carried her off to his lair on the isle of Lanka. Rama enlists the help of the monkey people and their general, Hanuman, as well as the mythical eagle, Garuda. Together, they rescue Sita and slay Rawana. Sita proves her purity after the abduction by entering a fire and emerging unscathed. In Nepal, Hanuman and Garuda – Vishnu's mount – are revered.

Krishna is the central figure in the *Mahab-*

Left, popular image of the terrifying Seto Bhairav. **Right**, a priest at Bisket ceremonies during the Nepalese New Year.

do so not out of love of destruction, but because man must respect the fact that all things eventually will come to an end, and from that end will come a new beginning.

Like Vishnu, Shiva takes different forms. He is Pashupati, who guides all species in their development and serves benevolently as the tutelary god of Nepal. He is Mahadev, lord of knowledge and procreation, symbolized by the *lingum*. And he is the terrifying Tantric Bhairav, depicted with huge teeth and a necklace of skulls, intent on destroying everything he sees – including ignorance.

One of Shiva's sons, by his consort Parvati (also known as Annapura, goddess of abundance), is the elephant-headed god Ganesh. It is said he was born as a normal child, but had his head accidentally severed, and the elephant's head was grafted onto his neck. It is Ganesh's responsibility to decide between success and failure, to remove obstacles or create them as necessary.

The idea of "new beginnings," made manifest in the doctrine of reincarnations, is what keeps the Hindu caste system strong. Hindus believe they must accept and act according to their station in life, no matter what it may be. Their birthright is a reward or punishment for actions – *karma* – accrued in a previous life. Their behavior in this life will help determine their next one.

Teachings of the Buddha: Brahminism was the dominant faith in India at the time of the

emergence of Buddhism in the 6th Century B.C. The religion's founder, a Sakya prince named Siddhartha Gautama, was born about 543 B.C. (the actual date is disputed) near present-day Lumbini in Nepal's western Terai. Raised in the lap of luxury in a royal palace, sheltered from any knowledge of the suffering outside its walls, he was married and fathered a child.

At the age of of 29, he convinced his charioteer to take him outside the palace grounds. There, the sight of an old man, a crippled man and a corpse – and his charioteer's acknowledgment that "it happens to us all" – persuaded him to abandon his family and his lavish lifestyle for that of a wandering ascetic.

For more than five years, Gautama roamed from place to place, nearly dying of self-deprivation as he sought a solution to the suffering he saw. He finally abandoned his asceticism, and while meditating under a *pipal* tree near Benares, India, oblivious to all distractions and temptations, he became enlightened. One must follow the Middle Way, he declared, rejecting extremes of pleasure and pain.

Now known as the Buddha, the "Enlightened One," Gautama preached a doctrine based on the "Four Noble Truths" and the "Eight-fold Path." We suffer, he said, because of our attachment to people and things in a world where nothing is permanent. We can rid ourselves of desire, and do away with suffering, by living our lives with attention to right views, right intent, right speech, right conduct, right livelihood, right effort, right mindfulness and right meditation.

The "self," said the Buddha, is nothing but an illusion trapped in the endless cycle of *samsara*, or rebirth, and created by *karma*, the chain of cause and effect. By following the Buddhist doctrine, the Dharma, he said, one can put an end to the effects of *karma*, thereby escaping *samsara* and achieving *nirvana*, which is essentially extinction of "self."

Gautama preached his doctrine for 45 years after his enlightenment, finally dying at the age of 80 and transcending to *nirvana*. Nepalis claim he may have visited the Kathmandu Valley with his disciple, Ananda, during his ministry.

In the centuries following the Buddha's life, many doctrinal disputes arose, leading to various schisms in the philosophy. Most important was the break between the Theravada or Hinayana school, which adhered more closely to the original teachings and today predominates in Southeast Asia and Sri Lanka, and the Mahayana school, which spread north and east from India.

It was Mahayana Buddhism which took hold in Nepal. One of the central beliefs of all Mahayanists is that one can achieve *nirvana* by following the example of *bodhisattvas*, or "Buddhas-to-be." These enlightened beings have, in the course of many lifetimes, acquired the knowledge and virtues necessary to enter *nirvana*, but have indefinitely delayed their transcendence in order to help other mortals reach a similar state of perfection.

The Buddhist emperor Ashoka of India's Maurya Dynasty made a pilgrimage to the

Two portraits: <u>left</u>, the Dalai Lama being paraded around the grounds of Bodnath, <u>right</u>, the Most Respected Tarig Tulku.

Buddha's birthplace near Lumbini in the 3rd Century B.C. He or his missionaries may have introduced some basic teachings while building stupas in the Kathmandu Valley. Nearly 1,000 years later, in the 7th Century A.D. the Tibetan King Tsrong-tsong Gompo invaded the Valley and carried back a Nepalese princess as his wife. Both the Nepalese lady ("Green Tara") and the king's Chinese consort ("White Tara") were Buddhists, and they persuaded him to convert to Buddhism.

Tibetan Buddhism: Since that time, Tibetan Buddhism has exerted a significant influence on Buddhist belief in Nepal. Altered in part by the earliest religion of Tibet, known as Bon, it has taken on a unique form in the world of Buddhism. The shamanistic Bon faith, ele-

pilgrimage among Tibetan people to discover where their leader was reborn immediately following his physical death. The correct child is determined by his recognition of possessions from his previous life.

Tibetans believe there are, at any one time, several hundred more *tulkus*, people identified in similar fashion as reincarnations of other important religious figures. These people generally go on to become leading monks themselves. There are four chief sects of Tibetan Buddhism, most important of which is the *Gelugpa*, or Yellow Hats. Although himself a Yellow Hat, the Dalai Lama preaches free access to all teachings, including the *Kargyupa* (Red Hats), *Nyingmapa* (Ancients) and *Sagyapa* (People of the Earth). Each of these

ments of which still exist today in Tibet and some remote corners of Nepal, has certain affinities with Buddhism. Bonpos (followers of Bon) claim their religion was carried from the west, possibly Kashmir, by their founder, gShen-rab, who (like the Buddha) endured great hardships and meditated to achieve his spiritual knowledge. In medieval times, interchange between Bon and Buddhism led to a mutual adoption of parts of each other's pantheon under different names.

The leading figure of Tibetan Buddhism – its pope, as it were – is the Dalai Lama. Every Dalai Lama is regarded as the reincarnation of his predecessor. Upon the death of a Dalai Lama, a party of elderly monks goes on a

groups has made important contributions to Tibetan Buddhist doctrine.

Tibetan Buddhism stresses the inter-relatedness of all things. Universal cosmic forces and the energies of the individual human being are one and the same, and through the faithful practice of meditation, one can learn to apply one's knowledge of these energies. This can involve an altered state of consciousness: skilled Tibetan monks are said to be able to levitate, to travel across land at the speed of the wind, and to perform other actions which Westerners tend to relegate to the realms of the occult.

Learning proper meditation, under the guidance of a personal teacher, is the first step toward understanding the doctrine of interdependence. The most important tools of meditation are *mantra*, or sacred sound, and *mandala*, or sacred diagram. In *mantra* meditation, chanting of and concentration on certain syllables, such as "*Om mani padme hum*," is believed to intensify the spiritual power of those indoctrinated to the meaning. *Mandala* meditation requires one to visualize certain circular images to assist in orienting the self to the total universe.

Another important aspect of Tibetan Buddhism is the perception of death and dying. Accounts of pre-death and post-death experiences are an integral part of Tibet's religious archives. Because mental and emotional states are believed to have an effect on afterlife and rebirth, the dying person – accompanied by family, friends and lamas – meditates through the period of transition from life to death. This makes it easier for his spirit, or consciousness, to give up its residence in the body.

The Tantric Cults: All of Nepal's religions, whether Hindu, Buddhist or otherwise, are strongly influenced by the practices of Tantrism, a legacy of the Indian subcontinent's medieval culture. While the Moslem conquest, the British *raj* and modern secularism largely eliminated Tantrism elsewhere, it has lived on in Nepal.

Tantra is originally a Sanskrit word, referring to the basic warp of threads in weaving. Literally, Tantrism reiterates the Buddhist philosophy of the interwoveness of all things and actions. But Tantrism, with roots in the Vedas and the *Upanishads*, pre-Buddhist Brahministic verses, is more than that. In its medieval growth, it expanded the realm of Hindu gods, cults and rites, and added a new element to the speculative philosophy and yogic practices of the time. Within Buddhism, it created a major trend called Vajrayana, the "Path of the Thunderbolt," which reached its greatest importance in Nepal.

The *vajra*, known as the *dorje* in Tibetan Buddhism, is a main ritual object for Tantric Buddhist monks. It is a scepter, each end of which has five digits curved in a global shape, said to represent the infinite in three dimensions. It is the symbol of the Absolute, a male instrument, and has as its female counterpart a bell or *ghanta*.

The prolific Tantric gods are presented in numerous human and animal forms, often with multiple arms, legs and heads as symbols of the omnipresence and omnipotence of the divine. Many of these deities have a terrifying appearance, like forbidding Bhairav, blood-thirsty Kali or ambivalent Shiva, who in the Tantric pantheon is both creator and destroyer. Their appearance is said to reflect man's when confronted with unknown forces.

Opposed to contemplative meditation, Tantrism substituted concrete action and direct experience. But it soon degenerated into esoteric practices, often of a sexual nature, purportedly to go beyond one's own limitations to reach perfect divine bliss.

Shaktism is such a cult, praising the *shakti*, the female counterpart of a god. Some ritual Tantric texts proclaim: "Wine, flesh, fish, women and sexual congress: these are the five-fold boons

that remove all sin."

At a higher level, Tantrism is an attempt to synthesize spiritualism and materialism. Practitioners seek to expand their mental faculties by mastering the forces of nature and achieving peace of mind. In the sexual act is seen wisdom, tranquility and bliss, along with – of course – the mystery inherent in human union.

The image depicting sexual union is called *yab-yum*, perhaps not entirely unlike the Chinese *yin-yang*, a symbol of oneness in polarity. In several locations in the Kathmandu valley, *yab-yum* and other erotica are carved in wooden relief on the struts of temples. The significance of these artistic expressions depends less on what they show than on who looks at them.

Left, Tantric erotica from the Halchok temple. **Above**, a sculpture of the god Shiva and his *shakti* Parvati.

The Valley of Kathmandu is a world in itself. In sharp contrast to the rural hills, where the only two directions are up and down, it is an oasis of flat land where life can move as it may.

Flying into the Valley, the hills suddenly open out. Green terraced hillsides descend stepwise down the Valley's rim to the flatness below. Three-hundred sixty degrees of blue hills encompass this emerald Himalayan gem. Red-tile roofs of tiny doll houses strike a pleasant harmony with the flat expanse of green below an azure sky.

Many thousands of years ago, the only inhabitants of this lush and fertile valley floor were *gopalas*, or cowherds. The Kiratis and the Licchavis, who followed them, left little lasting cultural legacy; but under the Mallas, there was a renaissance. Patronized by the nobility, Newar artisans constructed the temples, *bahals* (monasteries) and *chowks* (courtyards) that constitute the manmade environment of the Valley today. As time went by, the growing importance of the Valley as a trading post between Tibet and India laid the framework for the emergence of a unique culture. The exceptional fertility of the former lake bed contributed to the dominance of the agricultural population. Even today, Kathmandu's artisans, priests and traders maintain this intimate link to their precious land.

Building Close to the Land: The Valley's Newar settlements reflected this pattern. But there was something about these settlements that was unusual for an agricultural community – their compactness. Located on the spines of ridges, Newar houses clustered around sites of religious significance, expanding on the basis of the joint character of their family structure. Villages expanded laterally along these upland plains leaving the most fertile low-lying areas for farming. In this way, organic waste ultimately found its way to the farms, adding valuable nutrients to the soil.

The Gurkha invasion of the 1769 brought a concept of nationhood into this ancient and traditional milieu. With the establishment of

the capital of a united Nepal in Kathmandu, the tightly knit homogeneity of the Valley was interspersed with new values. The Gurkha settlers had more independent family units which spilled over the traditional urban precincts.

What one sees today in Kathmandu is precisely this mixture: a medieval township that finds itself in the midst of the 20th Century, a blending of the essence of the old Kathmandu with the effects of latter-day migration from outside the Valley. A charming air of rural life pervades even the city's commercial center.

The urban framework reveals a genuine sense of aesthetic perfection and a deep understanding of integrated social functions. Space is arranged, combined and organized into a subtle succession of buildings and courtyards, of ornamented facades and sunken fountains, of open spaces peopled with statues, monuments and decked temples.

Each new step opens unexpected vistas and perspectives. As you walk along the maze of narrow streets, you get glimpses of ancient courtyards through a succession of doors opening on dark passages. While statues of gods grin and groan, you pass open shrines, small temples set back from the street, and large

Preceding pages: heading to a distant well; men and beasts of labor; pilgrims at Pashupatinath; a Kathmandu lane; girl selling mustard oil in Asan. **Left and above,** images of childhood.

pagodas towering over the squares.

Chubby smiling faces appear fleetingly framed in dark rectangles of ornate windows. Painted eyes protect carved doors, as other eyes peer unobserved from behind trellised wood.

Everyone goes about his daily chores, working or playing, perhaps idling in the sun, shifting with its rays, seeking the shadow in times of summer heat and sunshine in the cold months.

The Divine in the Worldly: Lost in a maze of wondrous eye-catching detail, it takes time to realize how well thought-out is this integrated urban universe. It is a chain of neat architectural patterns reproducing the basic rectangular motif of the Newari house, with variations adapted to the configuration of the terrain and the needs of men and gods. In a valley where there are said to be more religious monuments than houses, it is sometimes difficult to tell the difference between the divine and the worldly. In fact, houses can be built only with divine permission, which must come prior to the foundation-laying ceremony and again after the roofing of the house. Concrete cubes are fast replacing the old mud-brick buildings that are being torn down in the heart of the city. But a great deal of construction following traditional building techniques is still taking place in Kathmandu's suburbs.

Bricks are manufactured near the construction site by a couple of men who dig the mud, mix it with water, stuff it into a simple wooden mold, and leave stacks of these bricks in the sun to dry. Although fire-baked bricks and cements are increasingly being used, they are more expensive, and it is the sun-dried "raw" bricks that mix best with the clay cement. The walls of buildings are made of a double line of gray bricks stuffed with clay. Beams and wood rafters are set in place and covered with planks, then are topped by a layer of mud on which the tiles are fixed. Though this mud is cooked to prevent tiny seeds from germinating, grass grows in roofs after a few monsoons have passed.

The Family Unit: Just as the house is the basic architectural unit, so is the extended Newar family the cornerstone of society. The family is both a support and a refuge, the main system of social insurance and security. From early age, the individual learns how to fit within the social nucleus and how to relate to the the clan and

caste, through respect for relatives and patron deities. Sometimes, joint families include three generations with 30 or more members. Family life is marked with rites and obligations that the individual does not dream of dodging.

If the family is the basic unit of Newar society, then the *guthi* is on a slightly higher plane and symbolizes a deep aspiration to community living. Often as night falls, you may hear voices and accordion notes pouring from the upper windows of ordinary houses. Inside, there is a *guthi* meeting where relatives and companions get together to have a good time, chatting, sucking at the *hookah* and generally relaxing.

Newars derive substantial advantages from belonging to various *guthi*. These brother-

hoods maintain local and communal services, organize feasts, festivals and processions, arrange burials, maintain family sanctuaries, care for the ailing and elderly, and even assist in the collective preparation of fields. *Guthi* are indicative of the social rank and the economic potential of each family. They also offer a channel for going beyond caste barriers. There is even a possibility of buying one's way into a better *guthi*. This institution, present in the Valley from the time of the Mallas, has been both a factor of social integration and a means of perpetuating cultural values and achievements.

Ceremonies of Daily Life: From birth to death, special rites and celebrations mark the impor-

Left, images of growing: classmates in a village school. **Right**, a makeshift brass-and-drum corps serenading outside a bride's house.

tant events of one's existence, assuring a symbiosis of body and soul with the divine. This deep relationship between man and god is reaffirmed through daily rites. In some, man symbolically becomes the god himself, strengthening his sense of sacredness and self-respect.

The birth of a child is supervised by a community midwife, and is a joyous affair. The midwife assists in the delivery, and after cutting the umbilical cord and shaping the child's head, anoints the newborn with mustard oil. This oil is regarded as therapeutic, and is used for massaging both baby and mother.

The *pasni* (rice-feeding) ceremony is the child's next important occasion. In the presence of family and priests, the seven-month-

old child is dressed in finery and fed rice presented on a coin by all members of the family. He is shown several objects on a tray: a heap of earth, paddy (unhusked rice), bricks, toys, rings, a pen and ink-pot, and a book. It is said his parents can tell the child's future profession from the object he first picks up.

The mother takes her baby everywhere, either on her back or in one of the many folds of the *patuka* around her waist. She takes the child to the fields, where it rides piggy-back while the mother works. But as soon as the baby can walk, the child is left in the custody of an elder brother or sister. The mother continues to go about her daily chores or prepares to have another baby.

Rites of Initiation: Childhood is a time of fun. Young boys push bicycle tires with sticks for hours on end, running alongside the street traffic. Girls play hopscotch on temple steps, keeping a quiet vigil on nearby toddlers. Kite season brings them all to the rooftops to try to catch the wind, or down to the streets to chase falling kites.

Initiation to adult life comes early for Newar children. All the girls in the family are "married" to the god Narayan before they reach puberty. They take a ritual bath and make a trip to the local Ganesh temple, where they undergo the symbolic rituals of a typical marriage – nails varnished red, vermillion smeared on the central parting of their plaited hair. The human marriage that will take place later, when the girl is in her teens, will be her second. Technically, this means that the girl will never be a widow and will also make divorce a mere formality.

The initiation of boys follows a different pattern. A lad of 13, draped in saffron robes, may clutch an elms bowl and a long curved stick as he makes his way from door to door in his introduction to Buddhist monastic life. If the child is Hindu and belongs to a Brahman or Chhetri family, this is the time of the sacred thread ceremony. He must wear this thread around his shoulders constantly, changing it only on the full-moon day of July, when the old thread is wrapped around the tail of a cow.

The Marriage Celebration: Marriage comes next. Traditionally, the parents make the match; but young Kathmandu urbanites are increasingly making their own free choices.

First, there is an official engagement ceremony, when the boy's parents send gifts of betel to the girl's parents. The girl's parents make a display of feigned reluctance, and the boy's representatives make very literary speeches extolling his virtues. After this hilarious exchange, and acceptance of the young man by the girl's parents, the wedding may proceed as planned.

Dates for weddings are fixed according to astrological calculations. Certain seasons are considered most auspicious but for marriage at short notice, an astrologer can be paid to "fix" a suitable date. Spring is the most popular time for marriage, and Kathmandu often resounds with the music of two or three marriage bands

<u>Left</u>, images of adulthood: family men share a *hookah* at a *guthi* gathering. <u>Right</u>, two businessmen engrossed in conversation.

making their way simultaneously along the New Road to or from the bride's house.

Weddings are long affairs and stretch on for the better part of a week. In Newar families, the groom sends a *pathi* (almost a gallon) of milk to the girl's mother as a token of compensation for the milk the girl sucked as a child. After dusk, the procession forms. Drummers and musicians make their way to the girl's house with the boy sitting at the back of a decorated chauffeur-driven car. (Before the advent of motor vehicles, he was carried in a palanquin). The visitors remain for a while at her home, sitting on chairs or in the courtyard chewing betel, that stimulating mixture of betel leaves, araca nut and white lime so popular in South Asia.

The bride does not show herself yet. She leaves at midnight and spends the night at a friend's house. It is only on the following day that she is received at her future husband's home. She distributes betel to each member of his household, lastly to her groom. Then the betrothed partake of the same food, and the bride bows down at the groom's feet.

The ceremony will last two or three more days, and each night the young woman goes back to her parents' house. On the last evening, after an offering of musk – believed to be an aphrodisiac – the marriage can at last be consummated. The end of the ceremony and the beginning of life in common is marked by a merry wedding banquet where the couple introduce their friends to each other. It is traditional that the bride should act shy and show herself aggrieved when taking leave of her parents . . . though not so upset that tears will ruin her makeup!

Old Age Death: In a country where death comes early (the average life expectancy is 44 for males and 47 for females), age is respected and celebrated. The old are venerated, and when an aged relative reaches the auspicious age of 77 years, seven months and seven days, there is a reenactment of the *pasni* ceremony that all children go through when they are seven months old. The old man is hoisted on a brightly decorated palanquin and paraded through the streets of the town. If he has a wife, she follows in a second palanquin and is carried around the village with respectful pomp. The old man wears a symbolic golden earring to commemorate this event, and carries it for the rest of his life.

When death finally comes, the deceased is borne on a bamboo platform to the banks of the river, usually in the pre-dawn hours. Traditionally, the dead must be carried to the cremation *ghats* by their survivors; nowadays, they sometimes make the trip in the back seat of a taxi. Occasionally, musicians precede the funeral procession, playing slow music.

At the riverside *ghats*, sons walk around their parent's corpse three times, carrying the butter lamp that will be placed on the face of the deceased. As the son sets the pyre ablaze, the dead person's relatives gets their heads shaved and ritually purify themselves with a bath in the river. The ashes are then scattered in the river. The priest carries the soul of the dead to the abode of Yama, the god of death, where it will merge with the divine.

Elsewhere in Kathmandu, life goes on. On the streets, in the *bahals*, in the temple squares and on rooftops, Kathmandu endures, caught in transition. It is a transition from old, to which the town clings with the tight bonds of Newari tradition; and a metamorphosis to the present, a reality that has come with the town's jet-age links to the rest of the world. Riding on this tightrope are Kathmandu's inhabitants, who are born, who live, and who die in the Valley world.

Left, images of death: an old woman breathes her last at a Bagmati River ghat. **Right**, a ritual cremation helps the soul to leave the body.

The great civilizations of the Kathmandu Valley are justly famous for the masterpieces of art they produced. In architecture, sculpture, painting, metalwork, literature, music and dance, the various groups of people who have made the Valley their home have left a marvelous legacy. Of the earliest settlements, little remains. There are the two great stupas of Swayambhunath and Bodhnath, whose origins are lost in time. There are the four stupas built at the cardinal points of Patan about the 3rd Century B.C., reputedly by the Indian Emperor Ashoka. The mounds are inviolable; they might contain relics of an unknown art form. Other remnants have vanished completely.

Licchavi Classics: The first golden age of Nepalese classical art, left to us in durable stone sculpture, dates from the Licchavi period of the 4th to 9th centuries A.D. Entirely religious in character and Indian in origin, it proclaims an age of amazing accomplishment – from the colossal image of the reclining Vishnu at Budhanilkantha to hundreds of beautiful small works of classic simplicity scattered about the Valley, all masterpieces of incalculable value.

Stone inscriptions at the ancient temple of Changu Narayan tell of King Manadeva I who – apart from commissioning places of Hindu and Buddhist worship – built a palace many stories high, a wonder of the age. Probably it was made of wood, for it has vanished without a trace. In fact, no early remnants of wooden artistry have been found, even though wood must have preceded stone as a material for construction, and certainly for carving. The carvings of the 12th and 13th centuries – the earliest known in the Valley – are masterly. These include the struts of the Hanuman Dhoka and the Basantapur Tower in Kathmandu, the Uku Bahal in Patan, and the Indreshwar Mahadev temple at Panauti, all of them almost Licchavi in their elegant simplicity.

But by this time, the golden age of classic Licchavi sculpture had come to an end, and an early Malla renaissance in stone, metal and paint, as well as in wood, had begun.

Preceding pages, Vajracharya temple dancing in classical Newar style. **Left**, an 8th-Century Licchavi stone carving of Vishnu at Changu Narayan.

This renaissance was spurred by the genius of the Newar people. Into the Kathmandu Valley crucible had been poured the culture and talent of people from India, Tibet, China, Mongolia, Central Asia and perhaps Burma. Their influences melded into a new, completely indigenous style. Religious symbolism, Hindu and Buddhist, was paramount. It decorated temples, religious courtyards, palaces and the homes of the rich, extolling the virtues of deities and of monarchs who had assumed divinity.

By the time of the Mallas, metal was preferred to stone for image-making, even for large-sized statues like the handsome golden kings of Kathmandu, Patan and Bhaktapur. These include the stately goddesses Ganga and Jamuna in the old royal palace at Patan, and the two exquisite Taras at Swayambhunath. Important temples were crowned with gold, fused by a mercury process. Goldsmiths, silversmiths, and workers in bronze and other baser metals developed their skills to a fine degree.

Other artisans likewise flourished: woodcarvers, ivory carvers, masters of terra-cotta, and brickmakers. Licchavi purity was smothered in amazing outpourings of ornamentation. During the centuries of Malla rule, Newar artisans touched almost every exposed surface of temples and important buildings with the magic of their many-faceted creativity.

Tibetan Influence: In the late 13th Century, a Newar architect and master craftsman named Arniko was invited to Tibet. He took a party of 24 assistants with him to build important stupas and cast historic images. So great was Arniko's fame that he joined the court of the Mongol emperor of China as "controller of the imperial manufactures." The multi-tiered pagoda-style roofs so much a trademark of East Asia owe their origin to this remarkable man. The modern highway of Kathmandu to the Chinese Tibetan border is appropriately named in honor of him.

Other Newari artists were also invited to Tibet, and in time, this new Tibeto-Newari style began influencing the art of Kathmandu. The gem-like Golden Gate of Bhaktapur (1754), renowned today as Nepal's most outstanding single work of art, owes its brilliance to this intercultural melange. Chinese and Tibetan symbols, like dragons and phoenixes, began appearing among familiar Newari symbols. Traces of Muslim influence can be seen in late Malla architecture, notably in the old royal palaces of Kathmandu and Bhaktapur.

While Bhaktapur produced marvels in wood and continued a virile tradition of stone sculpture, Patan was the city of metal workers. Their excellence is best seen in the 14th Century Kwa Bahal, or Golden Temple. So enchanted were Tibetan visitors to this city of artists, they called it Yerang, "Eternity Itself."

With the passing of the Malla dynasty in the 18th Century, Newari art floundered. It was even suppressed during the 104-year reign of the Rana prime ministers. Since the Shah dynasty regained power in 1950, there has been a revival of the arts. Much of the work done today is merely as a craft for tourist dollars, devoid of vision and grand purpose.

But for a short while in the 1970s, a true renaissance took place. The Valley's craftsmen displayed their latent abilities when UNESCO set about to restore the old royal palace in Kathmandu and the German government involved itself in the renovation of some important buildings in Bhaktapur. The old arts and crafts, indeed, are still alive. With adequate patronage, they can be very impressive.

Devotion Through Painting: Newari painting had its origin in illuminated religious manuscripts dating from the 11th Century. Done in simple natural colors over crude ink drawings on strips of palm leaf, or on the wooden covers in which manuscripts were bound, these earliest painting are Indian in style and Buddhist in inspiration.

Brahminical manuscripts began to appear in the 15th Century. Strong paper started to replace palm leaves some time later, and by the 19th Century, illuminated manuscripts were on their way out. Visitors must be beware of purchasing the many "old" manuscripts peddled on the Valley's streets and in some of its shops today. Almost all of them are fakes.

The Newars employed a miniature form of painting, distantly related to the Indian Pahari school. This style endured through a transition to painted scrolls in the 14th Century, and later to murals. The painting became highly sophisticated. Significant influence came from Tibet, where *thangka* or scroll painting was well established. Between the 14th and 16th centuries, Newar artists were invited to Tibet to paint scrolls and monastery murals. They left an indelible stylistic imprint on Tibetan art; at the same time, they themselves partook of the exotic styles of China, Kashmir and Central Asia that met and mingled on this high plateau. By the 18th Century, the Tibetan art of *thangka* painting had been introduced to the Kathmandu Valley.

Newari painting, known as *paubha* or *pati*, serves a variety of religious purposes: worship, meditation, glorifying deities, obtaining merit, recording festive events and consecrating temples. The detail of these paintings is so exquisite, the drawing so brilliant, that the Newar artists have left a clear record of the rituals, dress and customs of centuries past. The best examples of traditional painting, including the long scrolls often used for worship, hang in the museums in Kathmandu and Bhaktapur. Other fine 16th to 18th Century paintings are found in Swayambhunath, in Kirtipur's Bagh Bhairab, and in Panauti's Brahmayani Temple.

Thangkas for Tourists: The *thangkas* displayed in the Valley's shops are largely done for the benefit of tourists; painted by contemporary Newar and Buddhist Tamang artists, their colors are modern, and many are smoked to appear old. One shop in Bhaktapur sells *paubhas* painted in Patan. Otherwise, traditional Newar art is rarely seen. Hopefully, it will endure, because it has a rare charm and a smoldering beauty all its own.

Newar artists belong to a unique caste, the *chitrakar*. They are found most extensively in Bhaktapur, where some belong to a cooperative turning out modern *paubhas* and purely decorative pieces of art. Most of these artists are contracted to decorate temples and private houses with painted motifs for festivals and marriages. Some of them make and paint brightly colored papier-mâché masks representing popular deities. Once used only for ceremonial purposes, these masks are now made in all sizes for sale to tourists. They are even incorporated in a very recent innovation, string puppets.

Some Tamangs, calling themselves *lamas*, operate small ateliers in Kathmandu, Patan and Bhaktapur. Most of the *thangkas* found in the Valley's shops are turned out here. Many Tamangs paint in their distant villages until they have a sufficient number to sell in the Valley or to export to India.

Bronze temple guardians such as this fierce beast at Patan's Kwa Bahal are found everywhere.

Genuine Tibetan lama artists can often be seen painting at the great stupas of Bodhnath and Swayambhunath. A dedicated few strive to maintain traditional standards, using muted stone colors and time-honored laws of proportion and subject matter. There is a single Tibetan artist at Bodhnath who turns out appliqué *thangkas* of unusual beauty.

Outside of the Valley, there are as many styles of art as there are ethnic groups. In the distant Sherpa district of Khumbu, for instance, two brothers paint landscapes in *thangka* style. Elsewhere, brilliant artists may spend a lifetime unknown. One cloth painting, carried to Kathmandu, after having been purchased for a single rupee in a hill village, has been adjudged a masterpiece of Nepalese art.

In Kathmandu, the Nepal Association of Fine Arts has a large following of young artists painting in numerous styles and media. The NAFA has a permanent gallery, and holds regular exhibition of members' work.

Two Nepalese painters who have won recognition at home and abroad are L.S. Bangdel, working in Kathmandu, and Laxman Shrestha, resident in India. Their abstract canvases exude the essence of this country's mountains. In a strange, luminous way, their work can lay claim to the same ancestry as the *thangkas* and murals of traditional Nepal.

The Gilded Word: The written word in Nepal dates at least to Licchavi times. Chronicles of gods and kings, and later of royal achievements, laws, and life at court, were carved in stone in the Pali or Sanskrit languages.

Probably predating these rocks – no one can know by how many centuries – were the lyric odes passed orally from generation to generation. So rich is this particular art form today among the people of Nepal's mountains and valleys, it is easy to believe that troubadours composed and sang of their kings' battles and gods' love when the Licchavis were carving their masterpieces in stone.

The famous 17th Century King Pratap Malla of Kathmandu let himself be known as the "King of Poets," so presumably poetry flourished in his time. Even today, Nepal's kings and queens like to be known as poets and songwriters. Their creations are frequently recorded or played over Radio Nepal.

A classic example of Malla decoration, this intricate woodcarving serves as a roof strut in Patan's Mani Keshab Narayan courtyard.

Remarkably, it wasn't until the 18th Century that literati began expressing themselves in Newari, the language of the Valley, or Nepali, the lingua franca of the kingdom, introduced by the Gorkha conquerors. Early Nepali literature's brightest star was the 19th Century poet Bhanubhakta, whose name is a household-word wherever Nepalis are found. Two poets of almost equal stature are Motiram Bhatta, known for his gentle eroticism, and Laxmi Prasad Devakota, a recently deceased 20th Century poet of growing reputation.

The years of political unrest preceding the Rana overthrow in 1951 influenced a number of writers. Because of the threat of oppression, their writing was stilted and heavy with symbolism; besides, in a country where illiteracy was rampant, their words were aimed at a small educated elite. B.P. Koirala, the former prime minister who spent many years in jail or in exile, is the author of many short stories and novels belonging to this period and later. The works of Balkrishna Sum, a poet, dramatist, novelist and artist, also come from this era.

Today, late 20th Century authors tend to indulge in experimental styles and themes, and await the verdict of acceptance. They thrive despite the small audiences they command (mostly outside Nepal) and in spite of the lack of translation and distribution. As Nepalese literacy improves, the fame of some is bound to grow.

Songs of Life: Music is a main artery of Nepal. It is an important, hauntingly beautiful accompaniment to life itself. It follows a man from birth, through courtship and marriage, attends his religious ceremonies and harvests, follows him abroad and welcomes him home again, enriches his vocabulary of love and desire, tells of war and Gurkha heroism, and trails him to his death.

Everyone sings. Married women sing for the long life and well-being of their husbands. Young girls flock to the Teej dance festival and sing to attract worthy partners. During the festival of Tihar, bands of singing children, teenagers and adults "carol" through the streets, entertaining all who care to listen, collecting funds for some cause.

When you are in the city, you will hear music everywhere, from dawn worship to the late-night chanting of hymns. When you walk in the mountains, you will hear the throb of drums and distant echoes of song. So persistent is the Nepalese flute, you might think you are being followed through street, forest and field by

Krishna himself.

Professional musicians known as *gaine* were once found everywhere. Whole families traveled together, and one could almost watch the repertoire of songs being passed from grandfather to father to son. They sang old legends of gods and larger-than-life mortals, of love and impassioned happenings. To a song dedicated to Krishna and the *gopis*, they might add tongue-in-cheek twists – suggesting a certain tenderness between Queen Victoria and the first Rana prime minister, Jung Bahadur; or telling the story of the first ascent of Everest, with Tenzing pulling Hillary to the summit.

These delightful troubadours traveled from village to village, from festival to festival, accompanying themselves on four-stringed *saringhis* – a type of viola carved from a single piece of wood and played with a small horizontal bow to which tiny bells are sometimes attached. Their traditional function was for information as much as for entertainment. Among the illiterate masses, their religious songs conveyed a more immediate message than the teachings of priests or the carvings on temples and palaces.

Today, they are slowly dying out. Perhaps the young are turning to more lucrative means of living. Or perhaps they are wilting before the invasion of Japanese transistor radios and cassette players.

Religious music is played on a wide variety of instruments, from drums to cymbals, flutes to harmoniums. It is the preserve of the *damais*, whose normal occupation is tailoring. In recent times, these *damais* have grouped themselves into uniformed, cacophonous walking bands. They are *de rigeur* at large weddings, playing popular Hindi film music, often unrecognizably.

At the great stupa of Bodhnath, another kind of music can be heard. It is echoed in Nepal's far northern monasteries, wherever Buddhist lamas sit to pray or observe festivals with sonorous pomp. Huge, collapsible metal horns, smaller trumpets, thigh-bone flutes, cymbals and conches create sacred Tibetan music. Belching, tearing, grunting, wailing shafts of sound are held together by human chanting. There is also a happier Tibetan sound – folk music played on the colorful *damiyen*, a brightly painted ukulele-like instrument which sets feet stomping in rousing dances.

A Multitude of Dance Forms: Folk dances are everywhere in Nepal. They are performed in village clearings, in fields, in cramped houses, in temple courtyards.

At festival time, when hill people converge on Kathmandu, there are outbursts of folk dancing throughout the Valley cities. To the sound of simple musical acccompaniment – drums and voices, sometimes flutes or small hand cymbals, and the jingle of tiny bells worn around the dancers' ankles – an amazing variety of steps are executed.

Every clan has its own dances. These vary from the innocently naive to the sophisticated as when women form arabesques with brass platters in each hand, on which are placed lighted candles. In some of the dances, a distinctly Cossack influence is notable: performers squat on their haunches, kicking out their legs as they bob or spin up and down and around, setting on their haunches again without missing a beat.

Classical dancing is the domain of the Valley's Newars. The delicate dance of the *kumari*, which appears to have much in common with Indian Bharatanatyam and Thai dancing, is as fragile as the tinkling wind bells of the Newari homes and temples. The more vigorous dances of Manjushri and Vajra Yogini are an exciting contrast. Seldom seen today, these dances have been encouraged in recent years, and a revival is now taking place.

More frequently performed are the masked dances of Bhaktapur. These are at once primitive, lordly and aggressive. They tell of ancient battles between the gods and the forces of evil. Seen best by firelight, they are naively magnificent. These masked dancers are not to be confused with the Nawa Durga dancers. Tantric devotees don masks to walk, swirl and leap through the streets of Bhaktapur, Kirtipur and the village of Thecho. Considered by most to be possessed by the deities they represent, they are worshipped as such.

Centuries ago, a Malla king decreed that the dancers of Thecho must annually dance all the way from their village to his court at Patan, or be fined. Similarly, the masked Bhaktapur dancers appear in Kathmandu once a year at the festival of Indrajatra. Valley residents believe that as long as these sacred dances are performed in the streets, powerful deities will mingle with man, and the Valley will remain in the abode of the gods.

Storyteller spellbinds his audience during the Budhanilkantha temple festival. The oral tradition is still strong throughout Nepal.

Nowhere in the world can one find the same concentration of culture, art and tradition that exist in the Kathmandu Valley. To the majority of Nepalis, the Valley is Nepal. This concept, which stems from the land's early history, was magnified during the cultural heyday of the Mallas when the Valley flourished as a center of art and architecture. Later, the Valley's petty kingdoms were unified by Prithvi Narayan Shah, and the Valley then became the fulcrum of Nepalese power.

Due to its inaccessibility and the fact that it was closed to the outside world until the early 1950's, the Kathmandu Valley still remains a place of mystery. Although Western influence has made its mark on Kathmandu itself, it is easy to walk back into history and become totally immersed in imageries of the medieval period.

From The Outside In: There are two ways of discovering the Kathmandu Valley: from the inside out or from the outside in. We recommend the latter.

The typical visitor heads directly from the airport to his Kathmandu hotel and explores the Durbar Square from the safety of a private car. He will perhaps make excursions to Patan and Bhaktapur, marvel at the prayer wheels of Swayambhunath or Bodhnath, then depart to his next destination.

But the visitor who really wants to know the Valley, to feel its pulse and get to its spiritual roots, should start his exploration well beyond the city limits. In ages past, when the Valley floor was filled with water, the only settlements were near shrines and pilgrimage sites in the surrounding hills. They remain today, more ancient than Kathmandu itself.

These ancient shrines are the key to unlocking the mysteries of Kathmandu city itself. And they are not difficult to reach. Because of the Valley's compact size and its relatively flat terrain, one can travel by foot or bicycle – or if somewhat less adventurous, by car – to innumerable shrines and temples, each with a story of its own to tell.

In the following pages, we have presented the Valley's outlying shrines in a systematic fashion, by religious function. Thus the great Buddhist stupas are discussed first, followed by shrines to the important Hindu deities Vishnu, Shiva and Ganesh; then shrines to female deities; and finally nature sites.

With this background thus established, we take you into the cities of man, the metropolises of Kathmandu, Patan and Bhaktapur, and then the smaller villages which pepper the remoter parts of the Valley.

Following the descriptions of these destinations in Exploring the Valley is a section on various walks in the Valley. These excursions serve to tie some of the shrines to the villages and thus to the cities, providing the visitor a broad base of understanding of the residents of the valley.

Preceding pages: a Nagarkot roof with a view of Dorje Lakpa; a Newar farmer balances his daughter with cauliflowers; busy New Road; the many faces of Kathmandu postcards. **Left**, a flash of welcome from a novice monk.

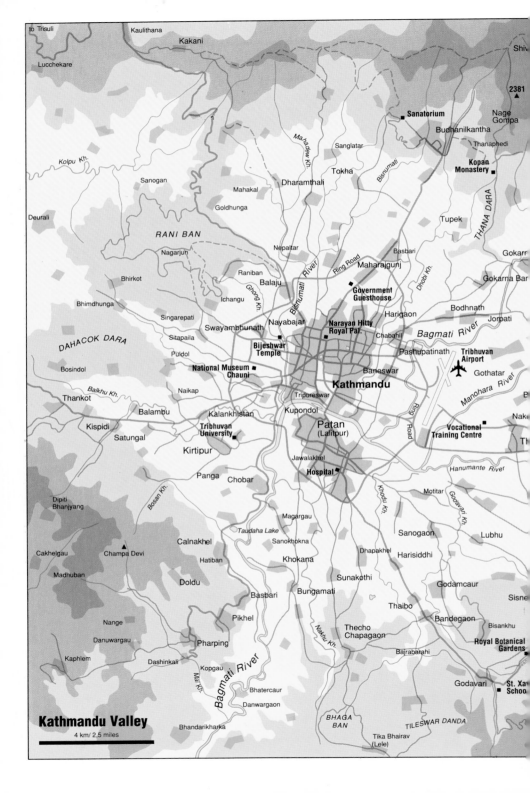

Kathmandu Valley

4 km/ 2,5 miles

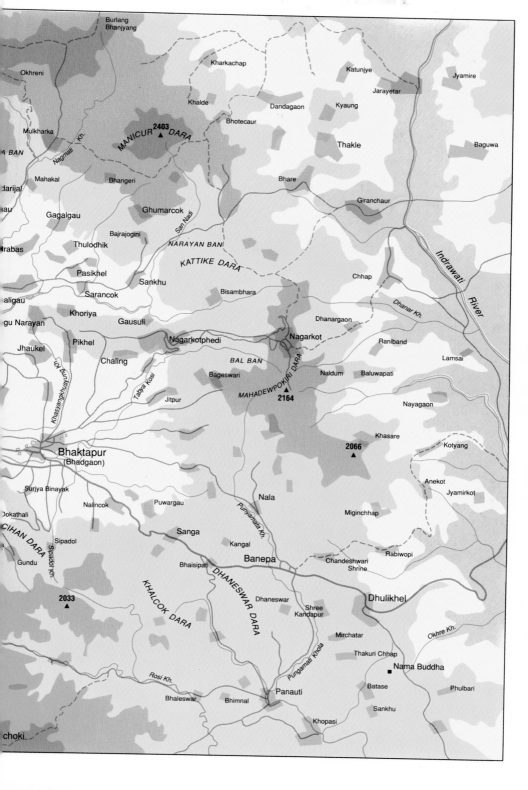

BUDDHIST SHRINES: THE EYES HAVE IT

Atop a green hillock west of Kathmandu, at the point where the legendary patriarch Manjushri discovered the lotus of the ancient Valley lake, stands the great stupa of **Swayambhunath**.

On all four sides of this ancient structure, looking out in all directions at the Valley below, are painted the eyes of the Buddha. Their gaze is one of compassion, an omnisighted stare from beneath heavy black eyebrows. Between them is a mystic third eye, symbolic of true wisdom. The nose, with the appearance of an incomplete question mark, is the Nepalese number *ek* or "one," a symbol of unity.

There is little doubt that this sacred site was established more than 2,500 years ago. Well before the advent of Buddhism, there must have been a monument here: a projecting stone which later became the central element of the stupa. Emperor Ashoka may have visited in the 2nd Century B.C., and an inscription dated at 460 A.D. says King Manadeva I carried out construction work on the site. By 1234, Swayambhunath was an important center of Buddhist learning, closely linked with Lhasa.

The shrine was destroyed by a Bengal sultan's troops in 1346. But it was rebuilt, and in the mid-17th Century King Pratap Malla made several renovations. He improved access to Kathmandu with a long approach stairway and a bridge across the Bishnumati River; he also built two new *shikharas* (temples) and added a big *vajra* (symbolic thunderbolt).

Today, 300 flagstoned steps lead to the terrace on which the stupa is built. Three stone Buddhas, daubed with yellow and red, sit at the bottom. At regular intervals up the steps are pairs of stone animals, the vehicles of the gods. These beasts are harmless; not so the monkeys, who slide down the stairway's metal handrails and pilfer anything visitors fail to protect.

The construction of a stupa adheres to specific rules, and Swayambhunath is a model of its kind. Each segment has a symbolic meaning. Its dazzling white hemispherical mound represents the four ele-

Preceding pages: Bodhnath at sunset. Below, The eyes of Swayambhunath.

116

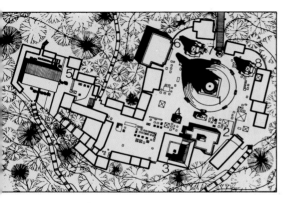

tone
uddhas in
e mist.

niche containing a fifth Buddha, facing the stairway. It is flanked by two pairs of benign, sculpted monks. At the sub-cardinal points are images of the Taras.

Around the stupa runs a row of prayer wheels, each turned by the faithful during a clockwise circumambulation. In their actions, Buddhist devotees symbolically turn the wheel of the law, representing the cycle of life and death.

In the *gompa* (monastery) facing the stupa, there is a daily service at 4 p.m. Onlookers are fascinated by the incense, the chanting and the deafening sound of trumpets. At other times, you will often see families exiting the *gompa* after meeting with the *rimpoche*. The father may be wearing a red ribbon around his neck. He takes his shoes off, kneels and prostrates himself several times in front of the main shrine. His wife and daughters, bejeweled and wearing their best saris, imitate him. They dot their foreheads with *tika*, the votive vermilion.

Images of the goddesses Ganga and Jamuna, masterpieces of Newari bronze art, guard the eternal flame in a cage behind the stupa. Here, on behalf of the

ments – earth, fire, air, water. The 13 gilded rings on the spire are the 13 degrees of knowledge, and represent the ladder to *nirvana*, which itself is symbolized by the umbrella at the top.

At the four cardinal points, four niches – richly adorned with repousse copper work – shelter the same number of Buddhas. These *dhyani* Buddhas are in four separate postures of meditation. One of these primary niches is abutted by another

faithful, a priest makes offerings to the sacred fire, symbol of the first appearance of the Adhi-Buddha.

At festival times, a human sea sweeps around the stupa. There is *puja*, *tika*, vermilion powder galore, the lighting of hundreds of small butter lamps, the making of offerings, and picnicking under the many trees.

A delightful legend tells how Manjushri had his hair cut at Swayambhunath, each hair subsequently becoming a tree, and the lice becoming monkeys.

On a neighboring hill stands another more subdued stupa, flanked by a *gompa* and a shrine dedicated to Saraswati, the goddess of wisdom and learning. School children bring their pen and ink here to be blessed during Basant Panchami, the festival of knowledge.

At the foot of the hill, the Tibetan refugee community has prospered. Many *gompas* have been built in triumphant shades of white, red and black. New houses, shops and carpet factories have spread amongst the brick factories and farmland across the ring road, under the all-seeing gaze of the stupa's eyes.

Bodhnath's Simple Beauty: The other great stupa of the Valley, and indeed, the largest in all of Nepal, is Bodhnath. Sitting on flat land as a crown above pastel-painted facades of shops and houses, its massive *mandala* design, supposedly a copy of Gyangtse in Tibet, dominates the northeast of the Valley with its size and power.

Bodhnath's great size and its red, white and blue-painted eyes, more remarkable even than Swayambhunath's, give it a striking appearance. The stupa combines planes and surfaces in a manner that can only be called simple, even austere; but it is done with a powerful effect. Built on concentric, gradually ascending, terraces – with the overall pattern of a *mandala* – the monument has a wide flight of steps leading to its base.

Along the stupa's base is a ring of 108 small inset images of the Buddha Amitabha. Surrounding the triple deck of platforms is an almost round brick wall with 147 niches, holding four or five prayer wheels each. Bodhnath's powerful silhouette is not interrupted by other structures; instead, the stupa shape is strongly emphasized by smaller stupas lying to its east, below the main stupa.

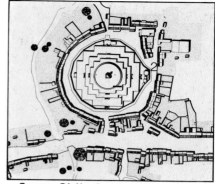

Goose Girl's Legacy: Worshipped mainly by Tibetan Buddhists, this stupa has always been linked to Lhasa. Its origin is a bit obscure. Legend says it was built by a woman named Kangma, born in supernatural circumstances as a swineherd's daughter after being banished from Indra's heaven for stealing flowers. In adult life, widowed with four children, she accumulated a fortune from her labors as a goose girl. She requested the king to give her as much ground as the hide of a buffalo would cover, so that she could build a temple to Buddha Amitabha. The king agreed. Kangma shrewdly cut the hide into thin strips, joined them, and stretched them out to form the square on which the Bodhnath stupa now stands.

A complete township has been built around Bodhnath. New monasteries great and small, chapels, private houses, shops, country liquor bars, lodges and carpet factories are all flourishing additions to the neighborhood. The small shops around the stupa are an inviting place for visitors to buy a variety of exotic items.

Mantras and Incense: At the start of the Tibetan New Year, normally in February by the Western calendar, people from far and near come to Bodhnath to watch *lamas* perform year-opening rites. Tibetans from the northern regions of Nepal, Buddhists from India and Ladakh, Sikkimese, Bhutanese and others arrive in traditional brown and dark blue dress, heavily decorated with corals and turquoise. Among the human tide, a few men sport Western garb but their fists wave smoking incense sticks. Professional beggars chant *mantras* and clap their hands.

Nearby crouch a few old women, their wrinkled hands mechanically counting the beads of their rosaries. On the stupa, the devout hoist long rows of multicolored

Lamas worship at Bodhnath.

prayer flags, blessing them first with juniper incense. They gather to pray in a colorful ceremony under the direction of magenta-robed *lamas* who blow great copper horns. At the climax of prayers, all throw fistfuls of *tsampa* (ground grain) into the air.

At the main entrance to the stupa, a dozen *lamas* position themselves in a double line. Other *lamas* walk majestically between them, holding a large portrait of the Dalai Lama under a canopy. People lunge forward to touch the portrait, tripping over themselves. The *lamas* retire into the monastery, some of them to prepare for hours of masked dances they will perform for spectators in a nearby field.

Other dances are performed in a monastery courtyard by professional troupes from Tibetan centers in India. There is much merriment and drink flows freely. The celebrations go on into the night, long after sunset fires the snow peaks and stars wheel about the soaring gold finial of the great stupa.

The Stupas of Chabahil: The stupa at **Chabahil**, about 1,500 meters west of Bodhnath, is basically of the same type as its towering neighbor, but is much smaller and more primitive looking. Its brick, stepped tower is too long for the rather plump, hemispherical mound on its narrow platform, but it is typical of the early stupas built in the Valley.

The village of Chabahil, just across the Dhobi Khola river from Kathmandu, has almost merged with the capital through 20th-Century urban sprawl. But during Licchavi times, it was an important rural settlement of its own account, situated at the junction of the Valley's two main roads – the one across the Bagmati River leading to Patan, and the one from the Kasthamandap running between India and Tibet.

King Ashoka's daughter Charumati, who lived here, is said to have been responsible for the construction of the stupa. She and her husband later retreated to two Buddhist monasteries they also built. One of those monasteries is supposedly the same one located nearby the stupa.

Around the Chabahil stupa are small votive Licchavi *chaityas* (reliquaries) in stone, with many of their small niches emptied of their Buddha images, and some

Celebrating Tibetan New Year.

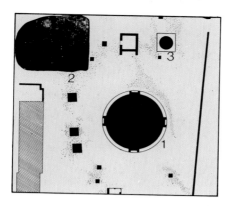

CHABAHIL
1-Dhando Chaitya
2-pokhari
3-chaitya

culture outside Tibet. Many Buddhist monasteries have sprung up recently in the immediate vicinities of Bodhnath and Swayambhunath.

Near Pharping, just outside the Valley southeast of Patan, Tibetans have built a white, castle-like monastery on a forested slope at the entrance to the **Gorakhnath Cave**, formerly a hermit's refuge now turned into a thriving center of Tibetan worship.

This cave bears the name of one of the ancient sages who meditated here. On the platform in front of the cave are his footprints, which according to the inscription, were carved in 1390. Tibetan Buddhists consider this site sacred to Padma Sambhava, the "second Buddha" who introduced Buddhism to Tibet. His image and those of other deities inside the cave date from the 18th Century.

Nearby, at the shrine of **Sekh Narayan**, sacred to Hindus, Tibetans have raised a monastery to commemorate the visit of the great Tibetan saint, Guru Padma Sambhava. Legend says he came here to meditate and to vanquish hordes of troublesome demons.

other classical Buddhist stone pieces. The most magnificent, one of the great sculptures of the Valley, is a 9th Century statue of a free-standing *bodhisattva* cut in black stone about one meter high, with smooth limbs and the tightly curled hair often seen on late Licchavi images.

Tastes of Tibet: With a community of Tibetan exiles estimated at about 12,000, the Kathmandu Valley has become one of the most flourishing centers of Tibetan

Rhapsody in blue at Chabahil.

VISHNU SHRINES: THE WIDE-STRIDER

Between the 5th and 15th centuries, Hinduism expanded around the trinity of Brahma, Vishnu and Shiva. Vishnu was originally a minor Vedic deity. In the *Vedas*, he allied himself with Indra to conquer demons. He fooled a demon by changing from dwarf to giant, encompassing in three strides the earth, the air and heaven, a scene often depicted in stone or bronze imagery.

By the time the *Mahabharata* epic was composed, the "wide-strider" had become "The One Being of All." In the epic poem, he helped the five Pandava brothers, assuming two incarnations as the black Krishna and his white brother, Balarama. As the flute-playing man-god who frolicked with the *gopis*, Krishna was a most popular figure.

A god with a thousand names, Vishnu comes in various forms and incarnations. In the earliest texts, he is identified with the lion, his vehicle. As the god Narayan, Vishnu is most often depicted lying on the cosmic ocean.

In the Kathmandu Valley, King Hari Datta established Narayan shrines not only as a means of veneration of Vishnu but also perhaps as a placement of political structure, a way to delimit his own kingdom. Later, however, the cult of Shiva predominated among the people. Later still, during the early Mallas, around 1390, King Jayasthiti Malla revived the Vishnu cult of the Vishnava sect, claiming to be an incarnation of Vishnu, a claim maintained until today by successive rulers.

Since that time, one simple Vishnu shrine has stood in front of each former royal palace in the Valley. There are other important Vishnu temples and shrines within towns, and half a dozen more sacred shrines dedicated to the god scattered in the Valley. None is more impressive than Budhanilkantha.

The Reclining Vishnu: In dreamless sleep, Vishnu as Narayan floated partly submerged in the primeval ocean, Nara, like a fetus in its maternal womb. A lotus grew out of his navel, issuing Brahma who then proceeded to create the world. This Indian

Preceding pages: The famous reclining Vishnu: 'robed' in red and below, in flowers.

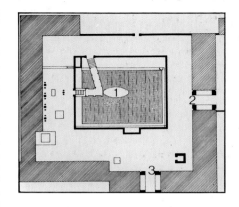

tale of the world's origin is Hinduism's most famous cosmic myth, a source of great inspiration for artists in the subcontinent. But nowhere else have sculptors translated it into stone so powerfully and so literally, as the Nepalis did at **Budhanilkantha**, a small hamlet nine kilometers (5½ miles) north of Kathmandu.

Some 1,400 years ago, a five-meter (16-foot) stone image of Narayan, the ultimate source and creator of life, was placed in a small pond at the foot of the Shivapuri Hills. Man had apparently dragged the huge black stone a long way, probably from outside the Valley, to this spot at the Valley's edge, where a small settlement had grown up by Licchavi times. This hamlet may have been a satellite of the famous nearby Licchavi town called Thatungri Dranga. Today only old bricks mark the site where it stood, a little northeast of Budhanilkantha.

Vishnu, as Narayan, reclines serene upon a bed made from the coils of a huge snake, Ananta. Eleven of Ananta's hoods rise up to form an elaborate oval-shaped outer crown encircling the god's diademed head. Even while he sleeps, Vishnu

open his eyes to the sky above.. He is placid and comfortable: his legs are crossed at the ankles and, aside from some large ornaments, he wears only a loose *dhoti*. His four arms hold four attributes: the discus (symbol of the mind) in the upper right hand, the mace (primeval knowledge) in the upper left hand, a conch (the five elements) in the lower left hand, and a lotus seed (the moving universe) in the lower right hand.

Worshippers descend a small stone walkway to the recessed water tank and perform their rituals from a wooden platform near the reclining figure. Every morning at 9 o'clock, a priest goes into the basin to wash the god's face and make similar offerings while attendants ring bells.

The Festival of Budhanilkantha is one of the big events in the Valley in Kartik (October-November), commemorating Vishnu's awakening. But even on ordinary days, pilgrims abound at this important and popular shrine. Unfortunately "restoration" has replaced the colored ceramic tiles with which the tank was lined and "protected" it with an intrusive concrete fence. Even so it is hard to detract from the power of the massive black sculpture in the cosmic ocean of the pond. The surrounding *paths* (shelters) and *dharmasalas* (rest houses) are full of activity, however, and there is a commanding view from the art deco south gates across the Valley.

The Licchavis sculpted at least three of these almost-identical Vishnu images, all of them lost for centuries. The one at Budhanilkantha, which is the largest, was the first to be found.

The second Vishnu image to be found was in Balaju. The third one, supposedly dug up near the central part of the Valley where the Licchavis once had their main settlement, was brought to the royal palace in Kathmandu for King Pratap Malla in the 1600s. This monarch had a small canal built in order to bring water in a constant flow from the natural spring at Budhanilkantha down to his palace.

A fourth reclining Vishnu image from the later Malla period is to be found within the sacred precincts of Pashupatinath, behind the main shrine.

A forecast of death forbids the kings of Nepal, themselves incarnations of Vishnu, from looking at the monumental image in Budhanilkantha, but the kings may view the other three Vishnu images, as they are believed – rightly or wrongly – to be only replicas of the Budhanilkantha original.

A beautiful pastoral walk leads through paddy fields from Budhanilkantha to Kathmandu.

The Priceless Treasures of Changu Narayan: The temple of **Changu Narayan**,

The great temple of Changu Narayan on a sunlit ridgetop beneath the clouds.

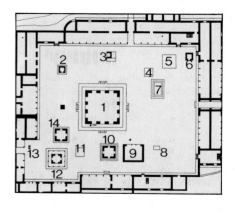

built on a hilltop some 12 kilometers (7 miles) east of Kathmandu, reached by road from behind Bhaktapur, was completely rebuilt after a fire destroyed it in 1702. Its origins go back to the 4th Century.

The traditional and most scenic access starts from the Sankhu road and proceeds across the Manohara River. It is a good 40 minutes' walk up the hill to the large temple bathed in sunshine. As you walk through the main entrance, you are greeted by a couple of stone elephants. You pass some small temples, then encounter a twin-roofed pagoda and the main two-tiered temple.

To the right, another temple has two important stones. These are an allegoric version of a lion-headed Vishnu Narsingh, dismembering the king of the demons, who is stepping on his fallen crown; and Vishnu Vikrantha, a dwarf with six arms.

Behind these, on a small terrace, is erected a slab of flat black stone with its top right corner broken. At its bottom is Narayan reclining on Ananta; in the center is Vishnu, with 10 heads and 10 arms going through the different layers of the universe. This beautiful priceless piece of the 5th or 6th Century is surrounded by half a dozen more images dating back to the 9th Century.

There is an image of Garuda, the mythical bird that serves as Vishnu's heavenly vehicle, in front of the main temple; it also dates to the 5th or 6th Century. Beside it is one of the oldest and most important Licchavi inscriptions in the Valley.

Apart from various Vishnu and Garuda

images, and graceful statues of Bupathin-dra Malla and his queen in a gilded cage, there is one more very interesting feature here. This is the paving of the temple-wide platform. In the central part, triangular bricks are used; in the periphery, old bricks with completely rounded edges are employed. The vast courtyard is surrounded by various buildings which are used as resthouses for pilgrims and a school.

From this sanctuary, there is a sweeping view over the surrounding countryside. To the east, a path slides down to **Changu**, which holds ruins of the Licchavi period. A very pleasant two-hour walk east along the ridge brings you to the Nagarkot road. The motorable road to Bhaktapur branches off to the right at the far side of the village.

The Cave Where Shiva Hid: Another spectacular view of the Valley is the main reason to visit the **Bishankhu Narayan**, which may be reached by a dirt road that branches off the Godavari road toward the east, beyond the village of Bandegaon. Although it is one of the most celebrated Vishnu shrines in the Valley, it is only a natural twisting rock cave, sitting in the saddle of a range that separates the Godavari

area from the Valley proper. A steep, narrow stairway cut into the rock leads to a wooden platform in front of a tiny opening to the cave, where free-formed stones are usually protected by a lattice of metal links.

The connection to Vishnu is through a legend: Shiva once hid here from the demon Bhasmasur, who had obtained from him the power to turn all living things into ashes and dust by a touch of the hand. Vishnu convinced the demon to touch his own forehead, and the demon turned himself to dust. The hillock adjacent to the cave is said to be made up of the ashes of Bhasmasur.

Laundry and Erotic Carvings: The rock temple of **Sekh Narayan** is located at the foot of the Gorakhnath hillock on the east side of the Pharping road, at the southern fringe of the Valley. At this point, the road twists at a sharp angle. There are four pools set at two different levels. By the bottom ones, women wash themselves and their laundry, some of which is spread out to dry in an abstract composition.

In the waters of a pond green with algae, a 13th-Century Surjya panel and an image of Surjya, the sun god often identified with Vishnu, are reflected half-submerged. Along the footpath, set into a wall, is a graceful early image of Shiva and Parvati.

Two stone stairways link the pool area with the Sekh Narayan temple, some 50 feet above the upper pool. It has been a place of pilgrimage since at least the early-15th Century. The temple sits snugly at the base of the ochre yellow overhanging cliff. It is a small, dark, single-story structure in wood and metal, with erotic carvings on its struts. Vishnu's stone-carved figure is the main image inside.

The 14th-Century bas-relief of Vishnu Vikrantha is the latest (and most inferior) of four sculptures found in the Valley depicting this particular incarnation. Here, one of his feet is raised to heaven, the other planted on earth. More powerful, probably older, but incomplete, is another stone sculpture of Vishnu next to the Vishnu Vikrantha. Vishnu's left leg is also raised but his knee remains bent.

The religious shrines throughout this area are superbly integrated into exceptionally beautiful natural surroundings. Near the top of the same hillock is the cave of Gorakhnath, and above it is yet another temple, the **Bajra Jogini**. Nearby is the

Submerged Surjya at Sekh Narayan.

Dakshinkali Shrine at the confluence of two streams.

A Fish in the Mustard Fields: Further west, in the immediate vicinity of **Machhegaon**, the neglected site of **Machhe Narayan** is reached from either Kirtipur or the Raj Path via a small foot-path meandering through mustard fields, bamboo groves and clusters of rural houses. Every third year, thousands of people from all over the Valley come to this shrine, which celebrates Vishnu's incarnation as a fish.

The small stone temple occupies the center of a sacred stone-walled tank shadowed by trees, with two simple public ponds flanking it. The gargoyles here are no longer spouting water, and the water in the ponds is stagnant and murky.

But in the sanctum, among images of other gods, is a sculpture of Machhe Narayan emerging from the mouth of a fish. Don't be surprised, however, if you are told – perhaps even by the priest himself – that "the priest is not here" to open the shrine.

Two Smaller Shrines: During the month of Kartik (October-November), thousands of worshippers begin a day's pilgrimage to **Ichangu Narayan**, then proceed to Changu Narayan, Bishankhu Narayan and Sekh Narayan. The Ichangu Narayan shrine is northwest of Swayambhunath, surrounded by clumps of trees and open fields. The two-story temple was built in the 18th Century on a site where, according to legend, King Hari Datta founded this Narayan temple in the 4th Century. The usual attributes of Vishnu can be seen within the walled compound. Note the stone pillars and carved struts. A Brahmin priest conducts daily worship. There is a lovely walk from here to Balaju.

Dhum Varahi, on the northeastern outskirts of Kathmandu, offers a weird scene on a windy day when leaves are blown away against a gray sky. On an open field overlooking the Dhobi Khola stand two huge trees, one of which – a pipal – crushes between its roots a brick shrine containing one of the most outstanding pieces of sculpture from the 6th Century Licchavi period – an almost life-sized stone sculpture of Vishnu's incarnation as a half-man, half-boar, rescuing the goddess Earth. A visit to this shrine can be incorporated in the walk from Budhanilkantha to Kathmandu.

Changu
Narayan.

SHIVA SHRINES: THE GREAT GOD

receding ages: At ashupa- nath: a isiting adhu. Left, king a dip the sacred agmati ver. Below ft, Pashu- atinath. ight, Shiva nd lingum.

Shiva is a composite god. He is both Destroyer and Creator, at once the end of things and the beginning of new ones. Terrible, he is Bhairav ("The Cruel") or Rudra or Ugra or Shava ("The Corpse"). Peaceful, he is Mahadeva ("The Great God") or Ishwara ("The Lord") or Pashupati ("The Lord of the Beasts").

Shiva is usually represented as a light-skinned man with a blue throat, five faces, four arms and three eyes. He holds a trident (the symbol of lightning), a sword, a bow, and a mace topped with a skull. Together with his son Ganesh, the elephant-headed god, he is the most helpful god in the Kathmandu Valley – if also the most awesome. In other representations, he may be seen wrapped in three snakes, one of which is considered to be the sacred cord of Brahmins. As Bhuteshvara, "Lord of the Evil Spirits," he haunts cemeteries; in fact, there still exists one Shaivite sect that eats corpses.

Sometimes Shiva is seen as a disheveled, unkempt holy man, the shame of the pantheon. Today, many of his faithful *sanyasins* and *sadhus* swarm from all over India and Nepal to celebrate the festival of Shivaratri at **Pashupatinath** in February or March. It is here, at this most sacred of all Nepalese Shiva shrines, that Shiva's dual aspects are best depicted.

The Shepherd of Fertility: Throughout the year, Shiva is worshipped at Pashupatinath as a *lingum*, or phallus. His vehicle, Nandi the bull, is regarded as an ancient symbol of fecundity. Indeed, Shiva as Pashupati displays only his sweeter side: a shepherd of animals and humans, and prime inheritor of original Vedic beliefs of fertility.

Perhaps the most interesting way to reach Pashupatinath, five kilometers (three miles) east of Kathmandu, is to follow the ancient route of pilgrims. This is a picturesque road which in ancient times was a symbolic link between the temporal power of the king and the spiritual power of Shiva. King Pratap Malla had it built as a flagstone highway.

Today, the route crosses the Dhobi Khola River by a steel bridge, closed to

traffic. It traverses the Pashupatinath Plateau, the probable site of the former Licchavi capital of Deopatan, then reaches a crossroads. Here you'll see a large *dharmasala* which opens onto an inner courtyard sheltering pilgrims and dying sacred cows. The road continues through a large expanse of brownish grass where monkeys prance through scattered trees. Eventually you pass through a hamlet. The approach to the temple is on the right-hand side of the road.

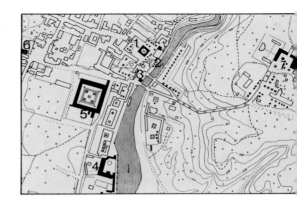

The main square in front of the temple is occupied by petty vendors and peddlers selling necklaces, rings, plastic bangles and toys, mirrors, small bowls full of tiny buttons, black stones inlaid with shells, tangerines and mangoes.

Entrance to the temple precinct is forbidden to non-Hindus. Notices on either side of the much-decorated gate make that abundantly clear, and policemen are there to remind you. But as you look from outside, you can catch a glimpse of the pigeons swarming on a huge structure of Nandi, and you'll also see a small Hanuman statue under its umbrella.

This large, gilded, triple-roofed temple was built in 1696. (Like many Valley temples, it has decorative roofs without corresponding floors.) Nearly 300 years earlier, there was a structure on this site, and its importance probably goes back long before that.

Immediately to the left of the temple, there is a ramp with a few steps of carved stone slabs, recycled from former Licchavi structures. The ramp leads to a small hill named after the famous Mount Kailash.

Visitors at Pashupatinath: left, pilgrims, and right, yogi.

From a grassy platform strewn with a few stone *lingas*, there is a good view of the whole Pashupatinath site.

The temple complex is a rather unhappy mixture of corrugated iron roofs clustered around the gilded triple roof of the temple. The sacred **Bagmati River**, which borders the complex, twists into a gorge on your left. Two bridges span the river and lead from the main village street of Pashupatinath to a stairway climbing the wooded hill on the east bank. Before the bridges to your left are *ghats* reserved for the cremation of royalty. Those *ghats* to the right are for commoners and are popular spots for bathing.

The *ghats* are a popular place for celebrations at various times of the year. Saturdays are particularly busy days. On votive days, and at the end of their menstrual cycles, women come here to purify themselves, changing into new *saris* afterward. This area is also noted for the local craft of block-printing textiles. In the hamlet, artisans dip their wooden blocks into green, black and red dye. They print square or lozenge patterns about 10 centimeters (four inches) wide. Pools of white cotton are put out to dry on mats along the streets. On the opposite bank, just in front of the temple, are 11 identical stone *chaityas* containing *lingas*. They are lined up at the foot of a terraced retaining wall stepping up toward the hill. Before the construction of the *chaityas*, there were hermits' and *sadhus'* caves here.

Along the road going around the grassy platform away from the river stands a small two-story 18th-Century temple. It is dedicated to Pashupati's legendary teacher, Guru Dakshina Murti, and has erotic carvings on its struts. Other erotic scenes and colorful Tantric representations can be found in the small two-roofed **Bachhareshwari Temple** of the 6th Century, located on the western *ghats*.

On the left bank of the river, near one of the bridges, is a beautiful Buddha bust probably dating to the 7th Century. Today it is half-buried, but is an important vestige of the past.

Further down the river, the **Ram Temple** with its extensive courtyard shelters yogis and *sadhus* during festivals – especially the Shivaratri celebration, when ten thousands of pilgrims flock to Pashu-

patinath. The government provides them with a free meal and firewood every day of the festival.

Pashupatinath is one of the four most important pilgrimage sites in Asia for Shiva devotees, closely linked to orthodox south Indian Shaivism since the visit of Shankaracharya during the high tide of Buddhism in the Valley. This famous Brahmin cleaned up the Pashupatinath shrine, threw out the Buddhists, and established the strong rule of orthodox Shaivite belief.

Guhyeshwari and Gokarna's Mahadev: Friendly monkeys may escort you up the stepped path climbing the hill, which has many votive *shikharas* and shrines topped by Shiva *lingas*. Farther on, the path descends to the **Guhyeshwari Temple**. It first leads to the **Gorakhnath Shikhara**, a tall brick structure flanked by a large brass trident and surrounded by *paths* and *lingas* on a wide platform.

The paved track meandering down the hill through shady trees eventually leads you to the Guhyeshwari Temple. This is a shrine of Shiva's *shakti* in her manifestation as Kali. Again, its entrance is forbidden to non-Hindus. Some child will no

doubt be quick to raise the alarm if you creep up the stairs to catch a glimpse of the beautiful gilded structure of the temple, ornamented with flags in front.

Beyond Pashupatinath and Bodhnath the road divides; go straight on to the Gokarna Safari Park entrance and eventually, Sankhu. Turn left to the village of Gokarna, on the banks of the Bagmati, and another important Shiva shrine: the majestic, three-roofed **Mahadev Temple**, now beautifully restored. This shrine sits atop three sets of irregularly shaped stone stairways, following the natural contour of the river bank. Shiva lies on a stone bed of cobras just above where the steps enter the water.

The temple was built in 1582. It is surrounded by a sort of outdoor "sculpture garden," featuring a multitude of gods and goddesses. Its upper gilt roof – which boasts a finial, trident, bells, pots and birds as decorations – glistens against a backdrop of green hillsides, fringed on top with tall trees. The inner sanctum houses a much-venerated *lingum*. On the approach steps is a small single story prayer hall, the Vishnu Paduka, built during the 19th Cen-

Guhyeshwari in the 19th Century.

KARNA
AHADEV
Mahadev
Vishnu
Paduka
Parvati

tury. It contains 16 metal plaques and displays Vishnu's foot-print embedded in the stone floor. This is an important place for after-death ceremonies.

None has the aesthetic power of Parvati, the finest and oldest image at Gokarna, standing inside a small isolated shrine between the temple and the main road. Sculpted in the 8th Century, Parvati holds in her left hand a lotus stem. Her figure, beautifully modeled with round, full, high breasts, slim waist and long limbs, rises from the simple oval of a lotus pedestal. Robed for protection from art robbers in glittering garments, adorned by fine jewels and a tall crown, the transcendent lotus goddess embodies the heavenly female. You can walk from here to Bodhnath.

The **Tika Bhairav** is a shrine of an altogether different register. It shows the darker side of Shiva as the terrible Bhairav.

To reach this shrine, you must travel outside the Kathmandu Valley to the Lele Valley, which adjoins it to the southeast. The shrine is situated on a peninsula made by the confluence of two rivers south of Chapagaon. Its site is marked by an enormous *sal* tree.

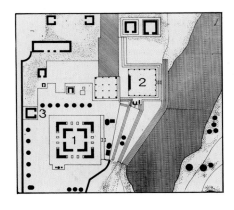

Don't look for a temple. Just walk past the few houses on the edge of the plateau, and continue to one of the most pleasant surprises in Nepal: a monumental, multicolored fresco showing a closeup of Bhairav's face in almost abstract design. The painting is on a three-by-six-meter (10-by-20 foot) brick wall. A simple brick platform constitutes the altar, and a dingy metal roof serves as shelter. Once a year, thousands of people come here to worship Bhairav.

GANESH SHRINES: GOD OF LUCK

Ganesh, the elephant-headed god, is one of the most popular divinities in Hinduism, and is certainly the most popular in the Kathmandu Valley.

Regarded as a god of good luck who casts obstacles aside, he is consulted by one and all before any task is undertaken – be it a journey, the building of a house, or even the writing of a letter. Ganesh must be invoked early every morning. Tuesdays and Saturdays are particularly propitious days to honor him.

There are differing legends as to his ascendency. Commonly believed to be the son of Shiva and Parvati, Ganesh is usually represented as a white-skinned deity with a fat, round belly. His elephant head has only one tusk, the other having been broken. His four arms hold a conch, a discus, a mace or goad, and a lotus or water lily. He travels on a shrew and is greedy for offerings of food, especially fruit. He has two wives, Siddhi and Buddhi.

Ganesh shrines are numerous in all Newar settlements in the Valley. Four shrines are particularly sacred: Chandra Binayak in Chabahil, Suriya Binayak near Bhaktapur, Karya Binayak near Bungamati, and Jal Binayak near Chobar.

Shrines for Disease Cures And Marriage Picnics: Two hundred meters (650 feet) west of the Chabahil stupa, in the middle of the village, is the **Chandra Binayak.** This double-tiered, brass-roofed temple houses a tiny Ganesh. The god sits on a golden tympanum, with twin flags and bells in front of him on either side. A brass shrew waits for Ganesh atop a big pillar in front of the shrine. Struts depict the eight forms of Bhairav and the eight mother goddesses.

People of all creeds come to this shrine to worship Ganesh. It is believed he can cure diseases and external bodily injuries.

South of Bhaktapur, halfway up the foothills in the southeastern part of the valley, is the **Suriya Binayak**. The Ganesh image here, merely a stone in the shape of the god, has been traced to the 17th Century. It is considered able to give the power of speech to children who are slow

Classic Ganesh image.

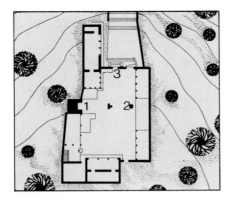

A tall brick and plaster structure marks the main sanctuary. There is also a *hiti* with a carved stone tap. Figures of devotees kneel nearby.

This is a favorite spot among the Nepalese for marriage picnics. If you encounter one here, you may be invited to join the guests for a hearty meal and heartier drinks. The bride and groom will be watching over the gathering from the first door of the *pati*, on one side of the rocky precinct.

Shrines for Completing Tasks And Strengthening Character: In a forest preserve between the villages of Bungamati and Khokana, south of Kathmandu, lies the **Karya Binayak**.

From the road linking the hamlets, a path leads uphill to a beautiful clearing and a small walled compound with a single-roofed shrine. Families often come here to ask Ganesh for help in completing difficult tasks.

In the shrine's altar is a free-shaped stone that takes significance in Ganesh cults as a symbol of the god.

A little below the shrine, and off to one side, is a brick building with a vaulted roof. Pilgrims are sheltered in the three

Shrine at Suryja Binayak.

to talk; this makes it a popular spot for family visits. The image is flanked by a pillar with representation of a shrew (Ganesh's vehicle) and a bell.

The path to the shrine starts from a bridge across the Hanumante River. It heads uphill, passes through a large gateway constructed by the Ranas, and leads up an open stone-paved stairway into a small enclosed space in the middle of dense forest.

arcades here. From this tranquil compound, where the only sounds one can hear are the babble of a nearby brook and the cries of crows in surrounding trees, there is a splendid view of the Bagmati Valley and the western foothills.

Jal Binayak: Those persons seeking strength of character go to worship Ganesh at **Jal Binayak**, situated outside Chobar Gorge. Whole Newar families, dressed in bright saris and smart suits, wearing perfume and jewelry, often make pilgrimages here. You may see them carrying small trays with offerings like flowers, eggs, powders or incense.

Pilgrims such as these may have been coming here for centuries before the present temple, with its three tiers of roofs, was constructed in 1602. A worn sculpture of Uma Maheshwar, carved about 500 years before the shrine was erected, can still be seen on the square base platform of the **Jal Binayak.**

The main image of the shrine is a massive rock. It extends outside the temple at the back; only a small part in front vaguely resembles an elephant tusk. Devotees apparently built the temple to shelter this

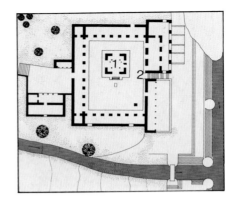

object of devotion.

On the struts are carved eight Bhairavs and the eight mother goddesses, or Ashta Matrikas. Ganesh always appears together with these goddesses.

Half of the struts on the lower roof depict Ganesh himself flanked by a beautiful damsel; lush branches above her figure suggest this may be a tree goddess. There are tiny erotic carvings below both Ganesh and the female.

Ganesh's shrew at Jal Binayak.

SHRINES FOR FEMALE DEITIES

Hindu mythology has no lack of female deities. But auspicious forms of goddesses are relatively few, and these will inevitably take on ferocious, fierce, bloodthirsty appearances. The most important of all these goddesses is **Devi** or **Maha Devi**, "The Great Goddess." As Parvati, Shiva's *shakti*, she follows the moods and forms of her male counterpart. But more than this, she actually dominates him.

Shiva is represented as being at peace with himself, totally passive. His *shakti* is the dynamic element of the relationship. When they engage in sexual intercourse, Shiva is at ease while Parvati is extremely energetic. When Shiva is depicted in his corpse form as Shava, his *shakti* is attempting to arouse him sexually. The image of the goddess as the active element has taken over in popular belief.

Shaktism as a cult devoted to the female is a return to the primitive cult of the cosmic mother goddess. When the Aryans conquered India, they overturned these phallic cults, reversing the female-male order with Vedic and Brahmin gods. But when the *Upanishads* were composed about 600 B.C., the neolithic Bronze Age goddess was depicted as having far greater wisdom than the patriarchal Aryan gods themselves.

Maha Devi the Terrible: The innermost shrine of a mother-goddess temple has a form symbolic of the female organ. There are many examples of this throughout the Valley. Even Buddhism, in its Tantric form, is not immune from the mood: "Buddhahood abides in the female organ," states one of its late aphorisms. Placing the human female in the center of the symbolic system, the Tantric Shakti cult makes each living couple a symbol – and hence, an incarnation – of Shiva and Parvati, thus justifying sexual coupling as a ritual to reach the divine.

Just as Shiva has thousands of names and incarnations, so does Maha Devi, his *shakti*. She is the black goddess Kali, "The Dark One," and Durga, "The Terrible of Many Names." From her womb, she is forever giving birth to all things. But Maha

Devi's stomach is a void which can never be filled. She craves for the ambrosia of blood – blood of demons, of animals, of human beings. In centuries past, human sacrifices were universally characteristic of cults of worship for the goddess. They were officially banned in Nepal in 1780 and in India in 1835.

There are many shrines in the Valley dedicated to the cult of female deities. Many more contain decorations or statues of such deities.

There are four principal shrines for *joginis*, or mystical goddesses. These are located in or near Sankhu, Guhyeshwari, Pharping and Vijeshwari.

Varahis – shaktis in the form of she-boars – portray the female aspect of the ultimate principal. They also have four main shrines which are scattered through the Valley.

Various other sites are consecrated to the Ashta Matrikas, the divine mother goddesses who attend both Shiva and Skanda, the god of war. They are frequently sculpted on the struts of temples, and are generally associated with the violent forms of the Tantric gods and goddesses.

Sankhu's Bajra Jogini: Hills encircle the ancient settlement of Sankhu in the north-eastern part of the Valley. They are covered with dense forests which hide a temple to a secret goddess, the **Bajra Jogini**. Halfway up the hillside, tucked away among tall, dark pines, her shrine is in a secluded spot fit for a Tantric deity.

Nepalese legend says the goddess has resided here from primeval history. She is credited with having persuaded Manjushri to drain the waters of the lake which once occupied the Valley floor.

To reach the shrine, follow a wide path, paved with stone, north from Sankhu for about 600 meters (0.4 mile). Then climb up a steep flight of steps to the temple. Along the stairway you will note a sanctum of Bhairav; it is marked by a large triangular stone with a gross Ganesh image on one side. Animal sacrifices are often made here.

The central temple is located amid a series of stupas containing four directional Buddhas. Its almost circular platform appears cut from rock. Built in the 17th Century, it has three roofs, struts with figures of various deities, and a golden

Goddess paraded to Sankhu Bajr

142

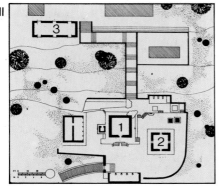

Sacrificial
Party at
Sankhu.

torana (rest over the door) portraying the Bajra Jogini as an unusually pleasant female figure. Within the temple sanctum, the goddess is flanked by her two traditional Nepalese companions, Simhini the lion son and Byaghrini the tigress daughter.

There is no god sheltered in the neighboring 16th Century, twin-roofed **Gunvihar Temple**, but there is a Swayambhu chaitya.

Behind this temple, a stone-paved path leads uphill to the **Bajra Jogini Dyochhen**. Locked inside the nondescript building are some of Nepal's most ancient and valuable sculptures. Among the most prized of which is a 7th Century head of the Buddha.

On the way to the *dyochhen*, you will pass a 10th Century water tank with a stone spout and a recessed, carved stone fountain at its center.

A chariot procession from Sankhu to the quiet site of this temple has been performed every year since the end of the 16th Century. You can walk from this area to Nagarkot.

The Temple at Pharping: Another temple of the same name and of the same period, a 17th Century **Bajra Jogini**, stands on a green hillside above Pharping, south of Kathmandu on the way to Dakshinkali.

A steep stone path from the village of Pharping merges into a stairway leading to the temple. Images of Bajra Jogini occupy two separate sanctums on the upper floor. She is also the central figure in *toranas* above her sanctums.

The Tantric goddess is identified by her awesome implements – the chopper with

a *vajra* handle and a skull cap. In all four representations here, her left leg is raised high, as if the artists who created her had been influenced by the much older Vishnu Vikrantha sculpture at the nearby Sekh Narayan Temple. Here again, against all "rules," Bajra Jogini has a pleasant face, pretty clothes, and as much heavy jewelry as any rich Nepali bride could want.

A path to the west leads to a small meditation cell. Above, the **Gorakhnath Cave** is marked by prayer flags hung from trees. In former times, this location was considered an ideal stopover place for pilgrims following a two or three-day walk from the Terai. From this hill, there is a fine view of the white Himalaya; below is Pharping, nestled on a plateau, with the wide expanse of the Kathmandu Valley beyond.

The Sacrifices of Dakshinkali: The most spectacular, regular, open religious worship performed in the Valley takes place where the main road south ends. Fittingly, this is at a shrine to the Dakshin, or "southern" Kali.

More animals are brought for sacrifice at the pit of Kali, situated at the bottom of

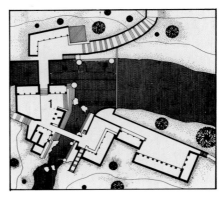

a long stairway, than to any other shrine. Twice a week, a large-scale massacre is staged; an even more incredible annual ritual is held during *Dasain*, with the image of Kali being bathed in blood.

The men who kill the buffaloes, goats, pigs, lambs, ducks, chickens and other animals – invariably uncastrated males – stand ankle-deep in their blood after slicing their throats or severing their heads. It is a gruesome scene to which visitors

Below, Dakshinkali sacrifice, gets a fearful glance from a Chhetri girl, right.

flock, packing the rest houses, shops and *patis*.

But the guided-tour atmosphere cannot break the spell created by the mystery of this dark spot. Situated in a natural recess between two ridges, at the spot where two streams unite between forested hillsides, it is a place of considerable beauty. Legends say that Kali herself commanded a 14th Century Malla king to build her this shrine here.

Now walled, it is decorated with brass tridents and a canopy adorned with snakes. Inside, the main Kali statue is of black stone. The six-armed goddess, trampling a male human, stands in the company of Ganesh, seven Ashta Matrikas, and a free-shaped stone of Bhairav.

The phenomenon of a "mother-daughter" shrine is notable at Dakshinkali. The path passing the lower shrine of Kali winds up a steep cone-shaped hill to the simpler shrine of her mother.

The eastern and northern slopes of the hillside on which shrines rest have grassy lawns, where worshippers often picnic – cooking and eating the sacrificed animals. Nearby, at the top of the stairs, where cars and buses are parked, the inevitable curio vendors do a thriving business. Peacock feather fans, bracelets, bangles and other trinkets are sold here.

A Tantric Temple: Of greater scenic, if not religious, interest, is the **Vajra Varahi Temple**. This site, one of the most important of Tantric origin in the Valley, is located in a small forest on a plateau east of Chapagaon.

The paths to the temple lead from Chapagaon through an interesting network of canals – some of them underground – with little round bridges, an exceptional indication of a sophisticated but long-forgotten irrigation and drainage system.

Beyond the canals are bright, open fields; you then pass through the dense cover of tall trees before reaching the temple.

The renovated Vajra Varahi was built in 1665, but the site existed long before that time. Various natural stones here are regarded as images of Ganesh, Bhairav and the Ashta Matrikas.

On the fringe of the forests are eight cremation grounds amidst vegetable

patches and mustard fields.

Shrine to a Demon Slayer: Outside the valley to the southeast is the **Chandeshwari Shrine**. From Banepa, the biggest settlement in the area, a path leads into a vale northeast of the hamlet. As you approach, you can see the shrine sitting on the right bank of a steeply sloping gorge. An annual chariot procession follows this route.

Legend says this entire valley was once crowded with wild beasts that the local folk regarded as demons. They called upon Parvati to rid them of Chand, a demon whom they particularly feared. When the goddess succeeded in her quest, she became known as Chandeshwari, "The Slayer of Chand."

In thanks, this shrine was built to her. It is a three-tiered temple in a wide precinct, with a lion and peacock on columns in front of the main altar. The *torana* and struts are richly carved with the customary eight Ashta Matrikas and eight Bhairavs.

In the sanctum is a free-standing image of the goddess Parvati, wearing rich silver ornaments. A multicolored fresco of Bhairav, painted on the western wall of the temple, is sometimes regarded as the shrine's main attraction.

Next to the temple is housed the image of Chandeshwar – in reality, Shiva, "The Master of the Slayer of Chand." He is recognizable by the image of Nandi the bull, Shiva's vehicle, facing the entrance. To complete the family gathering, Ganesh, the elephant-headed god, sits between the temple and Shiva's shrine.

Outside, just below the temple precinct, people come to wash and bathe in a pond by the brook. Three round *ghats* are located within a flight of five stairs near here; this is a place where the sick and the aged come to die.

Local folk look after them, and when the last moment nears, they prop the body up on an inclined plane between two of the *ghats*, so that the dying person's feet touch the sacred water of the stream and the head rests next to the tiny carving of Vishnu. Some of the holy water is given the dying person for a last drink, and he thus goes to a dignified death.

A bizarre fresco of Bhairav adorns the western wall of the Chandeshwari Shrine near Banepa.

THE VALLEY'S NATURE SITES

The Kathmandu Valley's first religious rites were associated with tangible natural landmarks, such as rivers and mountains, rocks and forests. The Valley's earliest inhabitants established their spiritual and ritual domain through this natural network. Each important site of worship is located on a propitious, if not grandiose, site. Swayambhunath, for example, is perched on a hilltop; Pashupatinath is hidden away in a gorge. Many other sites, no less sacred, are tucked into the lace of hills and forests surrounding the Valley.

Traditionally, it was the highest landmarks that became the most important centers of meditation and spiritual focus. Places that had remained above the waters of the primeval lake of Kathmandu were considered especially sacred. The smallest cave and the tiniest spring attracted meditating sages and legendary Buddhas. More prosaically, these uplands, draped in pine and fir, are tranquil scenic sites. Whether or not adorned by a stupa or a Hindu shrine, they are ideal for a stroll or a picnic.

The Legendary Gorge of Chobar: Your exploration of nature sites should begin with a visit to **Chobar Gorge**, through which – legend tells us – the waters of the lake of Kathmandu escaped after being released by Manjushri. This natural wonder, now much defaced with a huge cement factory, is located southwest of the city, where Chobar Hill, the highest point in a range of gentle hills, is sliced in two by the muddy waters of the Bagmati River.

The path to the top of this hill starts near the bank of the Bagmati at the hill's base. An impressive example of natural engineering and skillful design, the wide stone-paved track adjusts beautifully to the contour of the slope. After a series of steps and a pair of gates, it enters the courtyard of a Buddhist temple known as **Adinath Lokeswar**.

The most remarkable features of this triple-roofed structure – built in the 15th Century and reconstructed in 1640 – are the numerous water vessels, pots and pans nailed to boards all along the building. Below the golden *torana* depicting six Buddhas, the masked face of the Red Machhendra stares out from the main sanctum.

Facing the shrine, a stone *shikhara* is believed to be the entrance to a stone cave that cuts through the hill, emerging at the **Chobar Cave** below.

A suspension bridge, imported from Scotland and erected in 1903, spans the gorge. From halfway across, the view is impressive. On one side is the deep scar in Chobar Hill which legend says was cut by Manjushri's sword; probably, he had considerable help from an earthquake. Just to the south is the Jal Binayak shrine of Ganesh. Far below it, you can see women washing and bathing on a flight of stone steps which links two round cremation platforms.

Adventurous walkers can stop at Chobar en route from Kirtipur to Patan. Beyond the Chobar Gorge, the main road changes from bitumen to dust. It soon passes a small pond set scenically within open fields with small clusters of farmhouses scattered about. This is **Taudaha Lake**, which legend says was created by Manjushri himself so that the *nagas* (serpents) which had lived in the great

Preceding pages: religious sites 'flowered' in such towering forests. Left, the Jal Binayak temple at Chobar Gorge is a short walk from the mirror image at Adinath Lokeswar, right.

Valley lake could survive after he had drained it. Local folk believe the *nagas* still live here, and leave the pond's stagnant water to the wild ducks and the lotuses.

Summit of Two Trees: A beautiful mountain known as **Dinacho** ("Meditation Point") or **Champa Devi** rises here beyond the patch work of terraced fields. A single large tree crowns its summit; once there were a pair of trees at the top, and the peak still bears the nickname "Two Trees."

The Machhe Narayan temple complex is not much further west. It can be reached down the forested slopes of **Chandragiri**, "The Mountain of the Moon," capped by a small *chaitya* of Lord Buddha.

The road continues to the east, following the twists and turns of the Bagmati River from the heights. Contrasting panoramas unfold before it. In the foreground, sunshine brightens the ochre shades of a few houses resting in a fluctuating wave of green and mustard-yellow fields. In the distance, mist blurs the features of the Valley and the light blue peaks beyond.

Northeast of Kathmandu, the pilgrims' route that winds past Pashupatinath, Chabahil and Bodhnath soon skirts a forest grove preserved since before the time of the Licchavi monarchs. This grove, bordered by the holy Bagmati, was held sacred and spared from axe and hoe. It is said to be the place where Shiva himself once wandered, disguised as a beautiful golden deer under cover of the low forested hills.

Local people built a fine shrine, the Gokarna Mahadev temple on the river bank opposite the forest. Toward the end of the 19th Century, the grove was walled in and a deer park created. Known formerly as the King's Forest, the **Gokarna Safari Park** now operates a concession and visitors pay a fee to picnic or wander the roads and footpaths threading through the two-square-mile reserve. Several species of deer roam here, as well as black buck, monkeys and many colorful forest birds. There is even a caged tiger. Facilities include a scenic golf course and elephant and pony rides.

Several miles north of Gokarna, the Bagmati's nascent waters rush down the foothills above **Sundarijal** to be captured in a century-old reservoir encased by forested slopes and terraced, cultivated

Left, The Royal Botanical Garden. Right, Godavari Kunda.

**PULCHOWKI
MAI**
1-temple
2-Bhairav
 Shrine
3-Nau Dhara
 (tank).

**Doorway and
stone image
at Pulchowki
Mai.**

fields. This is one of the Valley's main water supplies. The approach road is particularly picturesque.

Where the road forks before the reservoir, the smaller trail leads east to a tiny rock cave. Inside is a 13th-Century stone image of Maha Devi, as well as free-shaped stones worshipped as **Sundara Mai** and the Ashta Matrikas. A later shrine housing a Shiva *lingum* honors Shiva and Parvati as deities of beauty; it is said they once rested in this simple cave when descending from their Himalayan abode on Mount Kailash-Meru.

Pulchowki and Godavari: Tallest of the foothills that encircle the Valley is **Pulchowki**, 20 kilometers (12½ miles) southeast of Kathmandu, beyond Godavari. A triple-peaked mountain culminating at 2,762 meters (9,062 feet), its name means "flower-covered hill." This it is, especially in spring, when pilgrims climb high to fetch blossoms – orchids, clematis vines and rhododendrons – for offerings to the mother of the forest, **Pulchowki Mai**, to whom two shrines have been built on the mountain.

One of these shrines is at the base of

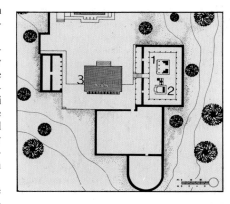

Pulchowki, not far from a roadside marble quarry. Built on a platform surrounded by dense forest, this three-roofed temple wears a dilapidated but attractive look. It is flanked by a single-story Ganesh temple and a grand 17th-Century *hiti* with nine spouts. The main icon within the shrine representing the goddess is only a free-shaped stone. As usual in a Tantric temple, the struts are carved with figures of the eight Ashta Matrikas.

This shrine is considered no more than

a lower-elevation substitute for the true **Pulchowki Shrine** above, at the apex of the mountain's central and highest peak. In this open shrine, the goddess is worshipped not only as mother of forests, but also as Lakshmi and Vasundhara, two goddesses of wealth, and as Varada, goddess of blessings.

The view from Pulchowki's summit can only be termed phenomenal. To the north, the whole Kathmandu Valley lies at your feet. Beyond, the snow-clad Himalayan range provides an incomparable backdrop. To the south, you gaze across the valleys of the lower hill ranges that lead into the Terai and India.

At the foot of Pulchowki, in the **Godavari** area, are located **St. Xavier's School**, one of two schools run by the Jesuits; the **Royal Botanical Garden**; the **Royal Department of Medicinal Plants**; and a fish farm. The botanical garden, entered upon payment of a small fee, has thatched-roof picnic shelters, lily ponds, rushing streams, and beds of seasonal flowers. Kept in greenhouses on the slope of the hill just above is a notable collection of orchids, ferns and cacti.

The path to the fish farm leads by a quiet spot with a *kunda*, a clear-water spring that emerges from a natural cave. Water collects in a pool at the bottom of a stepped brick wall, then flow through a series of carved stone taps into a pond in the outer courtyard. None of the images at this **Godavari Kunda** are especially old, but this natural site – where the sacred waters of the Godavari river pour from the mountains, is revered by Hindus as having magical power. Every 12 years, hundreds of thousands of pilgrims come here to bathe. To them, a dip in the Godavari Kunda is equal in merit to distributing six million cows to Brahmins.

The Lele and Matatirtha Kundas: Two other important *kundas* are situated in the southern hills. The first of these is in the tiny, dusty Lele Valley, a bumpy trip south from Kathmandu. The track winds its way steeply downhill through terraced fields, reddish-brown soil and a few green plots to Lele Village, where the arrival of a taxi is a major event for local children.

East of the village, a tiny, four-faced Shiva *lingum* stands in the wide expanse of a pond overshadowed by foliage. Past a **Festival at Matatirtha.**

small bridge, a storehouse bulges with dozens of bags of tea leaves to be carried by porters to Kathmandu. A lane leads to two temples in the midst of a lovely grove. The small structure on the east is the **Saraswati Kunda**. Its entrance is marked by a single-roofed Muktinath shrine built in 1668. The shrine contains a number of 16th to 18th Century sculptures.

Farther on, adjacent to the main **Lele Kunda**, stands the 16th Century *shikhara* style **Tileshwar Mahadev**. On the temple platform is an interesting carved-stone panel of Kailash Parivar, representing Shiva and Parvati surrounded by their entire family, dating to the 12th Century.

If Lele Kunda gives an impression of an almost hidden, intimate beauty, the wide-open spaces of **Matatirtha Kunda**, in the southwestern foothills of the Valley, give the opposite effect. There is nothing here of great historical interest, but the site has a wild charm of its own.

A wide, flagstoned pilgrimage track leads from the Raj Path near the village of **Kisipidi**, and opens onto a spacious open courtyard where grass grows over the flagstones. In the center is a recessed water tank with carved stone spouts, from which clear spring flows. The main *kunda* is in one corner of the courtyard, flanked by a small stone shrine containing a Shiva *lingum*. The site was established in the first part of the 18th Century; now devotees of all religions come here once a year to honor their deceased mothers.

The Images of Balaju: Although the reclining Vishnu at **Balaju**, Kathmandu's Industrial Estate a few kilometers north of the city center across the ring road, is probably not older than the one at Budhanilkantha, its position in the "Balaju Water Garden" is certainly more scenic. Set in a secluded tank and shaded by the sacred forested hill of Nagarjun, it enjoys a tranquillity missing from its more celebrated counterpart.

The Balaju tank is adjourned by a 14th-Century **Shitala Mai** image, housed in a 19th-Century twin-roofed temple. The area surrounding this small temple to Shitala, the goddess of smallpox, is a sort of outdoor sculpture garden. Many stone images are displayed here, including a 16th-Century Harihari, a composite half-Shiva, half-Vishnu god. At a lower level, a large

he Tika
hairav at
ele.

open water tank displays 22 stone water spouts in a row, more than any other *hiti* in Kathmandu Valley.

The wooded part of the hill behind Balaju, called **Nagarjun**, is a fine, walled forest reserve administered by the Royal Palace. Pheasants, deer, leopards and other wild animals live here amidst a great variety of trees. The eastern slope of Nagarjun has two caves, about a kilometer apart. A small image of the Buddha is kept in the lower one, while the upper cave, though smaller, has two Buddha images and a figure of Nagarjuna, a famed philosopher who lived in south India not long after the birth of Christ.

The top of the wooded hill can be reached in two hours by a footpath through the **Jamacho** forest reserve. At the summit is a Buddhist *chaitya*. Nepalis believe this is the point from where Manjushri surveyed the Valley whilst Tibetans say the Buddha preached a sermon here centuries ago.

Koteshwar's Sacred Confluence: If springs are holy places in Nepal, so too are the confluences of rivers. They are considered ideal places for worshipping, and hence for living.

At the spot where the three sacred rivers – the Bagmati, the Manohara and the Rudramati – meet, legend tells that Maha Devi once appeared to the demon king Shankhasur in the form of a Vishwarup Shiva with innumerable faces. Today, the **Koteshwar Mahadev** shrine commemorates this event. The worship of Koteshwar (*koti* means "millions" and *eshwar* means "gods") as the most powerful form of Shiva has traditionally been associated with having difficult prayers fulfilled.

The temple, a dome-roofed brick building, lies on a small plateau east of Patan near the rivers' confluence. It is marked by a few tall trees. Inside is a Shiva *lingum* said to date from the 8th Century. In adjoining courtyards are shrines to Bhagvati and to Gaganeshwar Mahadev. Further south, the **Kuti Bahal**, with its 15th-Century *chaitya*, stands at the place where relatives and friends gathered to bid farewell to Patan citizens traveling to Tibet.

Another confluence of streams in the western part of the Valley is the site of a double shrine. Here, where two rivulets join near **Naikap** village, a footpath between rice fields leads to a sunken altar. A 300-year-old stone tympanum and a *path* stand in front of it.

The open Mahadev shrine on the platform opposite the *path* is dedicated to Shiva. Two tridents are set beside a primitively cut, four-faced 6th-Century *lingum*. A standing 8th-Century Mahagauri is imbedded in a wall nearby the shrine; Mahagauri is armless, and the head set on top of the broken neck is probably not hers. Among the various stone images on the grass is a superb but headless 10th-Century Saraswati, carved from a large broken slab of stone. Her right arm and hand are mutilated; the absence of a head somehow adds to the aesthetic power of this masterpiece.

A carved *lingum* at Lele, and a pastoral scene near Bisankhu.

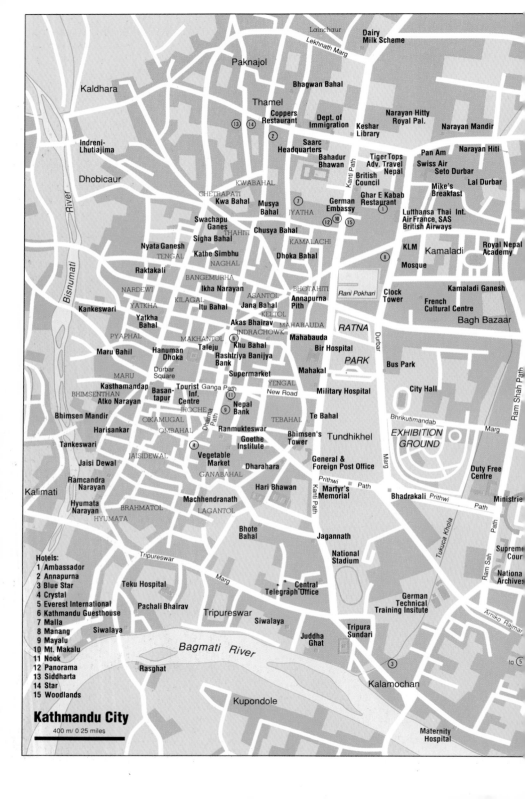

Lainchaur
Lekhnath Marg

Dairy
Milk Scheme

Paknajol

Bhagwan Bahal

Kaldhara

Thamel

Narayan Hitty
Royal Pal.

Coppers
Restaurant

Dept. of
Immigration

Keshar
Library

Narayan Mandir

⑬ ⑭

Saarc
Headquarters

②

Bahadur
Bhawan

British
Council

Pan Am

Narayan Hiti

Indreni-
Lhutiajima

TigerTops
Adv. Travel
Nepal

Swiss Air
Seto Durbar

Dhobicaur

KWABAHAL

Ghar E Kabab
Restaurant

Mike's
Breakfast

Lal Durbar

CHETRAPATI

Kwa Bahal

Musya
Bahal

⑦
JYATHA

German
Embassy

①

Lufthansa Thai Int.
Air France, SAS
British Airways

Swachapu
Ganes

⑫ ⑩ ⑮

Sigha
Bahal

THAHITI

Chusya Bahal

KAMALACHI

KLM

Kamaladi

Royal Nepal
Academy

Nyata Ganesh

Kathe Simbhu

Dhoka Bahal

⑧

Mosque

TENGAL

NAGHAL

Raktakali

BANGEMURHA

NARDEWI

Ikha Narayan

ASANTOL

BHOTAHITI

Rani Pokhari

Clock
Tower

Kamaladi Ganesh

Kankeswari

YATKHA

KILAGAL

Itu Bahal

Jana Bahal

Annapurna
Pith

French
Cultural Centre

Yatkha
Bahal

KELTOL

Akas Bhairav

MAHABAUDA

RATNA

Bagh Bazaar

PYAPHAL

MAKHANTOL

⑥

INDRACHOWK

Mahabauda

Maru Bahil

Taleju

Khu Bahal

Bir Hospital

PARK

Hanuman
Dhoka

Rashtriya Banijya
Bank

Durbar

Bus Park

MARU

Durbar
Square

Supermarket

Mahakal

City Hall

Kasthamandap

Tourist
Inf.
Centre

Ganga Path

YENGAL

Military Hospital

Bhrikutimandab

BHIMSENTHAN

Basan-
tapur

⑪

New Road

Atko Narayan

⑨

Nepal
Bank

Marg

OIKAMUGAL

IHOCHE

TEBAHAL

EXHIBITION
GROUND

Bhimsen Mandir

OMBAHAL

Te Bahal

Harisankar

Ranmukteswar

Goethe
Institute

Bhimsen's
Tower

Tundhikhel

Tankeswari

JAISIDEWAL

④

Dharahara

General &
Foreign Post Office

Duty Free
Centre

Jaisi Dewal

Vegetable
Market

Ramcandra
Narayan

GANABAHAL

Hari Bhawan

Martyr's
Memorial

Bhadrakali

Prithwi
Path

Ministrie

Kalimati

Hyumata
Narayan

BRAHMATOL

Machhendranath

Jagannath

HYUMATA

LAGANTOL

Supreme
Cour

Bhote
Bahal

National
Stadium

Nationa
Archives

Tripureswar

Teku Hospital

Central
Telegraph Office

Pachali Bhairav

Tripureswar

German
Technical
Training Insitute

Siwalaya

Siwalaya

Juddha
Ghat

Tripura
Sundari

Bagmati River

Rasghat

③

to ⑤

Kalamochan

Hotels:
1 Ambassador
2 Annapurna
3 Blue Star
4 Crystal
5 Everest International
6 Kathmandu Guesthouse
7 Malla
8 Manang
9 Mayalu
10 Mt. Makalu
11 Nook
12 Panorama
13 Siddharta
14 Star
15 Woodlands

Kupondole

Kathmandu City

400 m/ 0 .25 miles

Maternity
Hospital

TIMELESS KATHMANDU

eceding
ages:
ajestic
aks –
ery
ountain-
r's
light; a
iny day
reet scene.
ight, a
sident of
athmandu.

The founding of Kathmandu city is usually said to have taken place during the "Dark Ages" at the end of the Licchavi period and the time of the ascendancy of the Mallas. But it is almost certain that a conglomeration of small settlements existing prior to that time eventually united as one city.

One of the first known areas of settlement was at Deopatan, just northwest of Pashupatinath. A further settlement must have developed in the southwestern part at present-day Kathmandu, at the confluence of the Valley's two main rivers, the Bagmati and Bishnumati; river confluences have always been considered spiritually auspicious locations. In addition, several important Licchavi ruins are scattered about the Valley.

The hub of the city in medieval times, as today, was the area around the **Kasthamandap** (1). From this point, it was said, the city of Kathmandu spread in the shape of a sword, its handle to the south and its blade to the north. There is no way to trace this shape in the late-20th Century layout of the city, however.

According to legend, the Kasthamandap, "The House of Wood" (see History section), was erected at the crossroads of two important trade routes. This sizeable structure was used as a community center for trade and barter. It probably functioned very much as it does today. Decorated with red fringes and flowers, the Kasthamandap is on the itinerary of all visiting heads of state and royal guests. The name "Kathmandu" is a derivative of "Kasthamandap," giving certain proof that this building must have been its original center. Kathmandu city developed radially from this point, the Royal Palace and the Durbar Square being constructed soon after. Some theorize that the palace marked the northeastern boundary of the Old City.

Urban explorers who search the old and narrow streets leading toward the rivers inevitably discover buildings of great stature and quality that may have been past palaces. Along the river bank, one can find remains of early temples and shrines. A great deal of history still lies buried.

When the Valley was first unified by King Jayasthiti Malla in the 14th Century,

Kathmandu became his administrative capital. Considerable expansion took place from this time, with the fulcrum of activity shifting slightly toward the palace complex itself. Nevertheless, the old trade routes – particularly the diagonal road running from the Kasthamandap through Asan Tole – were thoroughly maintained and are still very much in evidence today.

The Ranas' Legacy: Architectural styles generally changed very little for centuries. Only a trained eye can differentiate between earlier and later artistry in traditional Newari buildings. It wasn't until the mid-19th Century, with the Ranas in power, that dramatic changes in architecture occurred. The leaders' travel in the outside world, from which the rest of the country was isolated, led to the introduction of many Western-influenced styles.

In Europe at this time, a great neo-classical revival was in full blossom. Jung Bahadur Rana returned from an 1850 visit to England and France with visions of grandeur in his head. The Western-style palaces he built as copies of European structures are in sharp contrast to the indigenous Nepali architecture of the time.

The culmination of this architectural style was the Ranas' palace, **Singha Durbar** (2). A building of gigantic proportion and size, it consisted of 17 courtyards and as many as 1,700 rooms, and was reputed to be the largest private dwelling in Asia, if not in the world. It took only 11 months to construct in 1901.

Sadly, all but the main wing containing the state rooms was damaged by fire in 1973. By that time, the place was being used as the government secretariat. An ambitious plan of renovation and repair of the main courtyard has been completed; it now houses the Prime Minister's offices and the National Planning Commission with other Government ministries in the same compound.

The Singha Durbar was only one of several hundred palaces that sprang up around Patan and Kathmandu during the Ranas' reign. With their decline in political power and the reemergence of the royal family, however, the Rana palaces have all become tarnished. Many of these grand buildings have been taken over by government or private organizations, stripped of their internal grandeur. Today, they are mere shells of their former splendor.

Also under the Ranas, Kathmandu's suburbs started to grow and expand. The traditional concept of the tightly-knit Newar city, designed to preserve every square meter of arable land outside the city, was broken. Western-style dwellings were built on the outskirts of the city, particularly to the northeast.

Recently a second period of Westernization has caused Kathmandu new growing pains, putting pressure on space and infrastructure. The gardens of the old palaces have been sold and subdivided and a spate of unzoned and uncontrolled modern architecture has sprung up. It is increasingly difficult to find within the ring road any sizeable cultivated areas, strongholds of the besieged Newar tradition.

New City and Old City: Because of the two markedly different styles of architecture, there are today two quite distinct parts of Kathmandu. There is the "Old City," flanked to the east by the **Tundhikhel**, a long open expanse used as a parade ground; and the expanding eastern area of mixed Western and traditional styles. The **Narayan Hitty Royal Palace**, built in 1962

Kathmandu city from th air.

by American and Indian architects, is aligned at the north end of the wide **Durbar Marg** which is the main area for travel and airline offices.

The two parts of town are basically divided by the north-south **Kanti Path**, or **King's Way**. This main artery skirts the Royal Palace, cuts across the **Lazimpat** district of embassies, and continues north as far as the reclining Vishnu of Budhanilkantha. On the outskirts of both Kathmandu and Patan houses, buildings and shops of various styles have developed along and beyond the ring road, joining the ancient cities into a single sprawling metropolis and enveloping previously cultivated land. Almost one million people live in the Kathmandu Valley and half of those in the city of Kathmandu itself.

The Old City has remained intact through the centuries, with the exception of one modification: after a major earthquake in 1934, **New Road** was constructed over the ruins. Running west from the Tundhikhel, it ends at Basantapur and the Durbar Square in front of the old palace. This wide street is the most vital commercial axis of the old city today. The diagonal cross street that in medieval times was the main route to Tibet today has kept its role as a center for traditional petty trade.

Old New Road: New Road – properly called Juddha Sadak – is the paradise of the new consumer society that has rapidly emerged in the Valley since Nepal was opened to the West.

You will find everything here, from the latest gadgets to antiques no older but certainly no cheaper than anywhere else. Moneyed people come here, window-shopping, parading in their latest Western outfits, buying French face cream, imported tinned food, Japanese stereo equipment, films, drugs, jewels, cigarettes, local and foreign magazines.

The road opens on a plain daubed stucco portico. About halfway down, a big pipal tree shades a small square with many *chaityas* where newsboys sell local papers. Intellectuals like to gather here and debate and this is the stronghold of the shoeshine boys. At the end of New Road, facing the Crystal Hotel at the corner, a large new supermarket has been built. Its bulk isolates a small, active, recessed shrine.

alute to the
ng on the
ndhikhel.

Where Have All the Hippies Gone?

Hardly had the Flower Children blossomed in San Francisco's Haight-Ashbury in the mid-1960s than they began taking seed in Nepal. The climate was perfect, cool and enchanted; the soil was rich, warm and understanding; and everywhere was the fertility of Shaivist Hinduism and Mahayana Buddhism, the mystic and the sublime, the indulgence of lotus eating (if also acid-eating), and the acceptance of a friendly people. Besides, hashish was growing wild and was sold in licensed shops, and harder stuff was readily available.

So while the Beatles and Jimi Hendrix sang of love with a whiff of smoke about it, while *maharishis* and newly discovered *rimpoches* gathered followings of the tuned-in and turned-on and the words "love" and "peace" took on new connotation, Kathmandu experienced an invasion the likes of which it had never seen before – and will almost certainly never see again.

They came bearded or shining-shaved, in boots and bare feet, heavily costumed or nearly naked, wearing beads or pierced-nose jewels, filthy or scrubbed-clean, under-nourished or well-fed, drug-dumb or highly articulate, wearing Buddhist saffron or Hindu

white, locust people who settled where they found their green and stayed until tolerance ran out.

Their monument remains: Freak Street, a lane within the long shadow of Basantapur, King Prithvi Narayan Shah's victory tower. The street is still gaudy if faded, and is trying hard to make a comeback. The velvet, satin, silk and Nepalese homespun fabrics still hang in shops. The well-thumbed second-hand books are there too, with the shoulder bags, the used shoes, the paper prints of gods and innocent erotica. In the perfumed shadows of evening, ghosts of days not long past linger at their old haunts. The music has

gone, the heavy beat and blare of acid rock pouring from smoky caverns named "Don't Pass Me By," "Yes, Yes," "Hungry Eye," "The August Moon." Their signs are down. They no longer exist.

On the trail of the hippies came Indian filmmakers. One movie became a contemporary Indian classic: *Hare Rama Hare Krishna*, featuring a song called "Dun Maro Dum," or "Smoke, smoke, smoke."

All that is gone now. It went so suddenly, almost as if it had never happened. Some say King Birendra's 1975 coronation took them like an epidemic. Or perhaps official tolerance waned with the prohibition of hashish and other drugs. Visas were refused and canceled. Free transport out of the country was provided for those without means. But there was no mass exodus, and no one remembers seeing them go. They just seemed to vanish in the smoky mist.

When the penniless hippies departed, their more well-to-do peers remained for awhile: artists, dancers, writers, poets who published with the likes of Archibald Macleish and Allen Ginsburg. And there were the mystics, those who could tell the future from the stars, from your palms, from the vibrations of the earth. Then most of them, too, with their capes and earrings and felt hats, left the Valley. More startlingly, perhaps, the familiar psychedelically painted coaches, vast in size and sometimes even double-decked, suddenly drove away. No more do buses carry labels like "London," "Paris," "Frankfurt," "Tehran," "Khajaraho," or "Goa," always Goa. Where is the Chapati Express now? The young people in Nepal today are primarily international budget travelers known as "Trippies." They are highly respectable compared to their predecessors: rarely a whiff of illicit smoke, and not a bare breast to be seen in public. Their haven is Thamel, at the north end of Kathmandu's Old City.

But even here, where colorfully named restaurants outnumber colorfully named lodges, and together they nearly outnumber nameless trekking-gear shops, the hippies' legacy can be seen. There are the pie shops, the print shops, the second-hand book shops with names like "The Tamang Tantric," "High" and "The Kathmandu Trade Post." The restaurants and lodges, many of which still offer rooms for next to nothing, rest on foundations established in the hippy era.

Cat Stevens sang a song about Kathmandu when it was one of the world's most famous hippie paradises, and Goa was at the other end of the rainbow. Today, Joan Baez's civil-rights era song would be a more appropriate theme: "Where Have All The Flowers Gone?"

The street going north to meet the diagonal axis of the Old City boasts the first commercial arcade in town. Behind a door, you find yourself in Hong Kong, Singapore or Bangkok, only to jump back 10 centuries when you step out. Narrow, paved side lanes are thrust between rows of wall-to-wall traditional houses. Here and there are a few modest restaurants, shady hotels and tiny, dimly-lit tea houses. A whole population wanders about or exchanges news to the whine of transistor radios. These alleys culminate in squares with corner *patis*, central *chaityas* and occasional temples.

Behind the Crystal Hotel, you can see the silhouettes of several temples. In the background is the Swayambhunath stupa on its hilltop, and the girdle of mountains in the far distance. At the crossing, pigeons anoint the statue of Juddha Shamsher Rana (prime minister from 1932 to 1945), under whose direction New Road was built. He would be amazed at today's honking traffic and one-way systems.

Forgotten Freak Street: As you walk further west, you soon come to a large space known as **Basantapur (3)**. It de-

rives its name from the biggest tower looming over the massive palace structure on the right. This square was once a courtyard where the royal elephants were kept. After the 1934 earthquake, when New Road was opened, new buildings were erected and the square turned into a marketplace. When the nation was preparing for King Birendra's coronation in 1975, the market was phased out and a brick platform erected.

People loiter here, talking in small groups, eager to warm themselves in the sun. Rickshaws cycle past, and street peddlers display assortments of local trinkets, bracelets, bangles, religious images, swords and knives. They sell their wares all over the square, as well as on temple platforms beneath the struts of the Hanuman Dhoka Palace.

Immediately to the left of Basantapur starts the famous **Freak Street**, once a favored hangout of long-haired travelers, today more often visited by tourists in search of the "hippies" who have long since moved to less conspicuous locales. Freak Street is a narrow lane with cheap hotels, dim taverns and a variety of shops.

New Road Gate.

The Living Goddess: Farther on, near a couple of modern schools, you'll note a white stuccoed facade with intricately carved windows. This is the house of the living goddess, the **Kumari Bahal** (a). This monastic courtyard was built in the mid-18th Century. Two painted lion statues guard the entrance steps, which have lintels carved with laughing skulls. Carved deities, peacocks and doves adorn the balcony windows.

But there are even more attractive sights to be seen inside the small courtyard, where the woodwork on all four walls is truly remarkable. After a donation per visitor has been offered, the *kumari* or living goddess appears at a window, either the one on the third floor opposite the entrance, or the second or third-floor window above the entrance. Taking pictures of the *kumari* is strictly forbidden, but you may freely photograph when she is out of sight.

Some consider the *kumari* to be the incarnation of the "virgin goddess" Kanya Kumari, one of the 62 names given to Parvati, Shiva's *shakti*. Others consider her a personification of Durga, another form of the same Parvati. Yet others say she is one of the eight Ashta Matrikas, or mother goddesses. This particular *kumari* is called the Royal Kumari, to distinguish her from past *kumaris* who live or have lived in Kathmandu, and several others who are worshipped throughout the Valley.

One legend tells of a girl of the Sakya clan in the 8th Century who claimed to be an incarnation of Kumari. She was exiled by the king, but when his queen became enraged, the repentent ruler brought the "goddess" back and locked her in a temple. Another legend says that a Malla king used to play dice with the goddess Taleju, who appeared to him in human form. One night he lusted for Taleju, and the goddess in great wrath told him she would never return. The king pleaded with her, and finally Taleju promised to return as an inviolable young virgin.

The living goddess is always chosen from a selection of girls four or five years of age, all belonging to the Sakya clan of goldsmiths and silversmiths. The *kumari*'s body must be flawless and must satisfy 32 specified, distinctive signs. The final phase of the selection process is a terrifying ordeal in the hall of the temple: men masked as demons try to scare the girls, and bloody buffalo heads are placed around them in the darkness. The girl who remains calm throughout this ordeal, reason the Nepalese, cannot be other than the goddess herself. She confirms her selection by choosing the clothing and ornaments of the previous *kumari* from among a large collection of similar items.

Once astrologers have assured that the girl's horoscope is in harmony with the King's, she is settled in the *bahal*, which becomes her home until she reaches puberty or otherwise loses blood, as from a small wound. She is allowed to leave only for various religious festivals, and then she must be carried, as her feet must not touch the ground. During the Indrajatra festival in August-September, men drag her flower-bedecked chariot through the city on three separate days. (See feature article on festivals.)

When her term as *kumari* has ended, the girl leaves the temple richly endowed and free to marry. But many would-be candidates are deterred by the prospect of a beautiful child, accustomed to years of utter idleness and adulation, being suddenly released to become a housewife and mother. Besides, some say, an ex-goddess brings bad luck to the household and early death to her husband.

Durbar's Forest of Temples: As you leave the *bahal* of the *kumari*, the **Temple of Narayan** (b) a three-roofed structure built about 1670 on a five-tiered plinth, is to your immediate left. You are now entering the **Durbar Square** (4). This wide area has less charm and less spatial cohesion than its counterpart in Patan. But it contains more than 50 important temples and monuments, dominated by the impressive bulk of the **Taleju Temple** (v), which houses the titulary divinity of the Royal Family.

The plinth of the Narayan temple and other surrounding stepped platforms are entirely covered by people during festivals. On ordinary days, curio or vegetable sellers requisition the first steps for their spreads of cheap goods. On the brick-paved square, farmers carry huge burdens on their backs or on shoulder poles, while rickshaws and taxis honk impatiently to penetrate the throng. Bicycle bells, children's shrill cries and hawkers' shouts add a dense bazaar atmosphere to the scene.

In the chilly hours of dawn, however, the Durbar Square and its neighboring

The Kathmandu Living Goddess with her attendants.

168

streets wake up to black and white-clad men who silently hurry to temples for early-morning devotions, and to traders unlocking their antique padlocks, removing their wooden blinds and unloading surplus goods into the streets from their crammed shops. Pigeons swoop to snatch the rice offerings, and the most sacred temples become aviaries.

Soon the flux and tide of human commerce sets alive the chiseled gods in this forest of temples that is the Durbar. Here in the square, and all along the ancient road to Tibet, is the heart of old Kathmandu. The lane slashes through the Old City in a diagonal southwest-northeast direction, following the course of the sun which casts raw blocks of deep shadow in the transparent atmosphere.

Although the lane will draw you eastward, reverse your direction. The best complete view of the Durbar Square is from its western end. Walk past a small stone Vishnu temple flanked by a beautiful statue of Garuda, and enter an area called **Maru Tole**.

The main feature here is the famed **Kasthamandap** (c) or "House of Wood,"

built about the 12th Century at the crossroads of the trade routes around which the city Kathmandu grew. Originally a community center where people gathered for ceremonies and other events, it later was turned into a temple dedicated to Gorakhnath. The god sits in the center of the platform in a little wooden enclosure. There are several other shrines for different gods in the building. Small carved figures around the first-floor cornice illustrate Hindu epics, and a pair of bronze lions guard the entrance.

Early morning is a good time to visit the Kasthamandap, which squats at the center of a rectangular open space. Porters, dressed in various earthy tones, sit here awaiting customers. Nearby, between the arcades of a rather low, two-tiered structure, petty vendors sell betel nuts, chilies, ginger, potatoes, onions, peanuts, dried fish, sweets, silver coins, votive powders and tressed wicks of incense.

Hidden behind the Kasthamandap is the small but very important golden **Ashok Binayak** shrine (d) of the Kathmandu Ganesh. Commonly called the Maru Ganesh, there is a constant flow of worshippers here; in particular, people who are leaving on journeys will pay a visit to ensure their safety.

Returning to the square, there is a **Shiva Temple** (e) on the left, with three roofs on a nine-step plinth.

Continue into a second square on the right. Just before entering this courtyard, note the **Shiva-Parvati Temple House** (f) on the left. The deified couple, carved in wood and crudely painted, looks benignly down from the center window of the upper balcony.

Set on a pillar at the entrance to this second part of Durbar Square is a statue of **King Pratap Malla** (g), who was responsible for the construction of many of the surrounding structures. He and his consorts were set up on a stone column facing the inner sanctum of his private prayer room, on the third floor of the **Degu Taleju Temple** (h). The northeastern corner of the square is taken up by post-1934 earthquake construction.

Opposite the entrance to the Hanuman Dhoka stands the **Krishna Mandir** (i) one of the few octagonal temples in Nepal. On the right-hand corner, a large wooden lattice screen hides an enormous gilded face of the **Seto Bhairav**, a fascinating masterpiece of popular art. The screen is removed only during the Indrajatra festival, when the fierce figure is showered with flowers and rice. Beer flows through his hideous mouth from a tank above him, and hordes of men jostle to drink this holy nectar.

Nasal, 'The Dancing One': Leaving aside, for the time being, the temples in the outer Durbar Square, you come to the entrance of the **Hanuman Dhoka** (j) the Royal Palace. On one side of it, a 1672 statue of the monkey-god Hanuman stands under a small umbrella. The deified animal is wrapped in a red cloak and his face is covered with a thick layer of *sindur*, red dust mixed with mustard oil. Hanuman, a hero of the epic *Ramayana*, is a congenial character reputed to bring success to military pursuits. Every morning, devotees bring him grains of rice, coins, burning incense, and sometimes errands written on small pieces of paper.

The palace gate, a surprising mixture of blue, green and gold, is flanked by two stone lions. The animal on the right is

mounted by Shiva, the one on the left by his *shakti*, Parvati. Note the highly colored group of characters in a niche above the gate: the Tantric Krishna of fierce aspect is in the center, flanked by Krishna the god of love and two of his favorite *gopis*, and by King Pratap Malla and his queen. The King and Krishna are both regarded as incarnations of Vishnu.

The gate opens upon the **Nasal Chowk** (k). Of 14 courtyards here, this is the one in which the actual royal coronation ceremony takes place. *Nasal* means "the dancing one;" the square owes its name to a small figure of the dancing Shiva placed on the eastern side of the square. Here is the entrance to the museum dedicated largely to the memory of King Tribhuvan.

The founding of the Royal Palace dates back to late Licchavi times. The Ranas made considerable improvements during their reign, but most of the structure dates from the Malla times. The construction was accomplished progressively over many centuries by successive additions – beginning in the north with the small **Mohan Chow**k (l) and **Sundari Chowk** (m), built for Pratap Malla in the 16th

Century, and continuing to the south.

After his conquest of the Valley in 1768, Prithvi Narayan Shah oversaw the renovation and completion of buildings around and to the east of Nasal Chowk. These included the nine-story **Basantapur Tower** (n) and the smaller towers of **Kirtipur** (o), **Lalitpur** (p) and **Bhaktapur** (q). All four are set in a square around and above **Lohan Chowk** (r). In this work, Prithvi Narayan Shah introduced the Valley to the concept of the fortified tower, such as he had previously built at Gorkha and Nuwakhot.

Later rulers made several additions and restorations. The area west of Nasal Chowk was constructed in the mid to late 19th Century by the Ranas, while the golden gate as it now stands was restored during the early modern Shah period. Nasal Chowk and all the four main towers were extensively restored prior to King Birendra's coronation, and today work still continues.

Immediately to the left of the gate is a stele representing Narsingh: Vishnu as a man-lion tearing apart his arch-enemy, the demon Hiranya-Kashipu. This image is **Towers of Nasal Chowk.**

followed by a gallery with a row of portraits of the present Shah dynasty rulers in full regalia. In the corner, the five round roofs of the five-faced **Pancha Mukhi Hanuman** (s) pile up high into the sky; this is one of only two such structures in Nepal, the other being in Pashupatinath.

After admiring the erotic carvings on the struts along the facade of Basantapur Tower, you can climb up through a maze of steep staircases and balconies. Here, you can peek into the Lohan Chowk to view its remarkable wood-carvings.

A Garland of Skulls: Leave the palace grounds and return to the central part of Durbar Square. You can see more erotic carvings, almost at head level, on the struts of the two-tiered 17th Century **Jagannath Temple** (t), the oldest structure in this area. Next to the Jagannath is the **Gopinath Mandir** (u), with three roofs and a three-stepped plinth; and a composite structure dedicated to Shiva, a white *shikhara* above a Newar-style temple.

Then you'll encounter a masterpiece: an oversized relief of the fierce-looking Kal Bhairav. Highly admired and revered, this **Black Bhairav** is indeed fearsome.

The black-skinned god wears red and yellow ornaments, plus a tiara and garland of skulls. His eyes and fangs protrude, and three pairs of arms are each armed with a sword, a severed head, a hatchet and a shield – all attributes of Shiva in his fierce form. Bhairav tramples on a corpse, symbol of human ignorance, and carries a ritual skull bowl into which believers put offerings.

The Black Bhairav, brought here in the second half of the 18th Century, is said to have been found in a field north of the city. People believe that the god punishes those who lie in front of him by causing them to instantly bleed to death. Many an argument is resolved with a challenge to "go and tell it to Kal Bhairav."

This northeastern end of the Durbar Square is dominated by the magnificent three-tiered **Taleju Temple** (v), built on a huge stepped platform amid a number of smaller temples opposite the main Hanuman Dhoka gate. Everything here is gilded, and thus is particularly resplendent at sunset. The walled precinct is off-limits to all but the King and certain priests, although Hindus are allowed access dur-

Hanuman Dhoka Palace.

ing the Durga Puja festival.

The goddess **Taleju Bhawani**, originally a South Indian deity, was brought to Nepal in the 14th Century and was enshrined as the ruling family's deity. She became a symbol of legitimacy for the sovereign; the rulers of Bhaktapur and Patan, in turn, set up their own shrines to Taleju in front of their palaces.

The present temple was restored in 1562 by King Mahendra Malla. Human sacrifices were performed here until, according to legend, the goddess became displeased when the usurper Prithvi Narayan Shah attempted to celebrate his victory with the customary slaughter of a conquered foe.

Nearby, protected by a fence along the white wall of the palace precinct, there is a long inscription in honor of the goddess Kalika. It is written in no fewer than 15 different alphabets and languages. Its text notes that it was carved on January 14, 1664, by King Pratap Malla, who prided himself on being an accomplished linguist and poet.

Massacre and Sacrifice: At the northwestern end of Durbar Square is an open courtyard called **Kot**, or "armory." It is surrounded by army and police quarters and barracks. While it is of little artistic appeal, it has great historical significance. Here, in 1846, Jung Bahadur Rana, the forefather of the Rana dynasty, perpetrated the "Kot Massacre," eliminating all the promising scions of the Nepalese aristocracy and paving the way for his seizure of power a few weeks later.

There is another mass blood-letting here every year during the Durga Puja festival, when hundreds of buffaloes and goats are sacrificed by young soldiers who must attempt to cut off the head of each animal with a single stroke.

At the entrance of **Makhan Tole**, a Garuda statue lies half buried in the ground. It must have once faced a temple that was destroyed long ago. As you pass to the right of the Taleju, cast a glance at the **Tarana Devi Mandir** (w). This low brick structure has three carved doorways, overpainted struts representing the multiple-armed Ashta Matrika mother goddesses, and a festoon of colored skulls.

There are other important structures nearby. The **Makhan Bahil**, a great

Left, Hanuman statue. Below, a curious Nepali. Right, the Taleju Temple.

monastery in late Malla times, features the remains of eight votive *chaityas* and a shrine with a *torana*, of Manjushri. The **Mahendreswar Mahadev** was built in the early 1960s and named after the late King Mahendra. It is dedicated to Shiva in his phallic form.

Centers of Commerce: The Makhan Tole is about six meters (20 feet) wide, flanked by facades of various colors, with wooden balconies and columns defining *patis* and shops. It leads into the **Indra Chowk**, an open space from which six streets radiate in all directions.

This area, traditionally dedicated to the sale of blankets and textiles, including soft woolen shawls known as *pashmina*, is particularly picturesque and animated. Crowds collect around cloth and flower sellers. A man selling flutes, which are inserted in a pole like the branches of a tree, strolls past a wayside dried-fish market. Tucked behind is the glittering magic of the bead market, where lengths of varied color combinations can be made up while you wait.

To the west stand three temples, all at street corners. The most important is the one on the south, a three-story house containing a highly revered shrine to Akash Bhairav on the first floor. The facade stands out with its white, purplish-red and green ceramic tiles. The house has yellow windows and two balconies, the lower one with four gilded griffins rearing onto the street. The shrine is active during major festivals, including Indrajatra, when the large image of Bhairav is displayed in the square. During this festival, a huge *lingum* pole is erected in the center of the square in place of the stones which normally occupy that position.

There are other important buildings in the vicinity. In a niche just before the house containing the Akash Bhairav shrine (5) is a tiny but tightly venerated all-brass **Ganesh Shrine**. Sellers and buyers of bundled cloth crowd the stepped plinth of the **Mahadev Mandir**. Women selling bracelets and cotton-cord ornaments for the hair squat at the foot of the **Shiva Mandir**.

The latter, a simplified version of Patan's Krishna temple, is a thick-set stone structure above a four-stepped plinth where carpets are displayed. Vines grow over the

Textiles for sale at Indra Chowk.

arches and pillars of the first level.

Beyond Indra Chowk, and as far as the oblong open space known as **Khel Tole**, is the most typical, oldest trading segment of the diagonal street. There is a constant coming-and-going of farmers, strollers, rickshaws, even cars forcing through the narrow line.

From the upper floors of traditional houses, women and girls watch the crowd scene below. At ground level are shops selling all manner of goods, though each seems to specialize: floor mats, warm blankets, shawls, saris, cloth, huge copper jars for ceremonies and festivals. Popular among visitors are the Tibetan-made carpets in various designs and colors, now one of Nepal's major exports.

The White Machhendranath: Past a small shrine smeared with fresh blood, turn left and enter one of the most venerated temples in the whole Kingdom. This superb construction, standing freely in the center of a monastic courtyard, is the **Seto Machhendranath** (6).

Two magnificent brass lions guard the entrance. Under the porch leading to the courtyard, musicians assemble in the evening to chant sacred songs. Take a few more steps into a splendid sight. Behind various steles, *chaityas* and pillars carved with deities and animals stands the famous temple. Note the gilt-copper roofs, the ornamental banners, the tympanum, the struts depicting the various forms of Avalokiteshwara, the girdle of prayer wheels around the pedestal, the lions and griffins guarding the approach steps to the shrine doorway.

The god within the shrine is Padmapani Avalokiteshwara, the most compassionate divinity in the Valley. Buddhist, but also worshipped by Hindus, this deity is known by the people as Jammadyo or Machhendra. The white (*seto*) god is taken out of its shrine once a year during the lively Seto Machhendra festival in March-April for chariot processions across the city.

The date of construction of this temple is unknown. It was restored in the early 17th Century. Its well-paved courtyard contains a variety of shops selling cloth, wool, string, pottery, Nepali caps, ribbons and beads, curios and paper prints.

Leaving the temple, you come immedi-

ruit vendor
t Indra
howk.

ately to the **Lunchun Lunbun Ajima** at the next street corner on the left. This well proportioned, small Tantric temple has three roofs, white ceramic tiles, a recessed altar, and portraits of the King and Queen between erotic carvings.

Proceed to the northeast. Somewhere to your left is the polygonal **Krishna Temple** (7), squeezed between private houses. Under its three roofs, the whole elevated ground floor is a *pati* where people sell ginger and potatoes.

Houses along this street have three, four, even five stories. One of them on the left is the first house to have glass windows in Kathmandu. Atop two shops, one selling vegetables, the other pipes and tobacco, the house is adorned with an interesting plaster frieze depicting a general riding in a column of riflemen, cavalry, dancing girls and color bearers.

All along the street, the tiny ground-floor shops overflow with goods. There is a whole shopping mall selling household utensils, then a stall specializing in Gurkha *khukris*. From cages in some of the shops, the songs of canaries filter through the lane.

Classical Asan Tole: Then you emerge on **Asan Tole**, the real heart of the Old City. This large open space features three temples, of which the all-metal **Annapurna Temple** (8), with its three levels of gilded roofs with upturned corners, holds a special fascination. Many passers-by ring its bell and pay homage at its shrine, containing no statue or stone image but a fine *kalasha*, or pot. Nearby is a smaller temple to a four-armed Ganesh, and a tiny Narayan shrine stands nearer the center of the square.

Asan Tole, besides being an important crossroads, is the traditional rice market-place and a center for hiring porters. The crowd here is dense. Continue down the diagonal axis and you will find the street less congested as the buildings become less typical, some of rather recent style. There is an area of bicycle repair and hire shops, then another area where rickshaw drivers traditionally congregate.

Finally, you come out at the asphalted Kantipath, the main north-south axis. In front of you is a large water basin, the **Rani Pokhari**. In the 16th Century, the wife of Pratap Malla had a temple built at its center in memory of her son who died young. The temple later collapsed, and a new shrine was erected. Beyond the fenced-in lake, you can see the clock tower of the **Trichandra College** built by the Ranas, and to your right, the wide expanse of the Tundhikhel and the landmark column of the **Bhimsen Tower**.

To see more of the northern part of the Old City, turn northwest from Asan Tole along a wider extension of the morning vegetable and fruit market. The street gets narrower as you proceed west, and is made even further congested by various food stalls.

To the left, an anonymous door opens into the **Haku Bahal** courtyard. An interesting projecting window balcony is supported by six small carved struts and an elaborately carved door frame, the *torana* which was dedicated in the mid-17th Century. At the center of the courtyard is a stucco *chaitya* which looks like an overbaked meringue pie. Houses in this area are compactly built, but many are in various stages of decay.

A few steps further on the same side of the road, facing a lane heading north, is a three-roofed temple of **Ugratara** (9), worshipped for relief of eye sores. Glasses,

Scene at Asan Tole, left, where porters count their earnings, right.

donated to the temple, have been placed on the walls.

The God of Toothache: Rickshaw drivers wait by the **Ikha Narayan** (10), a small two-roofed temple to your right. Its shrine houses a beautiful 10th- or 11th-Century four-armed Sridhara Vishnu, flanked by Lakshmi and Garuda.

Opposite, under a roof, a piece of wood is punctured with thousands of nails around a tiny gilded image of **Vaisha Dev**, the god of toothache. To plant a nail here is to get rid of pain by pinning down all evil spirits and influences. In case the nail doesn't do its job, the nearby lane is filled with dentists' parlors left and right. Some of them are open to the road, so all who wish can watch a tooth being filled or an extraction being performed.

Beyond, past a 400-year-old **Narayan Temple** on the north side of the square, is a remarkable 5th-Century image of the Buddha carved in a slab of black stone. Further north is a fine bas-relief of Shiva Parvati as **Uma Maheshwar** set in a brick case. This stone image represents Shiva holding the left knee of his *shakti* while sitting on Mount Kailash.

A short distance on the left, a lion-guarded passage lead to a monastery courtyard. In its center stands the famous **Srigha Chaitya** (11), commonly known as the Kathe Shimbhu, a smaller replica of the Swayambhunath stupa. Those too old or too ill to make the climb to Swayambhunath can earn the same merit by taking a pilgrimage here.

Return to the westward-leading street and pass a bicycle shop plastered with posters of Nepali and Indian singers and movie stars. If you continue, you'll cross the Bishnumati River and be on your way to Swayambhunath. Instead, turn south (left) into the lane returning to Durbar Square. You'll traverse an area of degenerating temples and *bahals*. People of mixed origins live in the area.

Crocodile Guardians: A variety of shops selling brassware, tin trunks, salt, *ghee* and cooking oil occupy the ground floors of houses as you head south. At the first crossing is the **Nara Devi** (12), a popular three-tiered temple dedicated to one of the Ashta Matrikas. Red and white lions guard the entrance to a spacious altar where women prostrate themselves. Colored ce-

If the god of toothache doesn't help below, perhaps a dentist will, right.

ramic tiles and paintings under the roofs are entrancing.

Across the square to your right, you can see the three roofs of the enclosed **Narsingh Temple** (13). To visit, you must walk through a gate, and weave through several courtyards to a small platform over the street facing the temple. Inside the shrine is an image of Vishnu with a lion's head.

Further down the main street, on the left, is the **Yatkha Bahal** (14), a Swayambhunath-like stupa which sits in a spacious courtyard. A *bahal* behind the stupa is considerably older than the recently constructed buildings around it. A *torana* over the doorway is wrought in the design of two crocodiles with upturned snouts forming an arch. The woodwork is excellent and well preserved, and the four 14th-Century female figures carved on the window balcony are exceptionally seductive.

Across the street is a metallic door painted with two figures. One stares at you with four eyes. Above its gilded tympanum, depicting the Ashta Matrika Chamunda, a pretty face pops out of an intricate woodwork window frame. This is a god-house to **Kanga Ajima** (15); it houses *jyapus*, or farmers.

Return to the Durbar Square, again passing the Kot. If you travel south from here, you can tour Kathmandu's most congested and rural-looking sector.

An Erotic Nucleus: Turn left and head south from the Kasthamandap, crossing an open space where peasants sell vegetables in the morning. The first building on your right, with its row of shops, was built to be used as a shopping center. Immediately after it on the left is the ceramic-tiled, three-roofed **Adko Narayan** (16), considered one of the four main Vishnu temples in Kathmandu. Vishnu's image is carved over erotic scenes on the struts below the second roof. The temple has a Garuda statue in front, lions in the corners, and small *chaityas* with images of the Buddha and Vishnu on *yonis*.

The street here is straight and fairly wide. Two- and three-storied houses face an enormous building in mixed Nepali and Indian Muslim style. Where vegetable and *chapati* sellers squat in the sun, the small **Hari Shankar Temple** (17) dedicated to Shiva is on your right.

Here you can taste the flavor of everyday life for many of Kathmandu's poorer residents. The street is busy with women wrapped in shawls, children and adults on bicycles, porters carrying wood. Small shops selling tea and biscuits do a roaring trade. One shop sells aquariums, another hundreds of bangles, and flies blacken a butcher's shop.

At a crossing, the three roofs of the **Jaisi Dewal** (18), a Shiva temple of the 17th Century, are piled atop a seven-stepped pyramid. Its struts have rather well-executed erotic carvings. Behind it, set in a *yoni*, is a huge *lingum* made from a free-shaped, erect slab of stone. This area is believed to have been the nucleus of the Valley during Licchavi times. Next to the temple, the roots of a tree hold together a small *chaitya*.

The composite structure of the **Ram Chandra Mandir** (19), in its own courtyard to the right, contains on its highly colored struts the tiniest erotic carvings to be seen anywhere in the Valley.

Further down the street, within the **Takan Bahal** (20), is an unusual stupa in ruinous condition dating from the 14th Century. It is a round stucco mound with a brick structure over it; the intricacy of a tree's roots have pushed the crown up.

As you approach the southern end of the city, you pass through an area occupied by the lower castes. To your right, a bridge spans the Bishnumati. Take the lane to your left, walking past an open courtyard where a Narayan *shikhara*, currently turned into a billboard, stands behind heavy *chaityas* and a fountain with a Ganesh shrine in the corner.

Past here, the street narrows and twists past run-down houses covered with painted stucco. A small lane to your right leads into **Musum Bahal** (21) which is an old and plain structure with four Licchavi *chaityas* and a well, protected by a cement enclosure with iron bars. Local legend maintains that a famous Tantric pundit, Juman Gubhaju, entered this well to end a drought in the Valley. A ceremony is held here every 12 years in remembrance.

Take a turn to the north, and you will emerge at an open crossroad, the **Lagan Khel**, where another **Machhendra Temple** (22) stands. This is a solid *chaitya* structure not more than 10 meters (33 feet) high. The popular god is covered with a red mantle within this shrine. During the Seto Machhendranath festival, the god's chariot must be driven three times around this temple as part of the final ceremony. The chariot is then dismantled here, after the deity has been returned to its principal temple near Asan Tole, borne in a colorful palanquin.

God of Traders and Artisans: To the west, half a dozen *bahals* can be visited in succession. With the possible exception of the **Lagan Bahal** (23), they have little appeal. Continue west, past traditional four-story houses where dyers once lived. Past the pyramid of Jaisi Dewal, the road descends. In a small walled compound on the left, behind and below the *path*, a deepwater conduit built at the end of the 18th Century was recently fixed up. *Lingas* in *yonis* and cacti in boxes beautify this active fountain.

A bumpy lane goes down to the river; you must turn right to return to Durbar Square. Past the Hotel Snug on the left, look downhill to a bulky, pale green school building. Take a few steps past a small recessed Ganesh shrine, next to a small fountain in an open courtyard, and you are back on the diagonal axis road. This is where the old trade route left the city, via the Bishnumati bridge to the left and on toward Pokhara.

At this strategic location is found the **Bhimsen Temple** (24), an important and prosperous shrine dedicated to Bhimsen, the god of traders and artisans. It is a large, rectangular, three-tiered structure. The ground floor is occupied by shops. The wooden lattices of the shrine on the first floor are built at the same angle as the struts. Bhimsen, a form of Shiva, has been popular in the Valley since the 17th Century. When there was active trade with Tibet, this image of Bhimsen was carried to Lhasa on the trade route every 12 years. Devotees come here to worship every morning. Curiously, the priest of this traders' temple is a member of the farmer caste.

Next to the temple are several four-faced Buddhist stupas and a small sunken *hiti* (water conduit) in a poor state of preservation. Quite different is **Maru Hiti** (25), one of Kathmandu's four primary conduits. It may be reached by crossing Maru Hiti Tole and proceeding through a narrow lane northwest of the Kasthamandap, not far from Durbar Square.

Erotic carvings on a strut of Basantapur Temple, Hanuman Dhoka.

WESTERN
SETTLEMENTS

When the old trade route between India and Tibet meandered through the western part of the Kathmandu Valley, settlements like Satungal, Balambu, Kisipidi and Thankot were common stops on that road. Today, as there is a motorable road where before there were only footpaths, these interesting communities are readily accessible from Kathmandu via the Raj Path.

The first three villages lie within a kilometer of one another, about six kilometers (3½ miles) west of the city. **Satungal**, with a population of slightly more than 1,000, is the first you encounter. It lies just south of the Raj Path. Satungal is believed to have been established and fortified in the early 16th Century as a bulwark against hordes of northern invaders. It is a rather poor village of mixed castes, and some of its landless peasants go to Kathmandu to find employment.

The main square of Satungal village is surrounded by *patis*. At its center is a two-meter (6½ foot) stone Buddha sitting on a free-standing platform. To the north, through a vaulted gate structure with two *patis*, and down several steps, you will find the **Vishnu Devi Temple**. It is of little artistic merit, but it nonetheless is a much frequented site.

Balambu, which lies north of the Raj Path, has more than 2,000 inhabitants. Several inscriptions found in and around the village attest that it was established during the Licchavi period, and later also fortified. Girdled by a row of trees, this community is even more rural looking than Satungal. Its main temples, notably the double-roofed **Mahalakshmi Temple**, are located in the central square. The square is lined with a row of three-story residences, among which the Ajima Devi god-house, with a beautifully carved *torana*, stands out.

A kilometer east of here is the Naikap nature site. To the southeast, a lane runs down to the Machhe Narayan shrine.

The hamlet of **Kisipidi**, with perhaps 650 residents, is a pleasant stop near Matatirtha. Lush green trees and small gardens are enclosed by stone walls, while

Taking a rest along the trail to Kisipidi.

traditional three-story houses are found on its eastern slopes. Kisipidi's main deity is **Kalika Mai**, who is honored with a twin-tiered temple in the village center.

The Village of Thankot: About two kilometers further along the Raj Path lies the sizable village of **Thankot**. This settlement is located to the southwest of the main road on an elevated sloping site surrounded by terraced fields. It was started under the Mallas, and turned into a military station by Prithvi Narayan Shah; hence its name, which means "military area." Thankot has about 3,500 inhabitants belonging to four different castes.

An uneven stone path leads uphill from here to the **Mahalakshmi Temple**, an impressive structure with two roofs, carved tympanum and columns, well-done erotic carvings, an open shrine, and kneeling devotees in petrified prayer facing it. There used to be a huge pipal tree in front of the temple; it was cut down to give way to a rather ugly L-shaped building.

From Thankot, a trail leads four kilometers (2½ miles) southwest to **Chandragiri**, "The Mountain of the Moon." A climb through a dense mixed forest of bamboo, pine and *sal* trees leads to the crest of the peak, where there is a small Buddhist *chaitya*. The view from the top of the 2,423-meter (7,950-foot) peak is impressive.

As you continue west along the Raj Path you pass on the right the dish of the British-installed satellite station, linking Nepal by telephone to the rest of the world. Further on is the monument of King Tribhuvan, built to commemorate the reestablishment of the monarchy after the Rana regime.

A panel by the roadside informs you that the Raj Path was built "by Indian engineers," and perhaps also by Nepali laborers, between 1953 and 1956. It was financed by India under the Colombo Plan. Before it existed, a triple relay of railway, ropeway and Tamang porters plied this route.

You can continue on the Raj Path to the pass at the entrance to the Valley. From here, the road winds down towards the Terai and India. Trucks trundle past, carrying loads of workers or goods, while overloaded buses painfully make their ways up the winding road.

statue of
ing
ribhuavn
alutes
avelers on
e Raj Path.

PATAN OF THE GOLDEN ROOFS

The city of Patan is located on a high plateau above the course of the Bagmati River, just south of Kathmandu. Sometimes called "the town with a thousand golden roofs" or "the city of fine arts," most local people know it as Lalitpur: *Lalita Pura*, "the beautiful city."

An essentially Buddhist city, Patan was built in concentric circles around its royal palace. Four main roads radiate from the palace to four directional stupas, earth and brick mounds said to have been erected by Emperor Ashoka himself. If true, this would make Patan the oldest Buddhist city in the world, dating to the 3rd Century BC.

Nevertheless, Patan has been an important town since very early times. Inscriptions from the 5th Century refer to King Manadeva's palace, the Managriha or "House of Mana," which might have been located in the area now called **Mangal Bazaar**, adjoining Patan Durbar Square. The city's great building period occurred under the Mallas, particularly from the 16th to 18th Centuries. Most of today's leading monuments were built or rebuilt at that time. With no fewer than 136 classified *bahals* and 55 major multi-roofed temples, Patan is really the cradle of arts and architecture of the Valley, a great center both of the Newari Buddhist religion and of traditional arts and crafts.

The town has only recently begun to sprawl beyond the limits marked by its stupas. It is at once more rural and more industrialized than Kathmandu. Many of its approximately 200,000 inhabitants are still farmers, and a majority of its population engage in small-scale home industries. The **Patan Industrial Center** has attracted some of the qualified manpower, contributing to the expansion of local skilled craftsmanship. Besides being a reservoir for labor for Kathmandu, local employment is provided by tourist hotels, UNDP headquarters and some of the commercial and private sector that have moved their offices from the ever-growing capital to the north.

The Royal Palace Complex: The north-south and east-west axis roads divide Patan

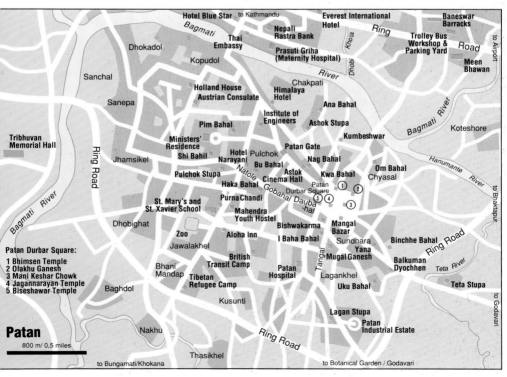

Patan Durbar Square:
1 Bhimsen Temple
2 Olakhu Ganesh
3 Mani Keshar Chowk
4 Jagannarayan Temple
5 Biseshawar Temple

Patan
800 m / 0.5 miles

into four geographic sectors, which meet at the **Durbar Square** and **Royal Palace** complex. This oblong space constitutes perhaps the most spectacular example of Newari architecture in any urban context. To the west, a dozen free-standing temples of various sizes and styles occupy a square framed on three sides by multi-story residences. To the east is the Royal Palace and its walled gardens.

The palace consists of three main *chowks*, or courtyards. The central **Mul Chowk** (a), built in 1666 for Srinivasa Malla, is the oldest. Two stone lions guard its entrance. The low two-story former residence of the Patan royal family, complete with *agam* house and king's prayer room, encloses a large square courtyard with a small gilded shrine, the **Bidya Mandir**, at its center.

Two tall, beautiful repousse brass images of Ganga on a tortoise and Jamuna on a *makara*, or mythical crocodile, flank the doorway of the **Shrine of Taleju**. The gilded *torana* depicts the Ashta Matrikas. On the roof over the shrine is a three-tiered square structure. Towering over this part of the palace, in the northeastern corner of the courtyard, is the triple-roofed octago-nal tower of the **Taleju Bhawani Temple** (b), built for Srinivasa Malla about 1666.

The smaller southern courtyard, the **Sundari Chowk** (c), holds in its center a masterpiece of stone architecture, the sunken royal bath called **Tusha Hiti**. The walls of the bath, created around 1670 and renovated about 1960, are decorated with a double row of statuettes representing the eight Ashta Matrikas, the eight Bhairavs, and the eight Nagas. Several of these statues are missing, perhaps stolen.

Two *nagas* girdle the top of the basin into which the water flows through a conch-shaped stone spout covered with gilded metal. Hanuman and the Buddha sit in front of this beautiful *yoni* basin while a live armed soldier stands guard.

The three-story buildings around the *chowk*, surmounted by the three roofs of a corner temple, offer fine woodcarvings, especially on the upper-floor window grilles. Stone images of Ganesh, Hanuman and Narsingh flank the outside entrance to this *chowk*. The central window above the entrance is of gilded metal, and those flanking it of carved ivory.

Shiva and Parvati, encased in a *torana*,

Patan's Durbar Square shows little change between the 19th Century, below, and today, right.

crown the much-admired **"Golden Gate"** gilded doorway leading to the third courtyard, the **Mani Keshab Narayan Chowk** (d). This northern *chowk* was completed in 1734 after 60 years of construction.

Between it and the central *chowk* is the temple of **Degu Talle** (e), the personal deity of the Mallas. Built for Siddhi Narsingh Malla in 1640, and rebuilt after its destruction by fire in 1662, this three-story building is crowned by a hefty four-roofed tower. The kings performed their sacred Tantric rites here in special ceremonial rooms. Beyond, in a small open space, dances and plays were performed.

Moghul Architecture: Facing the Sundari Chowk is the large, octagonal **Krishna Temple** (f), a stone *shikhara*-style building with a stairway guarded by two lions. To the west of this *shikhara* squats the ugly **Bhai Dega** (g), redeemed by a Shiva *lingum* within. To the north, an enormous bell hangs between two thick pillars; you may see porters, their baskets full of wood, resting on its sunny platform. Nearby, women crouch on the stepped base of the three-roofed 17th-Century **Hari Shankar** (h), all carved struts and *toranas* on arches

and pillars.

Immediately to the north of this temple, **King Siddhi Narsingh** (i), has been praying for more than 300 years, golden on his robust pillar. The *shikhara* behind him dates from 1590. On the other side of a small 17th-Century Narayan temple is probably the oldest surviving temple in the square – a two-tiered brick structure built in 1565 for the god **Char Narayan** (j), with struts depicting the *avatars* of Vishnu.

Facing the northern *chowk* of the palace is the **Krishna Mandir** (k), probably the most remarkable stone building ever raised in the Valley. It betrays influence of Moghul architecture from India. The first and second stories are made up of a line of pavilions in smooth black stone. A slender *shikhara* emerges from the second floor. On horizontal beams, episodes of the great Indian epics, the *Ramayana* and *Mahabharata*, are depicted with explanations in Newari. On the first floor, where the main divinity was installed in 1637, old people can enjoy music-making while watching the square below.

In front of the Krishna Mandir is a statue of Garuda on a high pole. The next

temple, the **Bishwa Nath Mandir** (l), is of the same age and style as the Hari Shankar but was badly damaged in a storm in 1989. The structure and damaged elephants are being replaced.

Ending the long row of temples is one of the most venerated and prosperous-looking temples, the **Bhimsen Mandir** (m), dedicated to Bhimsen, the god of traders. This three-roofed brick building with artificial marble facade from Rana times was erected in the late-17th Century. Its tympanums and struts are partially painted in silver, while the central body is gilded.

At the corner of the northern *chowk* of the palace, the lotus-shaped, deeply recessed **Manga Hiti** (n) has three beautifully carved spouts in the shape of crocodile heads. At certain hours, men and women queue up to refresh themselves with its clear water. Adjoining *patis* have old struts carved with mildly erotic scenes.

Rural Northern Patan: Leaving Durbar Square in an easterly direction, you first come to a small square, framed with traditional town houses containing shops on their ground floors. Here stands a small three-story **Olakhu Ganesh** with funny erotic carvings. Most of the people here are Hindu, mainly of the *jyapu* (farmer) caste. Farther to the north, a small lane opens on a large open space where women weave cloth on a row of bamboo poles.

The **Bhimsen Dyochhen**, an ordinary looking god-house, faces a larger open-square with a pond and a well. The street to the west leads past a small stupa to the **Unmatta Bhairav Temple**, flanked by a rice mill.

The eastern road leads into open fields and on toward the **Balkumari Temple**. You can turn north here in front of the **Naya Hiti**, an 8th-Century sunken fountain with two spouts. Immediately to your right is another larger, newer fountain, the **Chyasal Hiti**. On its top is a painted statue of the goddess Saraswati as a green-and-yellow woman riding a goose. This popular fountain also has many beautifully carved ancient stone images of the late Licchavi period.

A bit further is the small **Chyasal Ganesh Temple**. The path then narrows through rows of three and four-story houses. It turns twice, then enters a small square with an old stone *chaitya* in its

PATAN DURBAR SQUARE

Letters keyed to text.

a-Mul Chowk
b-Taleju Bhawani Temp
c-Sundari Chow
d-Mani Keshab Narayan Chow
e-Degu Talle
f-Krishna Temple
g-Bhai Dega
h-Hari Shanka
i-King Siddhi Narsingh
j-Char Narayan
k-Krishna Mandir
l-Bishwa Nath Mandir
m-Bhimsen Mandir
n-Manga Hiti

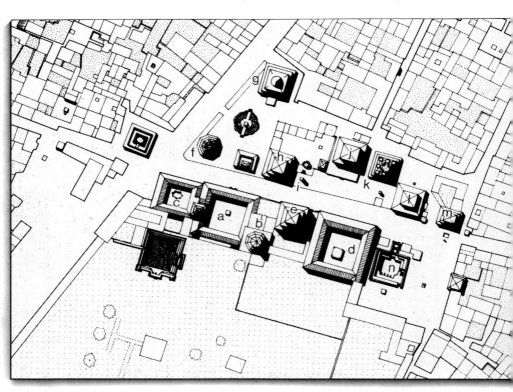

center, the **Om Bahal**.

The path leads north, then west, to join the main northern axis of the city. To the north, three adjacent *bahals* face the **Ashok Stupa,** a white plastered dome with a yellow top. Well preserved, it is surrounded by smaller *chaityas*. Beyond the precinct wall stretches a splendid view of the countryside, with mustard fields and patches of vegetables at your feet, an open field by the Bagmati River, and the city of Kathmandu slightly west in the distance. Prominent on the skyline is the Everest Hotel on the airport road.

The Kumbeshwar Temple: To the south of the Ashok Stupa is the towering **Kumbeshwar Temple,** which dominates this whole area of rural streets and houses. It and the Nyatapola Temple in Bhaktapur are the only temples in the Valley with five roofs, with the exception of the round, five-tiered Panch Mukhi Hanuman of Kathmandu's Hanuman Dhoka Palace.

Founded in 1392, the Kumbeshwar is also the oldest existing temple in Patan. Its struts, cornices and door frame are finely carved. Elegantly proportioned, it stands in a spacious courtyard surrounded by various Licchavi, Thakuri and Malla sculptures and steles. Notable is a figure of Ganesh that Giacometti would have been proud to have created. Like most Shaivite temples, the Kumbeshwar has a piece of grassy land adjoining its precinct; it is a grazing ground for the bull Nandi, Shiva's vehicle.

The platform also has two ponds, both filled with clear water during the Kumbeswar Mela in August. This water comes from a spring issuing from a sunken shrine within the compound; it is thought to originate from Gosainkund Lake, several days' walk north of Kathmandu. Persons who take an annual ritual bath here earn the same amount of merit as those who bathe in the lake.

During the Janai Purnima, in July-August, thousands of colorful pilgrims gather to brave a narrow catwalk and a possible dipping in the pond, to pay homage to a beautifully decorated silver and gold *lingum* that is placed on a specially constructed shrine set in the middle of the tank. Rice, coins and flower petals are thrown to the image. Men in loin cloths, boys in singlets, and women in dripping

eft, Char arayan; ght, rishna Mandir.

saris swim around the tank.

Brahmans and Chhetris, meanwhile, renew their *munja*, or sacred thread, which they wear around their left shoulder from the time of their initiation rite until death. Here and in other Shaivite temples, Brahmin priests – in exchange for rice and coins – tie a golden thread (*rakhi doro*) around the wrists of the faithful to protect them against diseases and evil spirits. During the Mela, drum-bearing sorcerers, or *jhankris*, wearing plumed headgear and white flared skirts, dance around the temple, working themselves into a trance to the increasingly frenetic rhythm of drums.

The southern part of the Kumbeshwar precinct, the **Ulmanta Bhairav**, a particularly important shrine for the Newar community, contains a four-faced brass Shiva *lingum*. Its sanctum is chiseled in silver. Bells and a blue, white and red garland decorate its black tympanum.

Pigs and Pastels: Outside the Kumbeshwar platform, past the large **Konti Hiti** where women often gather, beyond the **Konti Bahal** and the shock of huge Big Brother eyes in the inner courtyard, you enter an old section of Patan. Hindus and Buddhists live together here in more widely spaced houses and *bahals*. The atmosphere is definitely rural: a small cobble-and-earth lane, where pigs wallow in the mud and cakes of cow dung are stuck on house walls, wends downhill to the end of town.

Further to the northwest, the **Ana Bahal** has a naive facade of ceramic tiles in pastel colors and two stucco images in blue and orange representing the sun over the mountains. A few steps farther is one of the most beautiful water conduits still in use in the Valley, the **Alko Hiti**. Surmounted by five Licchavi *chaityas*, this conduit holds various other Buddhist and Hindu sculptures.

Legend claims this *hiti*, with three spouts shaped like crocodile heads, was built with the serpent king's blessings.

Return to the towering Kumbeshwar and head east, where you get lovely glimpses of brick bathed in sunshine, birds in vines, and small stupas in inner courtyards. The next major crossing has a fine **Krishna Temple**, two stone square-column stories on a stepped platform topped by an unfortunate brick and stucco dome of recent vintage. East of this is the **Dhum**

The gods never sleep

Bahal, a fine old house in ochre and violet, with prayer wheels on either side of its main door, struts carved in 1685, and a few statues of devotees. It serves members of the ironsmith caste who live nearby.

From the Krishna Temple, the main axis road returns south to the Durbar Square. The road is flanked by houses of fine quality with well-executed carvings. Keep an eye peeled for an opening to the left containing a small two-tiered shrine: known as the **Uma Maheswar**, it contains a beautiful Licchavi stone carving of Shiva and Parvati. Closer to the Durbar Square, on the left, is a two-tiered temple with a fine image of Garuda dated to 1706, a *naga* set into the paving, and a stone image of Vishnu with four hands. At the entrance to the Durbar Square, there are several shops selling curios and hawkers selling fruit.

Patan's Southern Sector: Return to the crossroads in Mangal Bazaar. The main southern axis road leads from here to the Lagan Stupa. Starting from the **Lakshmi Narayan Temple** built above shops, you first enter an area called **Hauga** which has several shops and workshops dealing in brassware. A side lane to the west leads to the **Bishwakarma Temple**, whose entire facade is embossed in copper. Above the *torana* crowning this shrine to the god of carpenters and masons is a fixed window, which shows a solar disc intersecting triangles. The brass and copper craftsmen living in this area keep it resounding with the clang of hammers.

About 200 meters south, at a crossing to the right, is a *chaitya*-shaped shrine of Lakshmi-Narayan in ruins, and an unappealing dome-shaped Shiva temple. Opposite them to the left is the famous **Baha Bahil**, one of the oldest monasteries in Patan, being built in 1427. Part of it is now in ruins; the rest houses a school.

The next small open space to the east has a sunken fountain, **Chakba Lunhiti**, with three spouts and an inscription dating it to the mid-11th Century. Restored in the mid-1960s, it is an important focal point of life in this area.

Behind it, two huge statues guard the entrance to the beautiful 16th-Century **Minanath Temple**, which is set in its own enclosure. A double-roofed shrine decorated in yellow and black brass, it has a huge prayer wheel in a cage to one side.

A basket seller and his wares.

Struts display multiple-armed goddesses. The divinity of this temple is closely connected with the adjacent Rato Machhendranath, and accompanies the Machhendra chariot in a much smaller chariot during the annual festival.

The Red Machhendranath: You will reach the **Rato Machhendranath** temple by turning west into the first lane from the main axis. The S-shaped paved path leads to a large, walled open space. Here is the three-story Patan home of the Red (*rato*) Machhendra.

Machhendra is the popular Tantric expression of the god Avalokiteshwara as well as of Lokeshwar. Venerated as Shiva by Hindus, he is worshipped by all as a god of rain and plenty.

A temple may have been built on this site as early as the 15th Century. The present structure dates from 1673. Pairs of lions guard the entrances to its four intricately carved doorways, while various animals on pillars face the main altar. Under the metal roofs, the struts depict Avalokiteshwara above the various tortures of condemned souls in hell. A row of prayer wheels underline the base.

The piece of dark red wood representing Machhendra is taken out of the shrine every year and paraded about on a chariot for weeks of processions during the Rato Machhendra celebration which begins in May. This is Patan's biggest annual festival. The celebration concludes when the chariot is taken to **Jawalkhel** at the southwestern entrance to Patan and dismantled.

But every 12 years – the next occasion will be in 1991 – the chariot is dragged to **Bungamati**, five kilometers (three miles) south of Patan. There, Rato Machhendra has a second residence in a temple in the center of the village where it resides for six months every year. The route from Patan to Bungamati is quite rugged, with a bumpy road surface and long uphill stretches; taking the chariot this way is a difficult undertaking. There is a saying that if the chariot fails to reach Bungamati within a certain time period, the god will be taken to Bhaktapur.

Ganesh and Narayan: The main road continues to the **Lagan Stupa**, the southern Ashok Stupa in Lagan Khel, through poorly constructed houses inhabited mainly by butchers and sweepers. Turning back north again, along a road parallel to that main axis, you go through an area

flanked on the west by open countryside, and on the east by houses of *malis* (gardeners), who tend the flowers needed for daily worship.

Soon you come to an open space with an interesting collection of buildings: a stone Ganesh Temple, a well-proportioned three-tiered **Bhairav Shrine** with rows of bells under metal roofs, and a 16th-Century **Narayan Mandir** in brick with nicely carved struts and a Garuda squatting in front of it. Craftsmen in the vicinity originally worked in ivory; some are now merchants and traders.

A few steps farther on, two huge stone "sofas" mark the entrance to the 17th-Century **Nayakan Bahil.** The Shrine's blue, white and green glazed tiles, added in 1940, are eye-catching.

Where the street meets the main east-west axis, a small, low **Mahapal Ganesh Shrine** juts out. Sticks of incense are kept burning in the empty shrine. This is a predominantly Buddhist sector where artisans produce woven items, mats, baskets, porter belts, and cane trays or *nanglo*, sold with gypsum stones in nearby shops.

Returning by the same route, you go back through Mangal Bazaar, skirt the Durbar Square and the palace garden walls, and enter the eastern sector of Patan.

Powdered Lions and Prayer Wheels: Through the open air bazaar, the road east leads to the grassy mound of the Teta Stupa, the east Ashok stupa which stands alone just across the ring road on the way to Lubhu. As the pavement narrows, note a brick platform similar to that at Basantapur. It used to be a vegetable market; now it houses shops in rows. Further along, three and four-story houses flank the route. They contain the workshops of silversmiths, goldsmiths and diamond cutters. Their craftsmanship is worth an extra look. Many people here smoke popular blend of tobacco and molasses in the *hookah chilim* as they work.

The herring-boned road soon leads past a workshop of artisans making *tablas*, traditional hand drums. In the open space facing a fountain are a couple of small temples. One of them, the **Hari Shankar**, exhibits corner struts with leaping griffins in green and violet; an important sculpture of Surjya, dated 1083, beside the door; and a kneeling Garuda in front. Siddhi Narasingh Malla is said to have had his residence in this *tole*.

Continue down the road, keeping an eye out for a lane which leads south to the **Guje Bahal**. The lions at the entrance, their heads copiously smeared with red and yellow powder, are linked by a flowery wrought-metal arch. Reconstructed in the mid-17th Century, this monastery has a fine-looking facade: a row of meditating Buddhas and a painted panel of Buddhist divinities decorate the upper stories. Behind the temple are a well and the **Guje Chaitya** stupa.

The lane to the left leads to the slender three-story **Yana Mugal Ganesh** built in the mid-16th Century. Its Ganesh image is painted in flashy orange. However, the metal *torana* pediment, a recent addition, depicts Bhairav.

Sundhara and Shikhara: An **Uma Maheshwar** *shikhara*-style temple is on the right as you continue. The main road opens into a square with various pleasant if slightly decaying temples, monuments and *bahals*. To the right, at road level, is a *sundhara*, a sunken fountain with a beautiful gilded water spout. This is an important local watering hole. Beyond it is another tall, thin *shikhara* dedicated to Uma Maheshwar; in the corner of the square stands a fine house with a wooden trellis on the ground floor and a completely carved facade. This square is important during the Rato Machhendra festival. It is the easternmost point of the Machhendra chariot's journey; from here, the god is carried south.

Leave the square and follow the road east through rural village houses. Note a fine three-roofed Ganesh shrine on your left. Opposite is the **Balkumari Dyoch-hen**, with circular latticed grilles on the ground-floor window frames. This part of Patan is inhabited by members of the sweeper caste. These low-caste people are shy compared to other *hookahs*, do not smile freely, and rarely answer the customary *"Namaste"* greeting.

Four hundred meters (a quarter-mile) away, past a deep sunken fountain and a little bridge, stands the eastern Ashok stupa, the **Teta Stupa**. It stands amidst a landscape of mustard fields spiked with brick and tile kilns. This stupa is smaller in circumference than either its western or southern counterparts. The Buddhist niches were added in the 19th Century.

The naked horse.

The Thousand Buddhas: If you continue east, you will soon come to a *jyapu* area. Turn left, off the main road, to find the large **Bhinchhe Bahal.** This monastery features a large, rectangular three-story shrine. You are likely to find men embossing *mantras* on a piece of brass to be rounded into a prayer wheel.

Of the various monuments at the northern limit of town, a three-roofed construction holds the visitor's attention because of a series of flaking paintings under its first roof. These depict a variety of weird scenes, perhaps taken from the *Ramayana*. One in particular is striking: it represents the silhouette of a horse made out of a jumble of naked human bodies.

Return south and west down an uneven village street full of cats. It is unusual to find that many elsewhere: cats are not at all popular with Nepalis, who believe they are the embodiment of evil spirits. Turn through the Sundhara square into adjacent commercial street and head towards a much-visited architectural masterpiece: the **Maha Baudha** or "Temple of the Thousand Buddhas."

Although the temple is not visible from the street, you cannot miss it. An arrow to your right points to a short lane overflowing with curio shops. Here, in a cramped courtyard, stands the tall structure entirely covered by terra-cotta plaques depicting the Buddha.

The temple is intended to be a copy of the Mahabodhi Temple at Bodhgaya in India's Bihar state. But if the construction principle is the same, the structure and details are substantially different – all the more so because this *shikhara*, built at the end of the 16th Century, was renovated after suffering severe damage in the 1934 earthquake. After the renovation, there were many "spare parts" left over, due to a reduction in the temple's original height. With this leftover material, a smaller *shikhara* was constructed adjacent to its parent temple.

From the roof terrace of a towering new house on the west side of the courtyard, you can get a plunging view of the monument and its surrounding rooftops. Various craftsmen working in precious metals live in the neighborhood.

Farther south is one of the most famous Buddhist monasteries in Patan, the **Uku**

ary boy,
t, eyes a
onze
ast near
e Maha
udha,
ht.

Bahal. This *bahal*, a large rectangular structure with two gilded roofs, has undergone a major restoration. As you enter, look on the right-hand side to see carved wooden struts of great artistic simplicity. These masterpieces, one of the earlier known works of this type, were in fact moved from the back of the *bahal* to their present "safer" location.

Chaityas and Bajracharyas: In front of the Uku Bahal are several *chaityas*, guardian lions and several other rather true-to-life animals, and a statue of a Rana maharaja in military uniform. The latter stands on a pillar like a displaced Napolean III in this 17th-Century compound. Behind the *bahal*, in the center of an open square with grass and trees, is the stone **Yatalibi Chaitya** stupa.

Return to the Patan Durbar Square and head west from the Bhai Dega Shrine. The main axis road is asphalted. It goes through two and three-story residential houses inhabited mostly by *bajracharyas*, the traditional Buddhist priest caste. The *kumari* or living goddess of Patan is chosen from among the daughters of the priests of **Haka Bahal**, a popular monastery which may have originally been located on the site of the Keshab Narayan Chowk in the Durbar Square. On the facade of the shrine is a row of 10 Buddhas set amid green, yellow, brown and white ceramic tiles.

If you continue as far as **Pulchok** the Narayani Hotel will be on your right and opposite you is the **Pulchok Stupa,** the west stupa of Ashoka and the most visible of the four. Climb up the steps behind the stupa to the newly-restored **Akshya-shore Mahavihar** on an early Licchavi site on the **Banagiri Hill**, from where there is a magnificent view.

Return south passing a two-story **Krishna Mandir** and skirt an oblong green-water pond to reach the interesting 17th-Century **Purna Chandi**. This shrine to Durga has three roofs and three *torana* crowned doorways, and is painted red with yellow and black spots. It holds only free-shaped stones. The struts depict Bhairav and the Ashta Matrikas.

Wander through a rural district, then leave the main east-west road to head northward. Glance at various interesting *bahals* and temples. You will see the highly adorned **Shi Bahil** with its three roofs,

Western Ashok Stupa provides grandstand for parade spectators.

pinkish facade and boards of ceramic tiles.

A Squinting Stupa: In an area called **Shiba Tole** is the beautiful little stupa of **Pim Bahal** a brick-and-stucco replica of Swayambhunath, overlooking a large pond; popularly believed to be the fifth Ashok stupa. But the earliest record is a 1357 inscription mentioning the restoration of the stupa after its complete destruction at the hands of Bengal Muslims seven years earlier. Note the stupa's painted eyes: they are definitely squinting.

Toward the northern end of a pond is a three-roofed **Chandeshwari Temple** with well-carved struts and crudely painted lions at the entrance. Follow the pond's longest side north, and come to the ancient looking, simple and beautiful wood structure of the **Joshi Agam.** This faces the 16th-Century **Mahadev Temple**, a small, two-roofed brick-and-wood shrine on a platform by a well.

Return eastward along the main road. Pass through a tall, arched gate and turn past a movie house; here you are surrounded by houses of mixed styles with occasional shops. Various monasteries are on either side of the road, including one with mural paintings representing death in the form of a phallic skeleton.

The houses become higher, finer and more compact, separated by narrow side lanes. One of these lanes on the north side leads to the enormous **Nag Bahal**, an open space which focuses on the life of 20 or more families. Half of the buildings around it have been rebuilt, and do not mix well with the older houses. Some have Western-style windows. In a corner, a sunken well is decorated with a statue of the Buddha. The building in the middle of the open space is used as a school. There is a special festival in this precinct every fifth and twelfth year.

You must return to the main road to reach the next courtyard, called **Ela Nani** from the name of its associated shrine, located to the left as you enter. Immediately to your right, the **Michhu Bahal** faces the same courtyard. Although both shrines have fine woodwork, they do not compare with the wonders of the adjoining inner squares to the east.

Here is the peaceful, vine-covered **Saraswati Nani.** This stocky single-story shrine is dedicated to Manjushri, the Bud-

mile from a young visitor t the Kwa ahal.

dhist god of learning, rather than his Hindu counterpart, the goddess Saraswati; tthe two are often confused in popular religion.

Next to it is the marvelous "Golden Temple," otherwise known as the **Kwa Bahal** or **Hirana Varna Mahavihar**. This Buddhist monastery is a large, rectangular building with three roofs and a facade richly embossed with gilded copper. The entrance is guarded by a pair of temple lions. Inside are several images, including some early bronzes of Gautama Buddha and Avalokiteshwara. The metalwork, especially that of the *toranas*, shows great detail and craftsmanship.

Take off your shoes and step into the lower courtyard. In its center is a small shrine, lavishly embellished with silver doors and images – many of them with a strong Hindu influence. The *gajur* which crowns the shrine is overly ornate, but a masterpiece nevertheless. A gilded frieze depicting the life of Buddha is situated immediately in front of the main shrine.

This is an ancient sanctuary. Legend connects its origin with a 12th-Century queen named Pingala of Marwar, although the earlier available records date from 1409. It is still actively patronized by Buddhist communities. Various groups stay at the monastery for a month at a time, observing very strict rules as they look after its maintenance.

A staircase leads to a Lamaist *gompa* on the first floor. If you ask one of the novice monks to guide you, he'll be happy to point out the interesting frescoes and other images of the Buddha within.

At the southwestern edge of Patan is **Jawalkhel**, site of the Valley's largest Tibetan refugee camp. This area is popular with visitors as a center of typical Tibetan handicrafts. In two large buildings, a couple of hundred men and women are always busy carding wool and weaving carpets. In the first building, five rows of women in traditional costume sit on the floor, one to three on a carpet weaving traditional patterns, chatting and singing. In the next building, old men and women comb the wool and loom it into threads. Shops display these handicrafts for sale. Portraits of the King and Queen of Nepal and the Dalai Lama look down from the walls on a maze of carpets, blankets, woven bags and small coats.

Below, many **Tibetans make their home in Jawalkhel.** **Right**, the **Golden Temple's courtyard.**

SOUTHERN SETTLEMENTS

South of Patan, various vehicle and walking tracks link settlements and sacred sites to the one-time capital. West of the Bagmati River are Kirtipur and its satellite hamlets, Panga and Nagaon. The twin settlements of Bungamati and Khokana lie on either side of the sacred Karya Binayak site. There is a road leading to the Lele Valley, and the road to Godavari and Pulchowki, passing through Harisiddhi, Thaibo and Bandegaon. And an eastern lane takes travelers to Sanagaon and Lubhu. The history of all these villages is linked to that of Patan.

Rocky, Neglected Kirtipur: Almost all Newar settlements in the Valley are on plateaus. **Kirtipur**, perched on a twin hillock about five kilometers (three miles) southwest of Kathmandu, is a magnificent exception. First established as a kind of outpost of Patan in the 12th Century, it later became an independent kingdom and the last stronghold of the Mallas which fell, after a prolonged siege, to Prithvi Narayan Shah in 1769-70. It is said the Malla soldiers taunted the Gorkha forces as they struggled up the fortress-like hill. After the conquest was complete, the vengeful Gorkha ruler had the noses and lips of all Kirtipur's male inhabitants, with the exception of those who could play wind instruments, cut off.

Remains of the original fortification wall can still be seen. The earlier fortified city had 12 gates, one for each ward. Beyond and below the fortifications live low-caste people. Many of the 20,000-plus inhabitants are farmers and others are merchants or commute to jobs in Patan and Kathmandu. The road to Kirtipur is through the **Tribhuvan University** which occupies some of Kirtipur's former farmlands; farmers seeking alternative jobs as laborers is now a familiar pattern with the ever-increasing urbanization of the Valley.

Besides farming, traditional occupations are spinning and weaving. The 900 handlooms of **Kirtipur's Cottage Industry Center** spin cloth for Kathmandu.

Kirtipur is neglected. Resting on a rocky saddle, it withstood the series of earthquakes that so damaged several other Valley settlements. But age has gnawed at buildings, and decay enhances a feeling of

walking back into Nepal's past. Some of the multi-storied houses still have exquisite carved windows; all the homes are laid out on stepped terraces linked by ramps and sloping paths.

One of the approaches from Kathmandu is up a long flight of steps. It enters the town near a huge pond, settled on the saddle between the two hills. The southern hill is surmounted by the **Chilanchu Vihar**, a central stupa surrounded by four small stupas, all with stone images set at the cardinal directions. Around it are houses and *dharmasalas* (resthouses), the former monasteries abandoned. The higher northern hill is inhabited by Hindus who have settled around the Kvath, a temple dedicated to Uma Maheshwar.

Where the two hills meet north of the central tank stands the famous **Bagh Bhairav Temple**, a place of worship for Hindus and Buddhist alike. This three-roofed temple, heavy within its enclosed courtyard of uninteresting facades, has a veranda on its ground floor and trellised balconies on its upper floors. The temple is decorated with swords and daggers presented by the Newar troops after Prithvi

eft, a
Thecho
voman.
Right,
hildren of
Kirtipur.

Narayan Shah's 18th-Century conquest. Within the temple is a famous image of Bhairav in his tiger form. Of particular interest is the upper *torana* above the main sanctum; it shows Vishnu riding Garuda above, and below, Bhairav flanked by Ganesh and Kumar. There are also some interesting if rather indistinct early wall paintings under the arcade, around the base of the temple.

The **Kvath's** setting and approach, up a flight of stone steps flanked by stone elephants, is more striking than the temple building itself. It commands a wonderful view of the Valley and the agricultural patchwork of green and yellow terraced fields. From the Kvath, you can see in the southeast how lower Kirtipur is spreading towards the two small villages of Panga and Nagaon. A path from Kirtipur leads into **Panga**, the larger of the two. Founded and fortified to cope with northern invaders during Malla times, it is an oblong settlement of about 600 houses. Most of its residents are Newari Buddhists, primarily farmers, with some carpenters and bricklayers. There are a half-dozen or so temples in the village, but none is particularly outstanding or older than the 19th Century.

The hill opposite Panga is capped by a large, rounded, earthen mound called **Mazadega**. This was planned as a stupa, but was never completed.

A path here leads to **Nagaon**, which it enters between a small pond and a water tank. This settlement, whose name means "newly settled village," has about 200 mainly Buddhist households.

Machhendra and Karya Binayak: The twin settlements of Bungamati and Khokana date from the 16th Century. The Malla ruler of Patan at that time wanted to control his land while preventing people from moving too far away from the city. He decided on two sites near the Karya Binayak shrine, amid very fertile fields.

But the area had to be sanctified. Legend says that at the time of a big drought, the king – accompanied by a Tantric priest – went to visit Machhendra in the rain god's temple in India, and invited the god to settle in the Valley. A shrine for Machhendra was established at the place where the village of **Bungamati** now lies. As early as 1593, the custom was established of **The streets of Kirtipur.**

leaving the Rato Machhendra in Bagmati during the winter months. The rest of the time he stays in his shrine in Patan; a palanquin carries him to and fro.

The approach road from Patan to Bungamati is dotted with small votive *chaityas*, appropriate for an ancient processionary path. The village of over 2,000 people is tightly clustered against a hilly riverside slope, surrounded by terraced rice fields and clumps of trees. Open ponds flank the paved path as it enters the village.

Past a Ganesh temple, a series of steps leads to a gate guarded by two lions and the head of a third one, which juts from a ramp built around the animal. Here is the powerful, *shikhara*-style **Rato Machhendranath** temple, with heavy columns and beautiful supports in its lower part. In the courtyard, cows, buffaloes and goats lie amid several *chaityas.* Through the grille of the wooden door of the nearby Lokeshwar Shrine, you may catch a glimpse of the huge head of Bhairav, with crooked nose, greedy lips and globelike eyes.

Ten minutes' walk away, past the important Karya Binayak shrine on a tree-covered hillock is the village of **Khokana**.

Slightly bigger than Bungamati, with a population of about 3,000 Newari Buddhist, Khokana is famous for its mustard-oil manufacturing. It is worthwhile to seek out one of the village's oil presses, which is located in poorly-lit factories with medieval atmospheres.

Khokana's streets are brick and stone-paved with central gutters. They are flanked by plain brick facades with no frills. The main street , built after the 1934 earthquake, is remarkably wide. The village's main temple is dedicated to the goddess **Shekali Mai**, also known as Rudrayani, one of the Valley's nature goddesses.

The Lele Valley Road: The road to Chapagaon and Lele, two villages which have greatly declined in importance since Licchavi times, is not often plied by casual visitors to Nepal. But this enchanting route unfolds picturesque scenes: black-and-white-clad civil servants going miles by bicycle every morning to their offices in Kathmandu; stands of bamboo drenched in sunshine; yellow mustard fields, green rice fields, misty blue hills, and a neat background of white snow-capped peaks.

The Machhendranath temple in Bungamati.

On a high, flat plateau on the verge of the next valley, **Sunaguthi** sits by the roadside. This settlement, founded in 1512, numbers about 2,500 people of various castes. The main shrine here, consecrated to the god **Bringareshwar Mahadev**, is not particularly beautiful, but it houses one of the 64 most sacred *lingas* in the Valley. On the same village square is a small two-roofed temple devoted to the Indian god **Jagannath**.

Gently winding uphill amid terraced fields, the path soon reaches **Thecho**, a larger settlement of more than 5,000 inhabitants of different castes. You may be inclined to stay awhile in this friendly town, watching the women washing clothes, scraping jugs and pots, or soaping their hair around greenish ponds.

Thecho's Balkumari Temple: In an open space surrounded by *patis*, a peacock stands on a column in front of the gaudily-colored **Balkumari Temple**. On the square below, grain and chillies are scattered on mats and dried. In the northern part of the settlement is the second main temple, this one consecrated to **Brahmayani**. Its two-roofed structure, guarded by familiar lions and a less familiar duck (vehicle of Brahmayani) on a column, overlooks another square. Framed Indian religious pictures hang below the first roof, and King Birendra watches the temple from a poster on a nearby communal house.

Two kilometers past Thecho, **Chapagaon** stretches along the main road. According to legend, a Malla king exiled one of his own sons here for siring a caste of his own, called *babu*. At the entrance to the village is a metal Ganesh shrine smeared with dry blood and a statue of Brahma beside a huge *yoni*. In the central square, beside two double-roofed temples to Narayan and Krishna, one of which has fine erotic carvings on its struts, is the **Bhairav Shrine**, a sacred single-roofed structure dedicated to the main deity of Chapagaon. This settlement of some 3,000 people looks fairly prosperous with a variety of shops and an effective drainage system. East of here is the fine Vajra Varahi Temple.

Immediately south of Chapagaon lie the two small satellite hamlets of **Bulu** and **Pyangaon**, peaceful rural settlements near the Valley's southern foothills.

Below, Thecho. Right, landscape near Lubhu.

BHAKTAPUR: CITY OF DEVOTEES

Seen from a distance in the early morning light, the long stretch of ochre brickwork blends perfectly with the landscape of gentle hills. Roofs are a double line of gray, and a single temple rises into the sky like a beacon. At the foot of the hill, the sacred Hanumante River draws the southern border of the city of Bhaktapur.

Bhaktapur – which is almost as well known by its alternate name Bhadgaon – is said to have been designed sometime in the 9th Century in the shape of Vishnu's conch by its legendary founder, King Ananda Malla. In fact, the backbone of the city is a double S-shape, directed east-west, opening on squares with temples, shrines and sunken fountains.

These open spaces were old village centers established along the ancient trade route to Tibet. Chroniclers of the time recall locations like Khopo, Khuprinibruma and Bhaktagrama, the latter name implying village (*grama*) status. After the

8th Century, these villages joined and grew into a town. This urban growth was the result of an evolutionary process rather than voluntary planning, or so legend would have us believe. Certainly, a concentric growth pattern, such as that of Patan, is absent in Bhaktapur.

The original center of Bhaktapur was the eastern square around the Dattatraya Temple. When the city became the capital of the whole Kathmandu Valley between the 14th and 16th Centuries, there was a shift from east to west with the development of a new palace area. There are indications that the town was fortified by the mid-15th Century, as the new focus of the city moved to Taumadi Tole with its Bhairav and Nyatapola temples.

A Medieval Showcase: Bhaktapur has preserved its character and identity better than the Valley's other two major cities. There are three main reasons for this: its independent development until the Valley was reunified by Gorkha invaders in 1768; its subsequent isolation and stagnation; and the greater attraction of Kathmandu for hill-tribe immigrants and 20th Century visitors. Indeed, with its 150,000 inhabit-

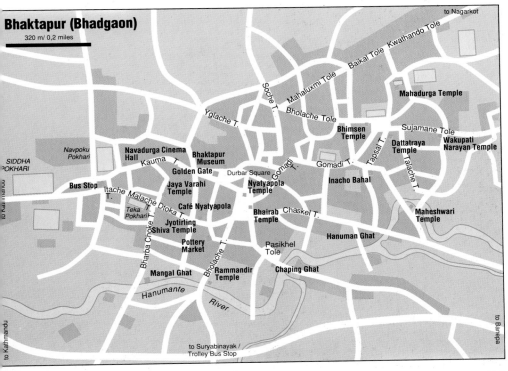

Bhaktapur (Bhadgaon)

320 m/ 0,2 miles

ants, Bhaktapur is regarded as showcase of "medieval" Nepal and has much benefitted from extensive restoration.

It is also the most self-contained and self-sufficient of the Valley's major settlements. Bhaktapur's own farmers grow its food. The city's own craftsmen build and decorate its houses, make its pottery and adorn its temple.

Its traders serve its commercial needs, and its people generally have preserved original traditions. The women's white shawls, and their red-edged black sari-like dresses (*patasi*), blend with the yellow and ochre of brick and wood. Streets are not crowded; life is unhurried but still purposeful.

The traditional approach road from Kathmandu passes through a grove of pine trees on a hillock, skirting the **Tundhikhel**, a large open field. It then passes alongside two reservoirs. The *pokhari* or tank on the northern side is the **Siddha Pokhari.**

It was properly excavated about four centuries ago, and used to be the largest clean water reservoir for Bhaktapur. Today it is far from clean, but it is neverthe-less sacred to people of all creeds: Shiva and Vishnu shrines and a small Buddhist stupa group can be found around it. There is a legend that a large serpent has taken up residence in this tank; to this day, people in the village are fearful of draining the tank for fear that they will expose the monster.

The Center of Bhaktapur: At this point, the road forks. The left-hand fork leads into the **Durbar Square**, which originally was outside the city proper. The square only became integrated during the reign of King Bupathindra Malla around the beginning of the 17th Century, and it was then linked to a lower square, Taumandi Tole, where the spire-like Nyatapola Temple stands.

If you were to take the right-hand fork, this would take you along the old east-west route through Bhaktapur. The street is lined with fine traditional houses, a scattering of roadside shrines, important temples and water taps. It eventually leads into the Taumadi Tole.

But for now, keep to the left. Entering the Durbar Square through the royal gate, you immediately become aware of the

Bhaktapur Durbar Square in the 19th Century.

**HAKTAPUR
URBAR
QUARE**

tters keyed to
xt.

main entrance
Rameshwar
mple
Durga temple
Bupathindra
alla
Sun Dhoka
Royal Palace
National Art
allery
Taleju Chowk
Kumari Chowk
Sundari Chowk
Durga
ikhara
dharmasala
-Tadhunchen
hal
Batsala Durga
Pashupati
mple
Chaysilin
andap

sparseness of temples, compared to the Durbar Squares in Kathmandu and Patan. In old prints and etchings, Bhaktapur Durbar Square was overcrowded with highly decorated buildings of all shapes and sizes. Today, by contrast, it is a vast open brick square.

The 1934 earthquake caused considerable damage here, entirely destroying two large temples which formed the focal point at the end of the square. One of them, the Chaysilin Mandap or "octagonal pavilion" (p), has been carefully reconstructed. The square, in fact, consisted of two smaller areas divided by a wing of barracks or *patis*. The buildings that remain, however, can impart a tribute to the former splendor of the Durbar Square.

It is said that Bhaktapur Durbar Square once contained at least 19 different courtyards. Legend claims there were, in fact 99 – though this is hard to believe. The August 1988 earthquake thrust Bhaktapur briefly into the world headlines as 180 houses were destroyed but its temples and palaces were unscathed.

A Walk Through Durbar Square: As you walk through the main entrance to the square, on either side of a small gateway (a) leading to the police head-quarters are a pair of very fine stone statues.

These represent the goddess **Ugrachandi Durga** with 18 arms and **Bhairav** with 12. Both wear necklaces of severed heads. Legend has it that their anonymous sculptor had both his hand cut off so that he could not copy these masterpieces elsewhere.

To the left, on the northern side of the square, are the remains of what was once a palace with multiple courtyards. Opposite the palace, on your right, are a series of minor temples: to Jagannath and Bhadri, to Vishnu, and a **Rameshwar temple** dedicated to Shiva (b). Adjacent to these is an interesting brick *shikhara*-style temple dedicated to Durga (c); it is decorated with sculptured images of Hanuman and Narsingh.

As you move into the Durbar Square, what strikes you immediately ahead is a life-sized gilded statue of **Bupathindra Malla** (d) seated on a tall pillar of stone. He is facing the **Sun Dhoka** or "Golden Gate" (e) leading through to the Taleju Chowk and the Kumari Chowk.

The Sun Dhoka is generally held to be the single most precious masterpiece of art in the Valley. Often equated with Ghiberti's famous Baptistery doors in Florence, Italy, this gilded copper gate was erected in 1753 by Jaya Ranjit Malla. It is a monument to the skill of the craftsmen who produced it.

The door frame illustrates many divinities. The *torana* exhibits a very fine example of Mahavaishnavi, and at its head is an excellent Garuda. The gate, set into glazed brickwork, is capped with a gilded roof, which has finials of elephants and lions over it.

Standing back from the gate, what remains of the former **Royal Palace** (f) can be seen on the right. The first important addition in the early-18th Century was the so-called "Palace of 55 Windows," painted black and red. In the 1934 earthquake, this palace was practically razed to the ground, and much of its artistry was lost.

To the left stands a "modernized" section of the old palace. It is still possible to make out some of the original Malla architectural features. The gateway, flanked by Hanuman the monkey god and Narsingh the man-lion, is the entrance to what is now the **National Art Gallery** (g). Within is a

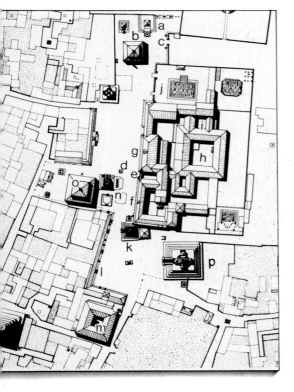

remarkable collection of *thangka* painting. This was no doubt the original entrance to the palace.

The Golden Gate, through which you now pass, leads to the religious and ritual courtyards. As you go through the gate, note a very small courtyard leading through an impressive guarded gateway.

Two Holy Chowks: Pass another small courtyard whose entrance is guarded by two beautiful Malla stone figures. Wind your way around to the back of the courtyard, where the opening to the **Taleju Chowk** (h) is found to the left. This small entrance, adorned with a magnificent woodcarving, is as far as a non-Hindu visitor may go: the two courtyards of the Taleju and Kumari *chowks* are sacrosanct.

But the military guards at the doorway can usually be persuaded to let you get a glimpse of the courtyard. In particular, try to look at the **Taleju God-house** on the southern side. Squint through the doorway to see, on the protective roof above, two dragons about to grab tiny elephants. A couple of lizards enhance the pointed roof, and a five-tiered umbrella crowns the whole. At the center of the *torana* over the entrance to the shrine, barely visible from the doorway, is an image of Taleju with four heads and eight arms. The doorway itself is flanked by two helpers of Ganga, and Jamuna on her tortoise.

Cast your eyes around the courtyard and see the richness of the carving and decoration. In the far right-hand corner is another small doorway that leads through to the **Kumari Chowk** (i). These two courtyards can perhaps be singled out as those most endowed with rare and beautiful artistic masterpieces, as well as representing two of the most holy shrines to be found anywhere in the Valley.

Before leaving this part of the palace, it is worth having a look at the **Sundari Chowk** (j), the ritual bathing courtyard of the Bhaktapur King. Unlike other bathing courtyards, this one is no longer surrounded by buildings. However, the tank itself is lined with stone divinities and is much larger than the one in Patan. From the center of the tank rises a magnificent *naga* or serpent, facing east toward another equally beautiful specimen. The water was supposedly piped from the hills beyond Bhaktapur through a lead-lined

The "Golden Gate."

conduit, but the tank is now dry.

Today, the Bhaktapur palace is still a place in which one should linger awhile: a place to contemplate the beauties contained in what may once have been the most impressive of all Durbar Squares.

Plinths and Pillars: Return to the bustle of the Durbar Square and turn east to reach the smaller of the two enclosed plazas that make up the square. Note the octagonal pavilion, the **Chaysilin Mandap** (p), which has been beautifully reconstructed from contemporary drawings on its original plinth, a gift from Chancellor Helmut Kohl of West Germany to the people of Nepal. It took three years to complete and the exquisite new woodcarving is a tribute to today's craftsmen. Note the inspired modern steel interior. On your left is a fine stone *shikhara* dedicated to Durga (k). Interesting animal guardians line the steps of the entrance to the shrine.

The square itself is framed on two sides by an L-shaped, two-story *dharmasala* (l), and on the north by the multi-level platforms of several temples ruined in the 1934 earthquake. In a corner beneath them, curio shops sell all kinds of traditional tourist trinkets, masks and puppets on strings. To the east, opening onto the street just beyond the square, is an unusual Buddhist monastery called **Tadhunchen Bahal** (m). It has retained the authentic look of a medieval *bahal*. According to an inscription, the cult of a human *kumari* was instituted here.

Reorient yourself to the praying king's pillar opposite the Sun Dhoka in the Durbar Square. Next to the pillar is a big stone bell erected in the 18th Century to call the faithful to morning prayer at the Taleju Shrine. Behind the bell, the stone *shikhara* of **Batsala Durga** (n) looks like the Krishna Mandir in Patan's Durbar. Many divinities are represented in stone carvings around the *shikhara*, as well as copper pinnacles and wind bells.

Farther on is a two-roofed shrine known as the **Pashupati Temple** (o). It is apparently a replica of the Pashupatinath in Deopatan, but is much less impressive because of the less striking setting. However, it is one of the oldest temples in the Valley, having been constructed toward the end of the 15th Century. Its black, carved woodwork depicts common men,

Malla King Bupathindra and Queen.

elephants, lions, *shardulas* or griffins, and finally two minor deities, Simhini and Byaghrini. Beyond this temple, a short street running east leads down to the lower **Taumadi Tole**, lined with shops.

Two Great Mystical Shrines: Here, the **Nyatapola Temple**, Nepal's tallest, stands more than 30 meters (98 feet) high. Carved wooden columns support five roofs and form a balcony around the sanctum. The temple is balanced superbly upon five receding square plinths. A steep central stairway is flanked by huge guardians on each of the plinths. Each pair of guardians is believed to have 10 times the strength of the pair on the plinth immediately above them. Thus, the two famous Malla wrestlers are 10 times stronger than ordinary people and themselves 10 times less strong than the elephants on the next plinth.

Power culminates in the Nyatapola's main deity, Siddhi Lakshmi, a mysterious Tantric goddess to whom the patron-king Bupathindra Malla dedicated the temple in 1702. The image of the goddess can only be seen in the dark of night by the temple's Brahmin priests. Exactly 108 colorfully painted wooden struts show the goddess in her manifold forms; other minor divinities are also depicted.

The Balance of Terror: On the surrounding brick platforms, there is a permanent fair. Farmers bring baskets full of vegetables, and chickens and goats to be sold for sacrifices. Curio sellers unfold treasures like knives, *saranghis*, *thangkas*, precious stone objects, masks, and prayer wheels.

The **Kasi Bishwanath Temple**, with its rectangular base resting directly on the square, is set at right angles to the Nyatapola. This three-tiered structure was completely rebuilt after 1934, using many parts of the previous temple. That in turn had been built in the early-18th Century on the foundation of what was probably an earlier structure yet.

This massive building is a perfect architectural foil to the spire-like, vertical Nyatapola. Both temples show the Nepalese version of the balance of terror: the Tantric goddess in her sacred shrine is counterbalanced by Bhairav's awesome powers, to whom this temple is dedicated.

Paradoxically, the image of Bhairav, which is taken out for chariot processions

Below, buildings restored to dignity displayed in 19th-Century painting, right.

across town during the Bisket festival, is hardly a foot high. It usually rests in a niche about one meter from the ground. A horizontal brass ledge cuts the central door in two; above it is a small hole through which offerings are thrust into the temple's mysterious inner space.

The real entrance to the Kasi Bishwanath is from behind, through the small **Betal Temple**. Betal, enshrined as a human figure in metal, accompanies Bhairav on his journeys in Bhaktapur.

The tile-roofed, three-story brick houses on the west side of Bhaktapur Durbar Square still have fine woodcarvings. The south side, by contrast, is mobbed with plain, post-earthquake houses. But behind them, a plastered-over, arched passage yields entry to the **Til Mahadev Narayan Temple**, one of the oldest temple sites in the city and an important place of pilgrimage in Nepal. An inscription attests to the fact that these premises have been sacred ground since 1080. The temple enshrines a 12th to 14th Century sculpture of Vishnu.

Near the shrine is a four-faced *linga* in a *yoni* under a cage. A jar is suspended over the *lingum*; water is supposed to fall drop by drop on the symbolic phallus. Many old women come to this compound to pay homage to the stone sculptures.

The Other Approach: If you return to the Siddha Pokhari tank where the road forks at the western entrance to Bhaktapur, and this time take the right or southern fork, you will soon walk under the city gate guarded by two stone lions. Three and four-story brick houses line the street, which slopes downhill, then uphill again. Attached to the houses are *patis* with carved wooden pillars that jut into the road. Radios echo each other along this rather narrow asphalted road, where city life and rural scenes alternate. This main axis of Bhaktapur winds its way in an east-west direction, roughly following the course of the sun.

Past a large open space on the right, you will come to another walled water tank, the **Teka Pokhari**. The painted murals of a low doorway to your left indicate a *bahal* within; this is the rather primitive-looking **Ni Bahal**. Its central image is Maitreya, the Buddha of the future.

A side lane to the right, brick-paved but muddy because of regular rainfalls and a

constant lack of sunshine, leads to one of the western *ghats*, the **Mangal Ghat**.

Ahead, on the left-hand side of the main road, a structure protrudes from the building line. Its facade looks like an *agam* house, with intricately-carved woodwork, overpainted figure struts of the eight Ashta Matrikas, and a row of small bells on the eaves. In fact, it is a temple consecrated to **Jaya Varahi**, Vishnu's *shakti* in his incarnation as a boar. Jaya Varahi's image can be seen on the *torana* above the middle window on the second story.

A small, tiled Ganesh shrine juts into the road almost next door; it has a beautifully worked bronze *torana*. Down the road are brass shops, several more *patis*, and another, smaller Ganesh shrine. Glancing down the lanes to the south, you can catch glimpses of ascending hills on the other side of the Hanumante River.

Pass a small brick-paved square, now almost a ruin, and a hodgepodge of various shrines. Soon you come to another square, this one dedicated to Shiva. The complex boasts a sunken *hiti* decorated with a 5th-Century stone relief of Shiva caressing his *shakti* Parvati. The water tank behind the *hiti* is a lovely pool used for bathing, swimming and laundry. Most interesting is the *shikhara* devoted to **Jyotirlingeshwar Shiva**. It has two separate sanctums. On the ground level is an ancient free-shaped stone considered to be one of the Valley's 64 sacred *lingas*; and hidden in the inner sanctum is an image of Nriteswar, the god of dance.

The Pottery Market: At the next crossing, the lane to the left goes directly uphill into the Durbar Square in front of the palace. The side lane to the right, paved with bricks, slopes gently downhill and merges with an open plaza. At the corner of the lane and the main road, a steep stone stairway leads up to a hill. There is a small Ganesh shrine here, a large pipal tree, and a lovely vista of the southern hills.

Take another set of steps on the other side of the hillock, and descend into one of the most fascinating corners in all of Bhaktapur: the **Pottery Market**. Thousands of pots dry in the open square. The huge potters' wheels, set up all around the plaza, are spinning all day long. As the men make pottery, their women pound grain, and children swarm about them all.

Potters at work.

220

A small shrine, with several images of Vishnu, occupies one side of the market square. Ganesh, the elephant-headed patron of potters, presides from his more showy double-roofed temple, the **Jeth Ganesh**. Its priest, quite aptly, is a potter. What's more, it was a local potter who donated this temple in 1646. From the pottery bazaar, the nearest lane south goes straight to the **Hanumante River**. Here is **Ram Ghat**, one of the bathing and cremation places serving the western part of the city. The lane across the river leads to the **Surjya Binayak Shrine**.

The Eastern Ghats: The eastern *ghats* are well worth a detour. Just before entering the Nyatapola Square is a small brick-paved plaza leading into a steep flagstoned lane. It continues south as a neat path with multi-purpose drains: these are used as a kind of railroad track for the religious chariots that are guided in an often uncontrolled manner down this street at Bisket time. This is the processional route followed by the goddess Bhadrakali and her spouse Bhairav once a year, symbolically joining the upper and lower parts of the city.

This path merges into the **Khalna Tole**. Unpaved except for one traversing road, this open space has three free-standing structures and one octagonal *pati* which shelters the Bhairav image during Bisket. From here, the **Chuping Ghat** along the river banks can be seen.

Every year the Bisket festival brings tens of thousands of people from far and near to Khalna Tole. Bhadrakali and Bhairav are there too, ensconced on a huge triple-roofed chariot to witness the extraordinary spectacle, with Betal hoisted prow-like in front.

A 25-meter (82-foot) *lingum* pole is erected in a circular stone *yoni* base. The *lingum* is hung with greenery and two large banners. When it is later pulled down, it marks the start of the New Year in the Valley.

The open shrine to the left along the river is dedicated to the Tantric goddess Bhadrakali. She is represented here by plain stones. When her image is brought here for the Bisket festival, it reveals only a headless standing female figurine.

To the right, just before the Hanumante bridge, is a large complex of temples,

small shrines and *patis* by the riverside. Across the bridge, the stone-paved road continues as a wide track.

This was Nepal's traditional main route to Tibet and the East. It's a short country stroll upstream to the **Hanuman Ghat**, a favorite bathing place for local people. Two arms of the Hanumante River come together here.

Past the next bridge, you come to two huge *linga-yoni* structures on raised platforms surrounded by other *lingas* and shrines. Here Hanuman, who usually serves as a mere gatekeeper in Nepal, is elevated to the role of principal god. An image of the monkey god in his red hood and cape stands beside a modern shrine dedicated to his master, Rama. The corrugated tin roof extends beyond the sanctum to form a porch supported by wooden columns and girdled by vines.

In the southern corner of the complex, Ganesh and the Buddha guard the entrance to a small, pleasant stone platform behind a riverside *dharmasala*. The recessed pit on this platform holds a sacred silver-plated *lingum*.

Women beggars here benefit from the many generous visitors who throw them rice. The old and the ill await death in *dharmasalas*; when the last moment nears, their feet are submerged in the sacred waters, and they are subsequently cremated on a small hill on the opposite bank.

The Old and the New: Further upstream, animal sacrifices are regularly performed at the **Maheshwari Temple** facing the *ghat* dedicated to the goddess with that same name.

The lanes going north from the Hanuman and Maheshwari *ghats* enter the oldest part of Bhaktapur, known as **Tachupal Tole**. You go through a maze of tiny lanes zigzagging passages, inner courtyards with chilies on mats, and corner *patis*, stepping over dozing men.

But suddenly you feel like pinching yourself. The pavement and the buildings around you are of the same old style, but somehow appear brand new. The ground, nicely bricked in a V-pattern, is so clean that even the women do not use mats to spread their grains for drying.

Indeed, the Dattatraya Square was the first part of the city to be restored to its medieval elegance by the West German Bhaktapur Development Project.

The square of Tachupal Tole slopes slightly upward to the east. There, standing on higher ground, is the *tole*'s main attraction: the **Dattatraya Temple** (a), tall and square, facing the rectangular and squat **Bhimsen Temple** (b) from across the whole length of the square.

The two-story Bhimsen, erected in 1605, has a simple *pati* for a ground floor. The austere image of the god, kept above, was molded from the earth. Behind the temple is a deeply recessed *hiti*. Facing the temple, a stone pillar supporting a brass lion shares a platform with a small double-roofed Vishnu temple. Roads branch in all directions from here: this area was the original site of Bhaktapur, and the square was its main open space.

Syncretistic Shrine: The Dattatraya Temple is probably the earliest structure on this site, dating from 1427. This is the only temple in the Valley dedicated to the syncretistic Dattatraya, a deity whose cult originated in southern India. Worshippers of Vishnu number Dattatraya as one of their Lord's incarnations.

Devotees of Shiva, particularly during the Shivaratri festival, venerate Dattatraya as Shiva's teacher. Local Buddhists, not to

DATTATRAY SQUARE

Letters keyed to text.

a-Dattatraya temple
b-Bhimsen temple
c-Pujari *math*
d-Salan Ganesh

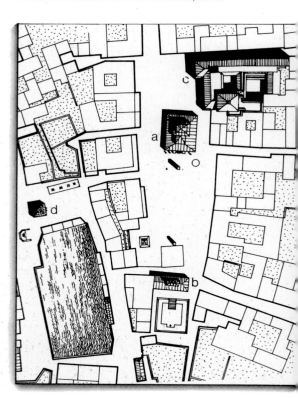

be outdone, consider Dattatraya to be Devadatta, a cousin of the Buddha, and they, too, offer gifts here to the deity.

The Dattatraya Temple is reminiscent of the Kasthamandap in Kathmandu, and like it must have served as a community hall for local citizens. Later a front section was added, accounting for its rather unusual form. Guarding the entrance are the same two Malla wrestlers found at the Nyatapola Temple; these are much larger in size, however. A few erotic scenes are carved around the base of the temple.

Priests' Houses And A Peacock Window: Within Tachupal Tole are 10 buildings which were formerly used as *maths* or Hindu priests' houses. The most famous, the **Pujari Math** (c) is located toward the south of the Dattatraya Temple. Built in 1763, it became so renowned that until this century, the government of Tibet annually sent a caravan laden with rich gifts. Today this old house with excellent woodwork is a museum of woodcarving and well worth a visit.

Many windows inside the *math*, especially those on the balcony of the ground floor of the central courtyard, are just as beautiful as the famed **Peacock Window** on the exterior, down a side alley; the *math* is best known for this work of art.

Within the Pujari Math, a Development Project map shows visitors that Bhaktapur's best-preserved houses line the main east-west axis on the north side of the city, and are also to be found around the Royal Palace. The highest density of population, more than 500 persons per hectare, is concentrated mainly on a vertical strip at the center of Bhaktapur, and in the whole newer eastern part of the city.

Standing in an open space north of the Tachupal Tole, the **Salan Ganesh** (d), erected in 1654, is a small but well proportioned and complete temple, lavishly decorated. Its sanctum has no icon, only a rock said to be a natural representation of the head of an elephant. Its struts depict Ganesh, Bhairav and the Ashta Matrikas, the mother goddesses.

Beyond, rural life takes over abruptly as the lane leads uphill to the **Nava Durga Dyochhen**. Inside, extraordinary, mysterious rites are performed. Tantric in origin, they are believed to be even more gruesome than ceremonial sacrifices fre-

attatraya quare.

quently carried out in the square in front of the shrine.

The Commercial Artery: A quiet brick-paved lane goes in a southeasterly direction from here and soon meets the main east-west axis of the town. At the corner stands a double-roofed, glided temple dedicated to Vishnu as **Wakupati Narayan**. In the merry month of *Magha* (February-March), which is propitious for weddings and ritual bathing, large groups of Newars pass here en route to the *ghats* – singing sacred songs, blowing conches and waving large flags with images of Vishnu. A 1408 chronicle mentions a Garuda pillar that was erected here by one of these families of bathers.

East along the main road is the **Brahmayani Mandir**, which marks the easternmost *ghat* of the same name. The landscape becomes progressively more rural, with a few potters' workshops, a loom, a fountain and a sawmill. The small brick temple of the *ghat* is built on a stone base and is flanked by two huge pipal trees, dwellings for crows eyeing worshippers' offerings.

Return to the main Dattatraya square

and exit via its southwestern corner, heading toward the Taumadhi Tole. Here the road is quite wide and runs downhill. Ground-floor shops sell groceries, bread, nails, tumblers, doorknobs, peacock feathers and temple offerings. This is, indeed, the commercial artery of the old town, winding gently to find itself again in the course of the sun.

Flying Angel Facade: At a crossing where two side lanes go down to the *ghats*, the small **Inacho Bahal** shows flying angels on a whitewashed facade. Then the main road skirts a large open space of the **Jaur Bahi**, a small single-roofed shrine which houses a Buddha in meditation. Although the shrine is modern, the elaborate doorway was taken from an old temple. A little further away is an ancient *dyochhen*-style building with a ground-floor shop selling brass and tin utensils.

At **Golmadi Tole**, the square is surrounded by several *patis* and is occupied by a plastered Buddhist stupa, shrines to Shiva and Vishnu, and a deep sunken *hiti*. There is also the triple-roofed, three-century-old **Gol Madi Ganesh**. Its 32 struts depict Bhairav Ganesh, a popular guardian of the Valley. Across the street, a charming miniature spire-like roof is perched atop a *dyochhen*.

Poetry in Colors: The dim road beyond here is lined with more shops displaying pottery, brass and other wares. Follow the elegantly-dressed local women, clad in their traditional red bordered black dresses (*patashi*), with white scarves (*patuka*) tied around their waists, into the interesting **Lun Bahal** to the left. Although rather dilapidated, it has a certain poetic air about it, and an unusual feature. This structure of Buddhist origin, built in the 16th Century, was later appropriated by Hindus. They placed a stone statue of Bhimsen, consecrated in 1592, within the sanctum. The god is seen here with brass ornaments and a brass mask of fierce expression.

Almost next door is a *math* with beautiful woodcarving, both on its facade and inside. This **Sukul Dhoka** has been recently renovated.

There are two routes you can take from here. The street going straight ahead leads, within 200 meters, to the eastern square of the Royal Palace. The main road turns south, passes more shops and a vegetable market, and returns to the Nyatapola Square.

Left, Nava Durga. Right, father and son.

TOWNS WEST OF BHAKTAPUR

Set upon a high plateau in the center of the Valley, about three kilometers (1.9 miles) west of Bhaktapur, **Thimi** – with 17,000 inhabitants – is the fourth largest settlement in the Valley. The history of this town goes back at least to the time of the independent Malla kingdom. Its name derives from *chhemi*, meaning "capable people," and was given by the Bhaktapur rulers to its farmers eager to help fight aggressors from Kathmandu and Patan.

Today, Thimi is renowned as the home of the Valley's most capable potters. Men and boys hammer and shape the smooth, moist and highly malleable reddish clay from the neighboring fields. They create cooking pots, water jugs and elaborate vessels for their favorite rice wine. Besides these, they produce charming and unique miniature elephants and peacocks for use as flower pots. Thimi is also known for its traditional painted masks.

Thimi's one main road runs from north to south, at right angles to the old road from Bhaktapur. It crosses several open spaces along the way. In the center of the southernmost square is the town's chief temple, a kaleidoscope of colors. Founded in the 16th Century, it is dedicated to Balkumari, one of the consorts of Bhairav, who in turn is represented by a brass image inside his own small domed shrine near his *shakti's* much more imposing temple.

Near the northern boundary of Thimi is **Nade**, a compact settlement of fewer than 3,000 people. From the south, the stone paved path leads uphill through a magnificent high-arched opening in the **Ganesh Dyochhen**. In an open space nearby is a locally famous temple of Ganesh. Small and well-kept, it has three roofs and an elaborate, colorful facade.

A large path from the old Bhaktapur road meanders through rice fields into **Bode**. You will be greeted by strong smells of manure as you cross two large open spaces; the second contains a pond, a paunchy *shikhara* and a stone *lingum*. Durga dances are performed once a year on the round stone platform here.

Straight on to the northern edge of town, you reach the **Mahalakshmi Temple** overlooking the Valley. This temple, of great local significance, has two roofs, the upper one of which is collapsing. Legend says that Bode was founded in 1512 after Mahalakshmi, who had a shrine at the site of the present village, appeared in a dream to the Malla king of Bhaktapur. The present temple was built in the 17th Century.

These three settlements are interdependent in their proper fulfilment of New Year's ceremonies. Every year on New Year's Day, the square around the Balkumari Temple in Thimi witnesses a spectacular gathering of 32 deities carried in elaborate multi-roofed palanquins under the shade of ceremonial umbrellas. During the journey, men throw vermilion powder – a sign of respect – over everyone and everything in their path. When several hundred men from Nade arrive with a palanquin bearing Ganesh, excitement reaches fever pitch. Later in the morning, many people rush to the Mahalakshmi Temple in Bode to see a similar but smaller possession.

Between Thimi and Bhaktapur is the small potters village of Nikosera, also known as **Sano Thimi** or "Little Thimi." Only a few families live here, but they create delightful objects of pottery.

Left, shaping clay in Thimi. **Right**, separating paddy from chaff near Bode.

EASTERN SETTLEMENTS

According to legend, the founder of the Bhaktapur dynasty, King Ananda Malla, created seven major settlements on the eastern side of the Valley in order to strengthen his new kingdom. Three of them pre-existed: these were Banepa, Nala and Dhulikhel. The other four, which he established, were Panauti, Khadpu, Chaukot and Sanga. Most of these settlements in fact lie outside of the Valley proper. Banepa and Dhulikhel took on increased importance with Ananda Malla's action, as they were located on the major trade route between the Valley and Tibet.

The trade route used to cut through the village of **Sanga**, which stands on top of the pass leading into the Valley from the east, five kilometers (three miles) east of Bhaktapur. The modern highway now bypasses it. After skirting Bhaktapur, the road climbs steadily past this community, then winds down rather steeply into the next valley.

A small lane to the north leads into Sanga with its distinctive police boarding school. The village, more scattered than most Newar settlements, enjoys a lovely setting. A little further to the east, a small, rocky boulder crowned by a patch of rubble offers a bird's eye view over the Kathmandu Valley.

The village of Sanga itself has no important religious or cultural buildings, but contains a historically interesting small shrine of Bhimsen. Legend has it that when the Valley was a lake, the god Bhimsen crossed it by boat, rowing from Tankhot in the west to Sanga in the east. A shrine to commemorate his voyage was erected in each settlement.

The Banepa Valley: After leaving Sanga, you pass through part of the lush Banepa Valley to reach the relatively large trading post of **Banepa**. This village also extends north of the highway, at the foot of a forested hill. A major fire some 25 years ago destroyed many of its buildings, but it remains an economically important headquarters for the distribution of goods to the surrounding hill areas.

The main Chandeshwari Shrine looks over the Banepa Valley from a hill on the northeast side of the town. To the north-west, a bumpy track cut by several brooks runs through terraced rice fields to **Nala**. It is said that one of the ancient Buddhas stopped here for his annual four-month meditation, as he was traveling from a visit with the Adhi Buddha at Swayambhunath to the home of the **Namo Buddha** at Namara.

This important meditation site and stupa is atop a hill three hours' walk east of Panauti; it is also possible to drive there from Dhulikhel.

The Buddhist shrine of Lokeshwar, called **Karunamaya**, is located about 100 meters west of Nala by the old Bhaktapur road. The temple is surrounded by buildings for pilgrims, and is marked by a water tank in front of it. Uphill from here, in the center of the village, a steep stone alley leads to a square dominated by the splendid four-tiered **Nala Bhagvati Temple**. Several processions take place around these two shrines during their colorful annual festivals.

From Banepa, the tarmac highway proceeds eastward to **Dhulikhel.** This village sits on a hilltop and is visible from a long distance away. On the main square is a

eft, a
1other at
ome. **Right,**
 father in
he fields.

Narayan Shrine and a pleasant **Hari-siddhi Temple**. Many of the old houses in Dhulikhel have been replaced with modern structures and office buildings.

As you climb a hillock on the north side of the village, you come to an open space. Here, a stone ramp and an arch mark the entrance to Dhulikhel's **Bhagvati Temple**, a three-roofed structure built on a heavy stone platform with ceramic tiles on its facade. Various attributes of Shiva are depicted nearby. From the temple, there is a fine view of the Banepa Valley and the Himalayan Range. The thatched roofs and mud houses at your feet are a precinct of low-caste people living on the fringe of the Valley.

Dhulikhel is the center of one of the major sub-sections of trade between the Kathmandu Valley, eastern Nepal and Tibet. More than 6,000 people live in the village, as many as in Banepa.

The Newar's Panauti: Fewer than 4,000 reside in **Panauti**, one of the finest all-Newar settlements in the region. The village is built at the confluence of two rivers in a small valley surrounded by mountains south of Banepa. It is predominantly agri-cultural and self-contained. Before the development of Banepa it was an important trade center, but today it has little trade. Nevertheless, shops do a thriving trade in food stuffs, electric goods and ritual paraphernalia.

The main village square, now often occupied by ducks, chickens and cows, used to contain a king's palace. A street branching to the south offers a view of the Roshi Khola river. Inside a walled open space are good examples of early temple architecture: a three-tiered **Indreshwar Mahadev Temple** built at the beginning of the 15th Century, and a **Narayan Shrine**. Both are being restored.

The Indreshwar Mahadev Temple is architecturally and historically one of the most important temples associated with the Newari culture of the Kathmandu Valley. Although the temple is said to have been founded as early as the 11th or 12th centuries, the present building dates from the early 15th Century, still making it one of the earliest extant structures. It is certainly a temple of fine proportions and exquisite carving, simple yet beautiful – a fine example of early Newar architectural style. The roof struts, showing incarnations of Shiva, are matchless in their serenity.

Shrines and Ghats: Outside the courtyard, you go past two shrines – one to Bhairav, the other containing a free-shaped stone representing one of the original nature goddess. At the point where the two rivers meet, on a peninsula, is a temple dedicated to Krishna. Several Shiva *lingas* sprout nearby. Adjacent to the temple is an important cremation *ghat*.

Across the **Pungamati River** stands the famous 17th Century **Brahmayani Temple**, which has undergone a major renovation. Brahmayani is the chief goddess of Panauti after Indreshwar Mahadev. An important chariot festival is held each year in her honor.

Archaeological findings may reveal the existence of a pre-Licchavi settlement in or around Panauti. This is the opinion of several specialists in regional prehistory; it is backed by a legend which mentions the existence of an old kingdom near the site of modern Panauti. Perhaps it is here, on the outer fringe of the Kathmandu Valley, that some of the missing clues will be found about this fascinating civilization's earliest aspects and antecedents.

Left, Indeswar Mahadev. Right, Panauti's Brahmayani.

EXPLORING THE VALLEY

Although compact in size, the Kathmandu Valley is so rich in terms of the temples, palaces and villages to be seen. This section serves to suggest how best your time can be used to get out and about.

Taking to your feet is the only way to see most mountain areas of Nepal but it is also the best way to see the Valley. The first section details various walks in the Valley to tie some of the shrines, villages and cities already described in the text. Take a packed lunch or some sandwiches and fruit and don't be in a hurry. Linger in the rice fields, wonder at the haunting views and enjoy the shy smile of a passing beauty. If you are short of time, arrange for a car to drop you off and pick you up.

Because every visitor to the Kathmandu Valley knows Nepal is the home of Mt Everest, the highest mountain on earth, and cannot fail to be curious about the amazing diversity Nepal has to offer, our section Beyond the Valley briefly describes some of the National Parks and what trekking in the Himalaya is all about. However for detailed information about the mountains, rivers and jungles of Nepal and how they can best be explored, see *Insight Guide All Nepal*.

Even for those limited by time or energy, something of the mountains can be enjoyed from the comfort of a Kathmandu hotel. Trips to the rim of the Valley and beyond to Banepa and Dhulikhel can give a glimpse of mountain life and still be accomplished in less than a day. One-day river trips on the Bagmati during the monsoon or the Trisuli from the Pokhara road are better than no river trips at all, though not as good as two or more. The mountain flight east to see Everest and the stunning range between takes its passengers to a different world and back, all in one hour.

Preceding pages: Dharma Guru, a Newar Tantric Priest, dramatizes the life story of the Buddha; the breathtaking Annapurna and Manaslu ranges; villagers at work; nature thrives on the sunny slopes of Kirtipur. **Left,** mountain biking on Shivapuri.

WALKS

There are many very beautiful walks within the Kathmandu Valley that combine cultural experience and natural heritage. To reach most of them, you have to hire a car or taxi. Most of these walks can be accomplished in a day and will take you to sites of great spiritual importance. You will sample the serenity of the countryside and the drama of mountain views.

1. Nagarkot to Changu Narayan. This three-hour walk is for those who do not like climbing hills. Start near Nagarkot village, where a gentle uphill grade leads through a pine-tree plantation. The trail then levels out, following a saddle that juts into the Valley, passing through several little Chhetri settlements. Soon, you'll see the gilded roofs of Changu Narayan above the village. The stone-paved street leading up to the temple is littered with stone sculptures. Marvel at the beauties of Changu Narayan temple, cross the courtyard and leave by a doorway on the west.

Ahead, is the meandering Manohara River, and just beyond it, the road at Bramhakhel. Aim for a point northwest of Changu Narayan where some small houses and a little tea room encourage you on your descent. On the river plain at the foothill, take off your shoes and wade through the soothing waters. Follow a dike through the maze of paddy fields back to the road.

2. Sankhu via Bajra Jogini to Nagarkot. A 12-mile drive past Bodhnath, skirting Gokarna forest on your left, brings you to the ancient and interesting little town of Sankhu, a post on the old trading route between Kathmandu and Lhasa. Walk northeasterly until the road peters out.

Climb up the hill to the important temple of Bajra Jogini. Then take the pathway east behind the complex, through a stand of pine trees. The trail wends its way, quite precariously, down the slope and back to the main trail between Sankhu and Helambu. The paths merge near a cluster of tea houses. Have a cup of *chiya* (tea) here.

There is a long climb ahead. Follow the main trail until you notice a well-worn side trail on the right, taking you in a southeasterly direction up a rather uninviting steep hill, across a rickety bridge, and

In parts of the Valley, foreign workers are still an unusual sight.

242

through a forest. As you come out of the Valley onto a grassy saddle, catch your first glimpses of the snow peaks of the Himalaya. A fairly well-marked trail follows the ridge; in the far distance is the army encampment on top of Nagarkot Hill. Soon the track dips and turns to the right, as it climbs a smaller ridge branching from Nagarkot leading to a large white cheese factory. Here many small houses have been converted into lodges.

You can easily find a secluded hilltop to watch the sun set over the mountains. This is undoubtedly one of the best panoramic views of the Himalaya – it would be possible to see Mount Everest, though it may appear small and unimpressive at the eastern end of the scenic vista. The drive back to Kathmandu takes 45 minutes.

3. Ichangu Narayan to Balaju. Begin by driving to Balaju. Here acquire tickets to enter the Jamacho Forest Reserve. Then take the Ring Road to the crossroads on the west of Swayambhunath, and turn onto the dirt road leading west, past the bus station, toward the stone quarries. Keep going by car as far as you can, past the scarred hillside up to a small saddle, then take the path leading to Ichangu. This is a wide,

well-worn trail bustling with activity. You might even witness the sacrifice of a goat at one of the small shrines along the way. Half an hour of walking brings you to the little temple-complex of Ichangu Narayan.

Beyond the temple compound, the trail narrows. It twists uphill through terraces of wheat and maize to a grassy saddle adjacent to the enclosure wall of the Nagarjun forest. A military guard will ask to see the entrance ticket to the Jamacho reserve. Follow the path in a northeasterly direction to the top of Nagarjun Hill, where there is a small white *chaitya* serving as a pilgrimage center during festivals at Balaju. On the hill's eastern slope are two small hermits' caves containing Buddha images. The descent to Balaju is fairly easy, with excellent views across to the Ganesh Himal range. Before leaving Balaju, it is worth paying the rupee entrance fee to visit the Licchavi reclining Vishnu and 22 water spouts in the Balaju Water Garden.

4. Budhanilkantha to Kathmandu. This pleasant afternoon's walk through the paddy fields northeast of Kathmandu begins with a visit to the reclining Vishnu of Budhanilkantha. From there, head east

Terraced fields near Nagarkot.

along the base of a wooded hill, then take a concrete bridge across a small river to a village. Follow the river's west bank to a steep gorge, where water-powered mills grind local corn. Then cross another bridge and climb a grassy slope past a two-tiered temple to the village of Tupek.

The trail skirts the southwestern edge of the village, where intensive rice cultivation takes place. A little further, at the village of Lasuntar, the trail drops down a rather precipitious gorge. At the bottom, a stream will lead you through a maze of paddy to the Dhobi Khola river. Cross the river, climb the hill on the opposite side, and proceed through another village to the Ring Road. Across the road is the shrine of Dhum Varahi, unmistakable in the clutches of an enormous pipal tree. Near here, the track turns into a motorable road which leads to Hadigaon, one of the oldest settlements encompassed in Kathmandu's urban sprawl. It is easy to catch a taxi from here.

5. Gokarneswar to Bodhnath via Kopan. This walk leads through one of the more remote parts of the Valley. Start at the Gokarna Mahadev temple. Cross a small bridge below the hamlet of Gokarneswar,

turn left (northwest), and follow a well-marked trail up a rather steep grade. Traverse paddy and maize fields and a bamboo grove to a saddle on a ridge marked by a pipal tree. The tea shops here will point you in the direction of Kopan.

Cross the main trail and head downhill to a grassy meadow. You will enjoy the superb views of the northern part of the Valley as you look toward Budhanilkantha. The path follows the edge of a forest plantation, crosses another main trail, then climbs a small hillock on top of which are the monastery and settlement of Kopan, well worth a visit. This is a Buddhist study and meditation center with as many as 120 young novices and a smattering of intense-looking Westerners.

The great Bodhnath stupa lies to the southwest of the monastery. Follow the motorable road down the hill and across a small river bed. Catch a taxi from here.

6. Kirtipur to Patan via Chobar. Take a morning taxi or bus to the town of Kirtipur, atop a rocky hill. Wander around this fascinating Newar settlement, then head off by foot toward Patan.

The ridge route leads from the southeast **Soaking in the scenery.**

244

corner of Kirtipur past a tumbledown stupa, then climbs slowly to the village of Chobar overlooking the Bagmati River (as well as a large cement factory). There are several important shrines here, including the Adinath Lokeswar. Leave by the southeast corner, cross the main road and make your way to the Jal Binayak temple complex at the mouth of the famous Chobar Gorge. Here you can cross the Bagmati – which drains the Kathmandu Valley – noting the chasm allegedly cut by Manjushri's sword.

The trail crosses a large grassy slope, a favorite picnic ground for area residents, then climbs a hill to meet the main trail from Bungamati and Khokana. You can follow this motorable track back toward Jawalkhel; on the outskirts of Patan; or cross the road and continue down into the beautiful Naku Khola river valley. A trail leads to southern Patan, where you can hail a taxi from the Ring Road.

7. Dhulikhel to Panauti via Nama Buddha. Have a car drop you early in the village of Dhulikhel, a one hour drive east of the Kathmandu Valley. The trail climbs on to a ridge from where you get stunning views all the way west to Annapurna. Wind your way up the trail for three hours to the important Buddhist pilgrimage site of Nama Buddha. Enjoy a packed lunch from this superb vantage point, having admired the shrine with the carving of Buddha offering himself to the hungry tigress and her cubs. The settlement of Namara has a stupa reminiscent of a small-scale Swayambhunath. The walk from here descends steeply to a lovely valley. Note the fine carved *paths* (shelters) for pilgrims and Ganesh shrines. Also explore the temples on the *ghats* and admire the woodcarvings on the Indreshwar Mahadev.

Valley Peaks: Three sizeable peaks surrounding the Kathmandu Valley are worthwhile hikes for the energetic. The six-kilometer trail to the top of **Phulchoki** (2,762 meters/9,062 feet) begins behind the St Xavier's school at Godaveri village. From Budhanilkantha, it is a steady three to four hours climb to the top of **Shivapuri** (2,732 meters/8,963 feet), capped by the remains of a fortified palace in a rhododendron forest. The summit of **Champa Devi** peak above Pharping, can be reached in only about an hour of climbing. There are excellent views from all these three peaks.

Soaking in the lifestyle.

ROADS

Other than the shrines and cities described in detail in the main part of the book, there are a number of villages perched on the rim and just beyond the edge of the Kathmandu Valley that must be included for their cultural or scenic interest.

A number of roads radiate from the city of Kathmandu like the spokes of a wheel. Exploring them by car provides a good opportunity to see the Valley, though you may have to walk to get to where you want to go. They are listed here clockwise.

The road north via Lazimpat, Maharajgunj and Bansbari leads through ribbon-developing rice fields to **Budhanilkantha**, home of the massive reclining Vishnu nestling at the foot of **Shivapuri** (2,732 meters /8,963 feet). A good three or four hours walk to the top through magical forests rewards the enthusiast with wonderful views. Budhanilkantha is growing even past the handsome walls of the famous School, run with British assistance along British lines, where the Crown Prince was once a pupil. The Newar ridge village of **Tokha** is reached by turning west about half way up from the ring road.

Northeast through **Chabahil** runs the ancient trade route to Helambu, passing the thriving township of **Bodhnath** for a quick round of prayer wheels, past **Jorpati** with its school and hospital, leaving the turning left to **Gokarna** and the scenic climb to **Sundarijal**.

Straight on the road passes the **Gokarna Safari Park**, the 650-acre King's Forest with its golf course, elephants and picnic spots. Winding on, notice the golden roofs of Changu Narayan perched on its ridge on your right before reaching the fascinating old town of Sankhu, once the last stop before climbing out of the Valley and beyond. Enjoy the friendly atmosphere of the town before the climb up to **Bajra Jogini**. From here the intrepid can walk up to Nagarkot.

A more conventional way to reach **Nagarkot** is by road due west of Kathmandu via **Bhaktapur**. A back route (take the first left after the ring road) takes you via the end of the airport runway and the Pepsi Cola factory to the fascinating old

Valley roads can be narrow and precarious.

township of **Thimi**. Note the tempting terracotta animals for sale by the road if you do not wish to walk to the main village. As you approach Bhaktapur, the road turns left to Nagarkot, past the rural backwaters of the city, alive with farming activity and ladies in their traditional red and black saris. A well marked turning to the left will take you winding up the hillside through the rice fields and the bamboo thickets to the important temple of **Changu Narayan**. Continuing on, you pass the "industrial estate" of Bhaktapur then, leaving the town past army camps and check posts, the road starts to climb to Nagarkot, seen towering to your right. Though not more than an hour to the top from Kathmandu (32 kilometres/20 miles) a night can be spent up here in one of the modest guesthouses to enjoy the spectacular view, extending all along the Himalaya range even up to Everest (with a little luck and imagination). Popular for early morning sunrise trips, at 6,886 feet (2,099 metres) this is the highest point that can be driven to on the rim of the Valley.

Continue on past Bhaktapur, noting the impressive view of the conch-shaped city to your left, past the trolley-bus terminal to the western edge of the Valley where the road climbs to **Sanga**. Pause to enjoy the panorama you are leaving before descending to the town of **Banepa**, distinctive with its statue of King Tribhuvan in the middle of the road. A detour left takes you past the Banepa Hospital and on to the **Chandeshwari Shrine**, notable for its startling fresco of Bhairav.

A 20-minute drive turning right in Banepa leads to the classic Newar village of **Panauti**, a little-visited treasure. Panauti is noted for its temples, *ghats* and desultory population. Particularly important is the 15th-century **Indreswar Mahadev** which has superb woodcarvings.

Another fifteen minutes from Banepa, an hour in total from Kathmandu, will bring you to **Dhulikhel** with its lovely mountain views and good facilities from which to enjoy them. The village and its temple are worth a visit and there are some pleasant walks from here three hours to the celebrated, sacred stupa of **Nama Buddha** on the hill of **Namara** where the lord sacrificed himself to a hungry tigress and her cubs. The hilltop stupa can also be

Maize and mustard fields.

reached by four wheel drive vehicles along a rough and winding dirt road.

You are on the Chinese built Arniko Highway, locally known as the "Chinese Road", leading eventually to the **Friendship Bridge** below the border town of **Zhangmu**. In theory you can drive all the way to Lhasa in Tibet, two long days away, but frequent landslides and problems with the road make the reality rather different. Check local conditions if you are planning on making the journey past **Barabhise**.

Opposite Patan, passing the most eastern of the four Ashok stupas which stands alone in fields, is the road to **Sanogaon** and **Lubhu**. Walks to the eastern side of the Valley can start from here.

"Eye of the Needle": More accessible is the tree-lined road to **Godavari** ten kilometers (six miles) east of Patan, which passes through lovely country and the unspoiled old Newar towns of **Harisiddhi** and **Thaibo**. From **Badegaon** on this road walk east to the little shrine of **Bishankhu Narayan** and test if you are pure enough of sins to fit through the alarming small "eye of the needle". The town of Godavari, at the end of the road, suffers from a disfiguring marble quarry on the lower slopes of **Pulchoki** (2,762 metres/9,062 feet), the highest hill on the Valley perimeter. Don't let that deter you. Up past the Jesuit boys school of St Xavier's, this is a good climb through indigenous rhododendron forests. The **Royal Botanical Garden** is a popular place for picnics, especially on a Saturday.

Close to the Godavari crossroads on the ring road south of Patan is the turning to the road that eventually winds its unpaved way to the remote village of **Lele** and the nearby **Tika Bhairav**. Passing through the rather charmless town of **Sunakothi**, enjoy lovely rural views until, after about ten bumpy kilometers, you reach the fascinating agricultural towns of **Thecho** and **Chapagaon**. The 17th Century Tantric temple of **Vajra Vahai** is set in trees to the east of the road at Chapagaon.

Continuing west along the ring road from the Lele turning, your next road on the left to the south is the seldom-visited dirt road to the sacred villages of **Khokana** and **Bungamati** a little beyond, the winter destination of the Rato Macchendra.

Trucks and buses have come to use the bridge over the Bagmati at the Kirtipur crossroads as a parking area. Turn south on the big road to **Dakshinkali**, one of the most impressively sinister of Kali's shrines, darkly huddled against a hillside just below **Pharping**. This historic area has a number of interesting temples and monasteries, particularly **Bajra Jogini**, **Sekh Narayan** and the **Goraknath Caves**. **Champa Devi** or Two Trees as it was affectionately called, is a pleasant walk from this road, passing the **Pine Ridge Resort** at **Hatiban** two kilometers (one mile) up the hill, commanding fine views across the Valley.

Soon after turning off the ring road to Pharping, imposing concrete gates on the right lead through the **Tribhuvan University** buildings to the fourth city of the Valley, **Kirtipur**. Perched high on a ridge, the temple roofs of Kirtipur are outlined against the sky. The road goes all the way up to the town's edge, from where it is best to explore this lovely old city on foot.

Below Kirtipur, straight on past the University is **Chobar**. Immortalised in legend by Manjushri, whose sword released the waters of the Valley, this site is now dominated by a belching concrete factory. The Ganesh shrine of **Jal Binayak** is just beyond the Gorge.

Traveling west on the ring road, you will note the old Rana ropeway, a relic from Afghanistan after World War I. Though replaced in 1960 it still sometimes works, linking the Valley (the depot is in Kalimati) to Hitaura. Before the Raj Path, this was the major way of bringing in supplies. The main road to Pokhara leaves the Valley to the west, and is by far the most heavily traveled by cars and buses as well as the big trucks that now supply Kathmandu from the Terai and India. This is the Raj Path, the main route into the capital. **Thankot** stands guard on the western edge of the Valley as the road climbs past the earth-satellite station and the statue of King Tribhuvan. It was he who inaugurated the Raj Path in 1956, thus first road-linking Nepal with the rest of the world. From behind Thankot the old foot trail into the Valley via the Chandragiri Pass to Hitaura and India beyond, is only two days walk. Today's road is aligned differently and crosses the rim of the Valley over a small pass, before dropping west amidst stunning views of Ganesh, Manaslu and Himalchuli and rolling, terraced middle hills. Excursions to Pokhara start along this road, as do those to the viewpoint of **Daman**, 80 kilometers (50 miles) towards Hitaura to the reservoir of **Kulikhani**, one of the Valley's major hydroelectric supplies; to the seat of the Shah kings, the palace and temples of **Gorkha**; with perhaps a side trip to the shrine of **Manakamana**, high above the Marsyangdi river.

Back in the world of the Valley, the western part is the least known as here are the fewest roads. The main artery through **Balaju** passes the Water Garden with the reclining Vishnu and the 22 water spouts before reaching the Queen's Forest of **Nagarjun**. Winding on upwards for an hour or so to the rim of the Valley, turn right to the small village of **Kakani**, from where you can admire the mountain view or enjoy a picnic. Glance over the fence at the Raj-style bungalow belonging, since the mid-19th Century, to successive British representatives in Nepal. For many years this was as far as foreigners were allowed to travel, progressing in style on horses and palanquins to glimpse the "beyond" that was officially denied them.

The road now drops to **Trisuli Bazaar and Dunche**, a six-hour drive from Kathmandu and the starting point for Langtang treks. An hour's detour to the historic fort of **Nuwakot**, Prithvi Narayan Shah's headquarters for his assault on the Kathmandu Valley, is interesting but rather long for a day trip from Kathmandu.

River trips can put in from this road, though normally the Trisuli is not deep enough for the rigged rubber boats, rowed or paddled, that are used for this exciting way of exploring the country. One-day white water trips are run on the Trisuli River from the Pokhara road, but they involve an unenviable amount of driving for a single day. Better to camp overnight by the river and three day trips will bring you, through the Himalayan foothills, to the jungles of Chitwan.

An appropriate way to explore the back roads of the Valley, avoiding roads and traffic, is by mountain bikes and fascinating one day trips can be devised. The recent popularity of these hardy bikes amounts almost to a craze. First developed in California, mountain bikes adapt well to exploring Nepal, combining cultural sensitivity and silence with the means of covering rough and even steep trails.

hapagaon.

Royal Nepal Airlines, the domestic flag-carrier, arranges a one-hour mountain flight east from Kathmandu every day to see **Mount Everest**, at 8,848 meters (29,028 feet), the highest point on earth. This "fly past" of the world's greatest peak is usually in the morning when the weather is most likely to be clear – your money is refunded if it is not – and is operated in either an Avro or Boeing aircraft.

This mountain flight gives an instant perspective of the extraordinary variety of terrain of Nepal. There is no better way to witness it.

Nepal has eight of the earth's fourteen 8,000 meter (26,250 feet) mountains either within or on its borders, and eight of the ten highest mountains in the world. All 14 are listed below in order of their heights.

Mount Everest, which bestrides the Nepal-Tibet border, is known to Nepalis as Sagarmatha (Mother of the Universe) and in Tibet as Chomolungma (Mother Goddess). It was named after George Everest, a British surveyor-general in late 19th-Century India. The world's highest peak was scaled on 29th May, 1953 by **Sir Edmund Hillary** of New Zealand and **Tenzing Norgay Sherpa** of India.

Nepal was not open to foreign mountaineers until 1949, and Nepalis were not interested in scaling the peaks. So it has only been in the most recent decades that the many peaks of Nepal's Himalaya have been explored and climbed. Everest, the great prize for mountaineers, has since seen many "firsts". These landmarks of exploration include **Nawang Gombu Sherpa** of India, who in 1965 became the first person to have climbed it twice; in 1975 **Mrs Junko Tabei** of Japan became the first woman to reach the summit; in 1978 **Reinhold Messner** of Italy and **Peter Habeler** of Austria proved Everest could be scaled without the use of artifical oxygen, a feat previously considered physiologically impossible; in August 1980 **Reinhold Messner** again made history by being the first person to make a solo ascent, from the Tibet side without using any bottled oxygen. This was also the first ascent ever

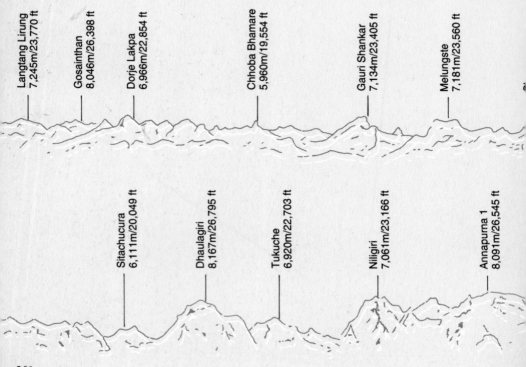

Langtang Lirung 7,245m/23,770 ft
Gosainthan 8,046m/26,398 ft
Dorje Lakpa 6,966m/22,854 ft
Chhoba Bhamare 5,960m/19,554 ft
Gauri Shankar 7,134m/23,405 ft
Melungste 7,181m/23,560 ft

Sitachucura 6,111m/20,049 ft
Dhaulagiri 8,167m/26,795 ft
Tukuche 6,920m/22,703 ft
Niligiri 7,061m/23,166 ft
Annapurna 1 8,091m/26,545 ft

made during the summer. In February the same year **Leszek Cichy** and **Krzysztof Wielcki** of Poland became the first persons to successfully climb during the winter. In 1990 **Ang Rita Sherpa** of Nepal became the first person to have climbed Everest six times. His feat still remains a record.

There is an exclusive, and ever growing, international "club" of persons who have stood on the summit of the highest mountain in the world. These number well over 300 persons, both men and women, from more than 20 different nations.

Annapurna 1 (8,091 meters, 26,545 feet) was the first 8,000 meter peak to be successfully climbed in the world, when in June 1950 a French expedition reached the top. The summiteers on this historic ascent were the team's leader, **Maurice Herzog**, and his climbing partner, **Louis Lachenal**. By 1960 all the remaining 8,000-meter mountains in Nepal had been scaled.

Even today, foreign mountaineers must gain permission from the Nepalese government who regulate which mountain may be climbed, by whom, by which routes and in which seasons. In addition to the formal permit granted by the authorities, expeditions are bound to provide specified wages and equipment for the Nepalis who assist them.

THE WORLD'S HIGHEST MOUNTAINS

1. Everest 8,848/29,028 on the Nepal/Tibet (China) border
2. K-2 8,611/28,251 on the Pakistan/China border
3. Kangchenjunga 8,586/28,169 on the Nepal/India border
4. Lhotse 8,516/27,940 on the Nepal/Tibet border
5. Makalu 8,463/27,766 on the Nepal/Tibet border
6. Cho Oyu 8,201/26,906 on the Nepal/Tibet border
7. Dhaulagiri 8,167/26,795 in Nepal
8. Manaslu 8,163/26,781 in Nepal
9. Nanga Parbat 8,125/26,657 in Pakistan
10. Annapurna 1 8,091/26,545 in Nepal
11. Gasherbrum 1 8,068/26,470 in Pakistan
12. Broad Peak 8,047/26,401 in Pakistan
13. Xixabangma 8,046/26,398 in Tibet (China)
14. Gasherbrum 2 8,035/26,362 in Pakistan

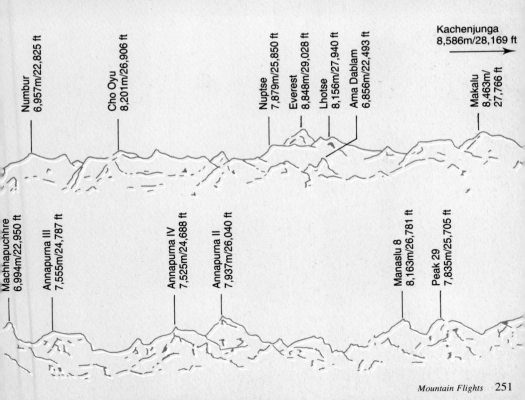

Machhapuchhre 6,994m/22,950 ft
Numbur 6,957m/22,825 ft
Annapurna III 7,555m/24,787 ft
Cho Oyu 8,201m/26,906 ft
Annapurna IV 7,525m/24,688 ft
Annapurna II 7,937m/26,040 ft
Nuptse 7,879m/25,850 ft
Everest 8,848m/29,028 ft
Lhotse 8,156m/27,940 ft
Ama Dablam 6,856m/22,493 ft
Manaslu 8 8,163m/26,781 ft
Peak 29 7,835m/25,705 ft
Makalu 8,463m/27,766 ft
Kachenjunga 8,586m/28,169 ft

Astride the long frontier between Nepal and the People's Republic of China lies the greatest concentration of high mountains on earth. Considered the consummate climbing challenge, the peaks of giants such as Mount Everest, Annapurna, Dhaulagiri, Makalu and Cho Oyu have long stirred the imagination of travelers and adventurers.

Rising from the glaciers on the flanks of these great mountains, a multitude of rivers plunge south to feed the holy Ganges. Cutting deep gorges, these torrential waters course through beautiful and enthralling country – verdant landscapes, thick stands of virgin forests, and villages steeped in ancient religions and cultures. Finally slowing as the waters meet the lowlands of the Terai, barely above sea level with hundreds of miles to go before meeting the sea, the rivers meander quietly through the plains and dense jungles rich in birds and wildlife.

Glimpses of the Valley: Fascinating glimpses of these wild regions are accessible to those willing to exert physical energy. One of the great charms of Nepal is that it is still largely without roads. Access to its interior – its villages and valleys, its mountains and hills – is by ancient foot trails and trade routes interlaced across the country. Only on foot can the traveler ever discover Nepal's true personality.

Outside of the Kathmandu Valley, there are four principal regions of interest to the visitor. From Pokhara, an important crossroads town west of the capital, one can explore the terrain of the Annapurna Massif or venture further west to Dhaulagari, Dolpo or Jumla and Lake Rara. Directly north of Kathmandu are the spectacular Langtang Valley and other isolated regions near the Tibetan border. East is the greatest of all mountains, Everest, and the homeland of the Sherpa people with the wilds of the Arun Valley and Kachenjunga further west. South in all directions, abutting the Indian frontier, is the Terai with its bustling border towns, its great national parks teeming with wildlife, its indigenous Tharu people, and its pilgrimage sites like Lumbini, the birth-place of the Buddha.

Almost ten percent of Nepal's total land area has been set aside as national parks, wildlife reserves and conservation areas, and these spots should be high on the list of priorities for explorers of inner Nepal. Tourism is encouraged in most of these sanctuaries, but a great emphasis is placed on its being compatible with conservation ideals, and in some cases, on its being economically beneficial to the local populations. Nepal's Department of National Parks and Wildlife Conservation administers seven national parks and three wildlife reserves whilst the Annapurna conservation area comes under the King Mahendra Trust for Nature Conservation. Under the patronage of the King and his brother, Prince Gyanendra, Nepal's park system is an example to the rest of Asia.

Nepal lies in the overlapping zones of Oriental fauna to the south and Palearctic fauna to the north. This factor, coupled with its dramatic altitudinal and climatic variation, has contributed to the kingdom's great variety of wildlife forms. For example, although the country contains only a fraction of one percent of the earth's land mass, about 10 percent of the planet's birds – roughly 800 species – can be found in Nepal. Its national parks, which represent three principal zones of terrain, trans-Himalayan, Himalayan and tropical, are set up to protect a representative cross-section of the land.

In addition to the mountain national parks of Sagarmatha (Everest), Langtang just north of the Valley and the Annapurna Conservation Area near Pokhara, most visitors tour the famous wildlife of Royal Chitwan National Park, just half an hour's flight from Kathmandu, and Royal Bardia National Park on the great Karnali river in the far west. These are the two famous Terai areas where substantial visitor facilities exist – now more than forty lodges and camps offer a variety of services – quite a change since 1964 when Tiger Tops first opened its, then, four rooms in Chitwan. More hardened travelers may venture west to Royal Suklaphanta wildlife reserve and Khosi Tappu wildlife reserve in the far east.

receding ages: a oyal hitwan ger. **Left,** ount verest.

River running down the famous rivers spilling through the Himalaya is another popular way of seeing the country. Since first pioneered by Himalayan River Exploration in 1976 running the river systems of Nepal is now a well developed industry and trips vary from the two weeks needed to run the Sun Kosi or Tamur rivers to several days on the Bheri, Trisuli, Seti or Kali Gandaki. The excitement of the white water, the unsurpassed scenery and the interest of passing villages makes for an unbeatable combination at the congenial speed of water.

Nepal Trekking: An increasing number of visitors to Nepal are now walking – or "trekking," as it is called here – into the interior. The word *trek* is Afrikaans in origin; South African Dutch pioneers used it to describe a long journey by ox-wagon in search of a new home.

But words change meaning when they travel, and in Nepal, where no ox-wagons could possibly traverse the rugged mountains, officialdom defines trekking as "a journey undertaken on foot for seeing natural and cultural scenes in areas where normally modern transport system is not available."

In late 20th Century Nepal, trekking is one of the most popular activities for visitors. By trekking, you will discover many new horizons: the haunting beauty of the Himalayan reaches and the peculiar warmth of the mountain peoples, far from the feverish pace of Western civilization. To trek in Nepal is to undergo an almost spiritual experience. It is to walk in communication with nature and man, beneath the world's most exalted mountains.

Trekking in Nepal, as it is known today, was established by a British citizen named Col. Jimmy Roberts. A veteran of numerous first ascents of Himalayan peaks in Nepal and Pakistan, as well as a provider of logistical support for other major climbing expeditions, Roberts founded Nepal's first trekking agency – Mountain Travel – in 1965. In doing so, he has created an industry which has benefited the mountain people and has grown to become one of Nepal's major foreign exchange earners. There are dozens of trekking agencies active in Nepal today.

Trekking need not be especially demanding physically. There are treks for every level of fitness, from short walks on relatively level terrain to rugged, demanding expeditions. Treks can last for a few days to a month or more. They can take the traveler to regions of anthropological or cultural interest, to areas of exceptional mountain scenery, into the jungle, over high snowy passes, or to expedition base camps on the lower levels of the highest peaks.

Seasons for Trekking: The best time for a trek depends upon the region to be visited but generally, the summer monsoon gives way to clear skies at higher elevations in late September. By mid-October, the rains are over in the middle hills and jungles, and the crisp clear days of autumn fill the country. In November and December, the weather remains predominantly sunny and clear, beginning to get cold at higher elevations.

January and February are the coldest months in the high Himalaya but the middle hills and lowlands are beautiful. Snow rarely comes lower than 3,350 meters (11,000 feet) and the land takes on a new enchantment.

March and April are excellent months for trekking throughout Nepal, although certain high passes are not safely open until mid-April. May can be beautiful at high altitudes although it may get hot below 1,200 meters (4,000 feet). With the onset of the monsoon in June, periods of rain are intermittent with bright, blue skies and the hills a brilliant green throughout the summer.

Trekking is allowed nearly everywhere in Nepal and all treks require a permit. Treks organized by agencies are highly recommended, especially if you are trekking in Nepal for the first time. Agents can tailor treks to your own pace, ambitions and interests and provide services to help you get the most out of your limited time. Arranging itineraries, permits, transportation, insurance, equipment, food, porters, sherpas and a *sirdar* (a sherpa leader) can be a frustrating and time-consuming experience – and sometimes a disappointing one – for the independent trekker.

Other beyond the Valley activities such as mountaineering, river running, wildlife viewing, hang gliding, mountain biking, kayaking, high-altitude skiing, marathon running and more adventure activities in Nepal are covered in the new *Insight Guide Nepal*. Compiled by a team of experts in the field, the book contains detailed information and useful maps.

Campsite en route to Khumbu.

केन्द्रीय टेलिफोन-भवन

TRAVEL TIPS

GETTING THERE

BY AIR

More than 90 percent of all non-Indian visitors to Nepal arrive by air at Tribhuvan International Airport, about 8 km (5 miles) from Kathmandu.

Many air carriers serve the Kingdom including the national flag carrier, Royal Nepal Airlines Corporation (RNAC), Bangladesh Biman, Burma Airways, China Airlines (CAAC), Dragon Air, Indian Airlines, Lufthansa, Pakistan International Airlines, Royal Bhutan Airlines, Singapore Airlines and Thai International.

Kathmandu can be accessed by flights directly from Europe (Frankfurt twice weekly and London once a week), Dubai and Karachi as well as the traditional route from the west via Delhi. From the east there are flights from Hong Kong, Singapore and Bangkok. Additional regional destinations served are Varanasi, Colombo, Patna, Calcutta, Dhaka, Rangoon, Paro and Lhasa.

FARES

All air fares must be paid in foreign exchange by foreigners in Nepal and there are a number of special fares available in Kathmandu. As air fares fluctuate with the exchange rate, check with a travel agent. Only Nepalese and Indian nationals may pay in rupees for any air passage between Nepal and India.

When coming from the west to Kathmandu on a clear day you will see close in succession the western Himalaya: Gurja Himal (7,193 meters), Dhaulagiri (8,167 meters), the dark deep valley of the Kali Gandaki River leading north to Mustang, the six peaks of the Annapurna Range, the pointed Manaslu (8,163 meters), and the three lumps of Ganesh Himal (7,429 meters) which dominate the Kathmandu Valley.

Coming from the east you can view suc-

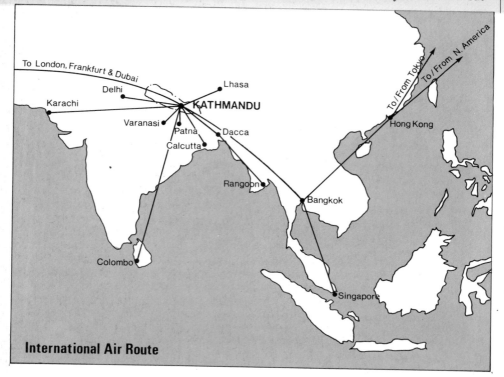

International Air Route

THE PROBLEMS OF A

HEAVY TRAFFIC.

You'll come across massive Thai jumbos at work and play in their natural habitat. In Thailand, elephants are part of everyday rural life.

FALLING MASONRY.

A visit to the ruined cities of Sukhothai or Ayutthaya will remind you of the country's long and event-filled history.

EYESTRAIN.

A problem everyone seems to enjoy. The beauty of our exotic land is only matched by the beauty and gentle nature of the Thai people.

GETTING LOST.

From the palm-fringed beaches of Phuket to the highlands of Chiang Mai there are numerous places to get away from it all.

OLIDAY IN THAILAND.

GETTING TRAPPED.

In bunkers mostly. The fairways, superb club houses and helpful caddies make a golf trap for players of all standards.

HIGH DRAMA.

A performance of the 'Khon' drama, with gods and demons acting out a never-ending battle between good and evil, should not be missed.

EXCESS BAGGAGE.

Thai food is so delicious you'll want to eat more and more of it. Of course, on Thai there's no charge for extra kilos in this area.

MISSING YOUR FLIGHT.

In Thailand, this isn't a problem. Talk to us or your local travel agent about Royal Orchid Holidays in Thailand.

Thai
We reach for the sky.

Herald Tribune
Reagan Calls on Moscow To Withdraw Support In Conflicts in Third World

Ask for it every day, everywhere you go.

Wherever you're going in the world, a copy of the International Herald Tribune is waiting for you. Circulated in 164 countries, on 70 airlines and in hundreds of quality hotels worldwide, the IHT brings you a view of the world that is concise, balanced and distinctly multinational in flavor. And you can get it six days a week, even when you're traveling.

INTERNATIONAL Herald Tribune

This region was the cradle of the **Insight Guides** and is their special domain. It all started on the enchanted island of Bali with the idea to create a very different guidebook — one that combines visual and intellectual insight. What is the magic of Bali, island of the gods? How do you avoid giving offence in Thailand? Does the nightlife of Bangkok live up to its reputation? Where do you find the best dining experiences in Singapore? **Insight Guides** provide the answers.

Bali
Bangkok
Burma
Indonesia
Malaysia
Philippines
Singapore
South East Asia Wildlife
Thailand
Vietnam

APA
INSIGHT
GUIDES

cessively the flat-topped Kanchenjunga (8,463 meters), the giant of them all, Everest (8,848 meters), Cho Oyu (8,201 meters), Dorje Lhakpa (6,966 meters), and Langtang Lirung (7,234 meters) standing above the Kathmandu Valley.

The twice weekly service to Lhasa flies directly over the Himalaya and must be one of the most spectacular and romantic flights in the world. Check local political conditions as these flights are seasonal and sometimes do not operate.

BY RAIL

Within India, trains are a convenient means of transportation but there is no railway to speak of in Nepal. A 47-km line was built in 1925 between Raxaul, India, and Amlekhganj, south of Kathmandu. Further east, a second line was built in 1940 between the Indian border and Janakpur, some 50 kilometers north. But that's all.

Combining Indian rail with Indian and Nepalese roads, it takes about three days to travel from Delhi to Kathmandu by way of Agra, Varanasi and Patna, crossing the border at Birgunj.

If you're coming from the Indian hill station of Darjeeling, you can take the train to Siliguri. From there, it's a one hour taxi journey to Kakar Bhitta, a Nepalese border post from where you catch a bus or taxi to Biratnagar.

If you are planning to travel overland from Nepal to Darjeeling by way of Kakar Bhitta, a special Darjeeling permit is required for all passports. An Indian visa is also required to enter India for foreigners, so if you are planning to commute once or twice between Nepal and India, it is advisable to obtain an Indian multiple-entry visa. This will save a lot of time and inconvenience.

BY ROAD

In addition to Tribhuvan Airport, there are only five official entry points. Check local political conditions as even these are sometimes closed temporarily. These points are:

Rani Sikiyahi (Kosi Zone), just south of Biratnagar.

Birgunj (Narayani Zone), near Raxaul, India, the most common point of entry for overland travelers.

Kodari (Bagmati Zone), on the Chinese Tibetan border, open to tourists with Chinese visas providing road access to Lhasa.

Sonauli (Lumbini Zone), near Bhairawa on the road to Pokhara.

Kakar Bhitta (Mechi Zone) with connections to Darjeeling and Siliguri, India (see above).

If you are entering Nepal by private car, be prepared to wait for several hours to get through any of the Indian border posts. Private vehicles are not permitted to enter China from Nepal. A *carnet de passage en douanes* is required for cars and motorbikes. These exempt the owner of the vehicle from customs duty for three months. A driver's licence is also required. Motor vehicles in Nepal are driven on the left side of the road.

TRAVEL ESSENTIALS

VISAS & PASSPORTS

Except for Indian and Bhutanese citizens, all passport holders require a visa for entry into Nepal.

A tourist visa can be issued by a Nepalese Embassy. This visa is valid for 30 days in the Kathmandu Valley, Pokhara and other parts of Nepal linked by highways.

A 15-day visa can also be issued on arrival at Kathmandu's Tribhuvan Airport for US$10 for all foreign nationals except British passport holders for whom the fee is UK£20. This can be extended to the full 30-day period at no additional cost.

For treks outside of the main highway areas, a trekking permit is required.

A single entry visa to Nepal costs US$10 for 30 days. Visas can be extended for up to three months at a rate of Rs. 75 per week for the second week and Rs. 150 a week for the third month. Longer stays will require the recommendation of the Home Ministry.

Extensions are granted at the Department of Immigration, Keshar Mahal, Thamel,

Kathmandu; tel: 412337 (open from 10 a.m. to 4 p.m. except Saturdays and government holidays; bring your passport and two passport-size photos).

You are also required to show that you have changed money (at least US$10 per day) to obtain a visa extension so bring your currency card or foreign Exchange Encashment Receipt.

Get a multi-entry visa if you are planning a short visit to Tibet or India within your three month period.

MONEY MATTERS

On entry, everyone is handed a currency card to be filled in with name, nationality and passport number but not the amount of currency imported.

Every time you exchange foreign currency for Nepalese rupees, the transaction must be recorded either on the card with the stamp of the bank, hotel or other authorized dealers or with a Foreign Exchange Encashment Receipt.

At the end of your stay, excess Nepalese rupees can be converted back into hard currency as long as what remains does not exceed 10 percent of the total amount changed.

Non-Indian visitors are not allowed to import or export Nepalese as well as Indian currency.

For currency exchange, there is an exchange counter at Tribhuvan Airport. The official rate of exchange fluctuates against all currencies.

US dollars are in high demand and there is a black market in Kathmandu. Buyers should be cautious and remember the currency card requirements.

The official exchange rate for all currencies is published daily in *The Rising Nepal* newspaper and broadcast every day by Radio Nepal in the Nepali language.

There are banknotes in denominations of Nepalese Rupees, 1,000, 500, 100, 50, 20, 10, 5, 2, and 1, and coins of Rs. 1.00 and of 50, 25, 10 and 5 *paisa*. There are 100 *paisa* to one rupee. Half rupee is 50 *paisa*, while 9s is called a *mohar*, and 25 *paisa* is referred to as a *sukaa*.

HEALTH

Visitors should possess a valid health certificate of inoculation against cholera and yellow fever, if coming from an infected area. Checking of health certificates is somewhat haphazard.

WHAT TO WEAR

Your wardrobe will depend upon when you are going to Nepal and what you intend to do there. Unless you are planning to meet Their Majesties, government or embassy officials, there is no need to bring anything but the most casual clothes.

From mid-September to March, light clothing is fine in the Kathmandu Valley. Avoid synthetic fibers which irritate the skin. For evenings and early mornings, a heavy woolen sweater or a padded anorak or jacket will be needed. Blue jeans, corduroy trousers or long skirts are in order and comfortable shoes are a must, even if you do not intend to go trekking. High-heeled shoes are out. Sneakers are ideal. Do not bother to bring a raincoat; it's too warm for it in the daytime, and a locally bought umbrella will suffice to bear the sun as well as the rain.

Special gear required for trekking can be hired or bought in Kathmandu or Pokhara, in standard Western sizes. The same applies for sweaters, ponchos, caps and other woolen or down clothing.

From April to September, only light clothes, preferably cotton, are needed in Nepal. That's true most of the year in the Terai, but in the cold lowland, nights in December and January make a sweater and jacket essential.

CUSTOMS

On entry, the traveler may bring in 200 cigarettes, 20 cigars, one bottle of spirits and two bottles or 12 cans of beer duty-free. Also duty-free are the following personal effects: one pair of binoculars, a camera with a reasonable amount of film, a record player with 10 records, a tape recorder with 15 tapes, a musical instrument, a transistor radio, one video camera (without deck) and a fishing rod.

Controls are quite strict at Tribhuvan Airport and customs officials must chalk all your luggage before you leave. Prohibited are fire-arms and ammunition (unless an import license has been obtained in advance from the Ministry of Foreign Affairs, or the Home Ministry), radio transmitters, walkie-talkies and drugs. Special permits are required for 16mm cameras. Customs are also quite sensitive about video and 8mm movie cameras and these may be recorded by them in your passport.

You must also clear customs when you are leaving the country. To avoid hassles, be aware of the following:

1) **Souvenirs** can be exported freely but antiques and art objects require a special certificate from the Department of Archaeology, National Archives Building, Ram Shah Path, Kathmandu. It takes at least two days to get it. It is forbidden to export any object more than 100 years old. If you are in doubt, obtain a certificate.

2) **Precious and rare commodities** are strictly forbidden to be exported out of Nepal. These include precious stones, gold, silver, weapons and drugs. Animal hides, fangs or wild animals may not be exported either. Live pet animals such as Tibetan dogs may be taken out.

3) **Currency** – Have your currency card ready for inspection and keep receipts for any handicrafts or purchases you have made.

Upon departure, do take note that a Rs. 300 airport tax is payable upon check-in on all departing international flights.

GETTING ACQUAINTED

GOVERNMENT & ECONOMY

Nepal is a constitutional monarchy headed by His Majesty King Birendra Bir Bikram Shah Deva. Following widespread demonstrations and riots in early 1990, the ban on the multi-party system was lifted on April 8, 1990 and a democratic constitution proclaimed on November 9, 1990. The Prime Minister, Krishna Prasad Bhattarai, heads an appointed interim government and Council of Ministers and prepares for a general election. The King (born Dec. 28, 1945) and Queen Aishwarya Rajya Lakshmi Devi Shah (born Nov. 7, 1949) have three children; the older, His Royal Highness Crown Prince Dipendra (born June 27, 1971), is heir to the throne.

Nepal's population is almost 19 million, nearly 50 percent of it under the age of 15. The annual rate of population growth is 2.7 percent. Nepal is classified by the UN as one of the world's least developed nations with one of the world's half dozen lowest per capita incomes at about US$160 per annum.

The overwhelming majority of the population is dependent on agriculture for their livelihood and much of this is subsistence farming on small plots on terraced hillsides. Only a mere 2 percent of the workforce are employed in industry.

The majority of imported goods come from or via India, Calcutta being Nepal's official point of entry. This makes Nepal particularly vulnerable as was demonstrated by the problems that arose with India when the trade and transit treaties expired in 1989.

Tourism is the single largest source of foreign exchange at US$65 million in 1988 with revenue from the export of hand-made wool carpets close behind, reaching US$57 million in 1989.

Nepal is heavily dependent on foreign aid for its economic development as it tries to provide basic necessities for all its citizens by the year 2000. Two-thirds of its development budget comes from foreign aid, both bilateral and multilateral. The foreign aid commitment for 1989/90 was between US$400-$500 million.

Literacy is very low with less than a quarter of the population being able to write their names. Health care is minimal with one doctor for every 25,000 population and with only 3000 hospital beds in Kathmandu. Infant mortality is "very high" and one child in every six dies before his fifth birthday. Life expectancy for adults is little more than 50 years, with women usually having a lower life expectancy than men.

TIME ZONES

Nepal is 15 minutes ahead of Indian Standard Time and five hours, 45 minutes ahead of Greenwich Mean Time. Thus, international time differences are rather staggered as follows:

Kathmandu
12 Noon

New Delhi
11.45 a.m. today

Paris
7.15 a.m. today

London
6.15 a.m. today

San Francisco
10.15 p.m. yesterday

Hawaii
8.15 p.m. yesterday

Sydney
4.15 p.m. today

Tokyo
3.15 p.m. today

Hong Kong
2.15 p.m. today

Bangkok
1.15 p.m. today

Rangoon
12.45 p.m. today

CALENDARS

Five different calendars are used simultaneously in Nepal. These include the Gregorian calendar familiar to the West and the Tibetan calendar.

The traditional ones are the Sakya Era calendar, which began counting years in A.D. 108 , and the Newari calendar, starting in A.D. 879-880.

The official calendar is in the Vikram Sambat calendar, named after the legendary North Indian King Vikramaditya. Day One of Vikram Sambat was February 23, 57 B.C. Hence, the year 1990 of the Christian era is 2047 of the Vikram era.

This system is the only one you'll find in newspapers, public service and the world of government bureaucracy.

The Nepalese celebrate their New Year in mid-April, according to the Western calendar. The fiscal and budgetary year begins in mid-July.

The Nepalese year is 365 days long, same as in the West, with 12 months ranging in length from 29 to 32 days.

These calendar months are called *Baishak* (31 days), *Jesth* (31 days), *Asadh* (32 days), *Srawan* (32 days), *Bhadra* (31 days), *Ashwin* (30 days), *Kartik*, (30 days), *Marga*, (29 days), *Poush* (30 days), *Magha* (29 days), *Falgun* (30 days) as well as *Chaitra* (30 days).

The number of days in a month in a Nepalese calendar is never constant as it is dependant on the solar movement.

The seven days of the week have been named according to the planets. They are *Aityabar* (Sunday), the Sun Day; *Somabar* (Monday), the moon day; *Mangalbar* (Tuesday), Mars Day; *Budhabar* (Wednesday), Mercury's day; *Brihapatibar* or *Bihibar* (Thursday), Jupiter's day or the day of the lord; *Sukrabar* (Friday), Venus day; and *Shanisharbar* or *Shanibar* (Saturday) which is Saturn's day.

CLIMATE

From the eternal snow of the higher peaks to the tropical expanses of the lowlands, Nepal enjoys an extreme variety of climates. Altitudes and exposure to sun and rain are the most influential factors.

Sitting at an elevation of about 1,350 meters (4,400 feet), the Kathmandu Valley knows three seasons. The cold season – from October to March – is the best time to visit the country.

The night time temperatures may drop nearly to freezing point, but the sun warms the atmosphere by day, so that the morning hours see the mercury climb from 10°C to 25°C (50°F to 77°F).

The sky is generally clear and bright; the air is dry and warm. Nippy mornings and evenings are invigorating. In the winter, there is frequently an early-morning mist – a result of the rapid heating of the cold night air. October and February are particularly pleasant.

The weather is noticeably warmer in the Pokhara valley, where temperatures rise to 30°C (86°F) at midday in the lower altitude.

In April, May and early June, the weather becomes hot and stuffy, with occasional evening thunderstorms.

Nature is in full bloom but the brightly colored landscapes are often shrouded in heat mist. Daily temperatures in Kathmandu fluctuate between 11°C and 28°C (52°F and 83°F) in April, and between 19°C and 30°C (66°F and 86°F) in June, with maximum temperatures of 36°C (97°F).

By the end of June the monsoon arrives, heralded by pre-monsoon rains which normally start in May. The rainy season lasts three months, during which time the Himalaya usually remains out of sight though the rains create some spectacular lighting effects. Violent downpours create some flooding but it is still possible to visit the Kathmandu Valley. Trekking stops with the proliferation of leeches (*jugas*), and the lowlands are cut off by swollen rivers and occasional landslides.

The monsoon ends around mid-September. Autumn brings clearer skies, cooler nights and a symphony of brown and gold to the land.

CULTURE & CUSTOMS

What is a foreigner? By definition, he or she is wealthy. Think how many bags of rice the plane ticket that got you to Kathmandu is worth. The postulate of foreign wealth has been deeply ingrained in Nepalese minds.

CHARITY

Its consequences can be a bit unsettling for the visitor; the corollary is that the Nepalese should try to get a little of that wealth. Foreigners have often been extremely generous with sweets, goods, clothing and cash. As a result, a little blackmail is not unusual from porters and guides on mountain treks for those who go it alone. One often gets requests for free medicine, or encounters beggars in the tourist-trodden parts of the Kathmandu valley.

Children frequently chant the magic words "Rupee! Paisa!" with palms extended. It is mostly a game. Ignore them and they will smile and romp away. Should they insist, grown-ups will shout and scatter them, for there is pride in the Nepalese be it in the valley or in the hills.

On occasion, rowdy crowds of unruly children will throng you. Take care of your belongings, make sure your bag is zipped up, your camera equipment secure. Mostly, they will annoy you by popping up between your camera and the statues you want to photograph. Let them be: children can give a sense of proportion to a picture. Ask a friend to distract them. Or else give up, or pretend to, until they are busy somewhere else.

One can go about almost everywhere in complete confidence. Women can walk on their own without being bothered.

RELIGION & SUPERSTITIONS

A source of bad feeling may arise if you are asked not to enter a certain precinct or not to photograph a shrine. Comply with good grace. The reasons for enforcing a taboo are as evident to the local people as they are obscure to you.

Nobody will ask you to forgo your own values and standards as long as you don't expect them to be followed by everybody. Respect and open-mindedness are essential. The apparent familiarity with which the Nepalese behave towards idols should be no invitation for you to imitate them by riding on statues or other such nonsense.

The Nepalese understand that Western values are different from theirs. Even if they are shocked or stunned by your behavior, they will explain it as primitive barbarianism, and will not pursue the matter as long as they don't think the gods are offended.

In Nepal, superstition and religion merge and diverge until they become indistinguishable. But the beliefs, whether stemming from religious dogma or pure superstition, are deep-rooted and ever present. It would be impossible to fully comprehend and adapt to the implications of these beliefs without becoming a thorough initiate of the regions, customs, traditions and rituals of the Nepalese people. However, an attempt is made here to list some important ones which, if you remember and heed, will help to establish a congenial rapport between the Nepalese and yourself.

First of all, know and accept the fact that

you are a foreigner and therefore ritually "polluted." Thus some seemingly innocent act on your part, which could have been tolerated of a Nepalese, might have unpleasant repercussions.

Some rules of etiquette: don't step over people's feet or body (walk around them) and don't make the mistake of offering to sharewhich you have tasted or bitten into.

Lack of toilet paper has led to the customs (which has eventually become a ritual) of using water and the left hand to cleanse oneself after a bowel movement. Therefore, nothing should be accepted, and especially offered, with the left hand only. If you offer or accept anything then do so with both hands (if it is practical to do so). This will please your Sherpa, or some Nepali whom you have met, very much. Using both hands to give or receive signifies that you honor the offering and the recipient or giver.

You will notice that most Nepalese take off their shoes before they enter a house or a room. It would not be practical to suggest that you unlace and take off your hiking shoes/boots every time you enter a village house. It would be helpful, however, if you were to avoid entering a house unless you wished to spend some time in it (to eat a meal or drink some tea, for example).

The kitchen area or the cooking and eating area are to be treated with the utmost of respect. On no account should you go into the kitchen or cooking and eating areas with your shoes on. You should avoid intruding into these areas unless you are specifically invited there – remember that the hearth in a home is sacred.

Nepalese often eat squatting on the ground. Do not stand in front of a person who is eating, because your feet will be directly in front of his plate of food. If there is something you have to tell him, it is wiser to squat or sit by his side.

TIPPING

Tipping has become a habit in hotels and restaurants patronized by foreigners. A hotel waiter or porter will expect a one to two rupee tip. Taxi drivers need not always be tipped but when they have been particularly helpful, about 10 percent of the fare is in order. A 10 percent tip is also customary in Westernized restaurants. Elsewhere, please do yourself and the country a favor, abstain from tipping.

WEIGHTS & MEASURES

Nepalese use the decimal system, but for specific purposes stick to traditional measures. As elsewhere in the Indian subcontinent, they count in *lakh* (unit of 100,000) and *crore* (unit of 10 million). Heights are usually measured in meters but sometimes also in feet. (One foot equals 0.305 meters; one meter equals 3.28 feet). Distances are counted in kilometers.

Weights are measured in kilos (kilograms), with the following exceptions:

For rice and other cereals, milk and sugar: one *mana* equals a little less than half a liter; one paathi, about $3^3/4$ liters, contains eight *manas*; 160 *manas* equal 20 *paathis* equal one *muri*, about 75 liters.

For vegetables and fruits: one *pau* equals 200 grams; one *ser* equals four *paus*, or one kilogram; one *dharni* equals three *sers*, or 2.40 kilograms.

For all metals: one *tola* is equal to 11.66 grams.

For all precious stones: one carat equals 0.2 grams.

The term *muthi* means "handful", whether it be of vegetables or of firewood.

ELECTRICITY

Major towns in Nepal have been electrified using 220-volts alternating current, though some fluctuation is normal. On festive occasions, Kathmandu is ablaze with lights at night. A few large hotels have their own power generators, as there are frequent power cuts. The rural electrification program has a long way to go before it can phase out the poetry of candles and firesides. A small flashlight is useful.

BUSINESS HOURS

Government offices are open from 10 a.m. to 5 p.m. Sunday through Friday for most of the year. They close an hour earlier in the winter. Saturday is the rest day in Nepal, Sunday being a full working day for offices and banks. Only embassies and international organizations take a two-day weekend; they are generally open from 9 or 9.30 a.m. to 5 or

5.30 p.m. during the remainder of the week. Shops, some of which remain open on Saturdays and holidays, seldom open before 10 a.m. but do not usually close until 7 or 8 p.m.

HOLIDAYS & FESTIVALS

Festival dates vary from year to year because of the difference between the calendars and because many are determined only after complex astrological calculations. It is often difficult to know in advance when any festival will take place, as the uncertainty is considered part of the mysticism, but this list will give you an idea. Rely on local knowledge after you arrive in Kathmandu as the festival grapevine works very well at short notice. Refer to the "Land of Festivals" for details.

MAGHA (JANUARY AND FEBRUARY)

Magha Sankranti
Basanta Panchami
Magha Purnima
Maha Snan

FALGUN (FEBRUARY AND MARCH)

Losar or Tibetan New Year
Democracy Day or King Tribhuvan Jyanti
Shivaratri
Holi

CHAITRA (MARCH AND APRIL)

Ghorajatra
Pase Chare
Chaitra Dasain
Seto Machhendranath or Rath

BAISAKH (APRIL AND MAY)

Bisket – Bhaktapur
Bal Kumari Jatra – Thimi
Matatirtha Snan – nr Thankot
Buddha Jayanti

JESTH (MAY AND JUNE)

Sithinakha

ASADH (JUNE AND JULY)

Tulsi Bijropan

SRAWAN (JULY AND AUGUST)

Ghanta Karna
Bhoto Jatra – culmination of Rato Machhen-
dranath
Krishna Jayanti
Raksha Bandhan or Jani Purnima
Naga Panchhami

BADRA (AUGUST AND SEPTEMBER)

Gaijatra
Indrajatra
Gokarana Aunshi or Father's Day
Teej

ASHWIN
(SEPTEMBER AND OCTOBER)

Dasain or Durga Puja

KARTIK
(OCTOBER AND NOVEMBER)

Tihar or Diwali and Lakshmi Puja
HM The Queen's Birthday
Haribodhini Ekadasi

MARGA
(NOVEMBER AND DECEMBER)

Yomari Purnima

POUSH (DECEMBER AND JANUARY)

Constitution Day or King Mahendra Jayanti
HM The King's Birthday

RELIGIOUS SERVICES

Roman Catholic church services are held at 9.00 a.m. on Sunday mornings and 5.30 p.m. Sunday evenings at St. Xavier's College in Jawalakhel, tel: 521050 and at 5.30 p.m. on Saturdays at the Annapurna Hotel tel: 221711.

Protestant services are held 9.30 a.m. on Sundays at the Lincoln School, Rabi Bhawan tel: 216603.

For Jewish services contact the Israeli Embassy tel: 411811.

For Moslems the main mosques are in Durbar Marg.

COMMUNICATIONS

MEDIA

NEWSPAPERS & MAGAZINES

There are several newspapers published in English in Kathmandu, as well as dozens in Nepali. They are somewhat controlled, although Nepali dailies and weeklies – when read between the lines – express various shades of opinion. In English, *The Rising Nepal* has a wider coverage of foreign news than the more parochial *Motherland*. Both dailies and weeklies devote a lot of their front pages to the King's activities.

The International Herald Tribune can be found at newsstands and hotels. (It arrives one day late). Also available are *Time, Newsweek, The Far Eastern Economic Review, Asiaweek* and *India Today*. There are few foreign news publications to be found in Nepal, except Indian newspapers which arrive daily on the morning flights.

RADIO & TELEVISION

Two news bulletins in English are broadcast by Radio Nepal daily at 8 a.m. and 8.30 p.m. There is also a "tourist program" from 8.15 p.m. to 9 p.m. in the evening. Bring a shortwave radio if you are addicted to international news.

Early in 1986 television arrived in Kathmandu. Nepal Television presents 4$^{1}/_{2}$ hours of programs daily and they have plans for future expansion.

The English news is on Nepal Television every evening at 9.40 p.m. – check the programs daily in the *Rising Nepal*.

POSTAL SERVICES

The **Central Post Office** in Kathmandu has three sections. Fortunately, they are located closer to one another at the junction of Kanti Path and Kicha-Pokhari Road.

The so-called **Foreign Post Office**, tel: 211760, deals only with parcels sent or received from abroad. Avoid sending or receiving any during your stay.

To buy stamps, send letters or receive them through Poste Restante, you must go to the **General Post Office**, tel: 211073 (open 10 a.m. to 5 p.m. daily except Saturdays and holidays). During the months of November to February, it is open only till 4 p.m. Please ensure that stamps on letters and post cards are franked in front of your eyes. If you use Poste Restante, ask your correspondents to either mention only your family name on the envelope, or to write it with a big initial. Main hotels will usually handle your mail. This is certainly the easiest way.

TELEPHONE & TELEFAX

For telephone and cables, there is the **Telecommunication office**, Tripureshwar deals with telephone calls and telexes. Its telex service is available only during government working hours at the Central Telegraph Office.

International telephone connections are now excellent with the installation in late 1982 of the British earth satellite station. Dial 186 for international operator. Dial 187 for calls to India. Dial 180 for internal trunk calls and 197 for enquiries.

For dialing into Nepal note the country code is 977, the Kathmandu area code is 1, and Pokhara area code is 61.

Telefax has reached Nepal though it is only found in the more progressive offices for the time being. Ask your travel agent or hotel if a public service is available.

EMERGENCIES

KEY PHONE NUMBERS

It is useful for the traveler to jot down a few essential telephone numbers that might prove to be handy in the event of an emergency.

Service	Dialing Direct
Police Emergency	216999
	216998
Bir Hospital	221119
	221988
Patan Hospital	521034
	521048
	522286
	522278
Teaching Hospital	412303
	412404
	412505
	412808
Ciwec Clinic	410983
Nepal International Clinic	412842
Fire Brigade	221177
Telephone Enquiry	197
International operator	186
Operator for India	187
Internal trunk calls	180
Telephone maintenance	198

HYGIENE

Although there is no more danger to health in Nepal than in many other countries, elementary sanitary precautions are in order. Health requirements are lax for entry, but the traveler is advised to get injections against typhoid and meningitis and to have gamma globulin against hepatitis. Make sure your routine tetanus and polio inoculations are up to date. Cholera inoculation is not required or recommended.

Never drink unboiled and untreated water and do not trust ice cubes anywhere except in the best hotels. Avoid eating raw vegetables and peel fruit before consuming. Never walk barefoot and wash your hands often. If you follow these guidelines you should avoid many of the intestinal infections which lead to diarrhea.

Nevertheless, it is not uncommon for minor problems to occur soon after arrival in the country especially after those long intercontinental flights. "Travelers tummy" should clear up after a couple of days but if it is particularly severe and persistent or interferes with your travel plans, get a stool test and medical assistance.

The foreign-staffed CIWEC Clinic at Baluwatar opposite the Russian Embassy, tel: 410983 is particularly convenient and experienced with travelers.

MEDICINE & PHARMACIES

Most medicines that you will require during your visit are readily and cheaply available in Kathmandu without a prescription. Do not rely on the pharmacists but ask for medical assistance when making a diagnosis. Look out for the well known brand names manufactured under licence in India but check the label carefully as contents may be different from those you are familiar with back home.

Pharmacies can be found in all the major towns of Nepal. For trekkers or those venturing off the beaten track be sure you have what you need with you before you leave Kathmandu.

HOSPITALS

For more serious problems, there are doctors attached to the big hotels, the American-staffed CIWEC Clinic, Baluwatar, tel: 410983, and the Nepal International Clinic, Naxal tel: 412842. The major hospitals are:

Bir Hospital
Kantipath
Tel: 221119, 221988.

Patan Hospital
Patan
Tel: 521034, 521048, 522286, 522278.

Teaching Hospital
Maharajgunj
Tel: 412303, 412404, 412505, 412808.

GETTING AROUND

MAPS

The green map of Nepal and the orange street map of Kathmandu published by Himalayan Booksellers will complement the maps found in this *Insight Guide*.

Regional trekking maps are also available, though most are not entirely reliable. The best are those prepared by Erwin Schneider, even though they cover only eastern Nepal and the Kathmandu Valley. *Apa Maps, Nepal,* covers the country from Dhaulagiri to the eastern border.

FROM THE AIRPORT

For travel from Tribhuvan Airport to Kathmandu, a bus service is theoretically provided by RNAC and by Indian Airlines. Passengers arriving on other airlines are left at the mercy of taxis.

Indian Airlines, Durbar Marg	411997
Japan Airlines, Durbar Marg	412138
KLM Royal Dutch Airlines, Durbar Marg	224896
Korean Air, Kantipath	212080
Lufthansa, Durbar Marg	223052
Northwest Airlines, Kantipath	226139
Pakistan International, Durbar Marg	223102
Pan American World Airways, Durbar Marg	225292
	228824
Qantas Airlines, Kantipath	213772
Royal Nepal Airlines, Kantipath	220757
Saudi Airlines, Kantipath	222787
Singapore Airlines, Durbar Marg	220759
Swiss Air, Durbar Marg	222452
Thai International, Durbar Marg	225084
Trans World Airlines, Kantipath	226704
Adventure Travel Nepal, Durbar Marg	223328
	221729
Annapurna Travel & Tours, Durbar Marg	223940
Everest Travel Service,	
Gangapath	221216
Gorkha Travels, Durbar Marg	224896
Himalayan Travels & Tours, Durbar Marg	223045
Kathmandu Travels & Tours, Gangapath	222985
Malla Travels, Malla Hotel	410635
Marco Polo, Kamal Pokhari	414192
Nepal Travel Agency, Ramshahpath	413188
Natraj Tours & Travels, Durbar Marg	222014
Shankar Travel & Tours, Lazimpat	422465
Sherpa Travel Service	222489
Tiger Tops, Durbar Marg	226173
Trans Himalayan Tours, Durbar Marg	224854
Universal Travel & Tours, Kantipath	214192
World Travels, Durbar Marg	226939
Yeti Travels, Durbar Marg	221234

The taxi ride from the airport should not cost more than Rs. 45 by meter. Taxis can accommodate three passengers. Often the driver is assisted by an "interpreter." When traveling from Kathmandu to the airport, buses depart from the RNAC building at the beginning of New Road.

DOMESTIC AIR TRAVEL

Flying is the best way of moving around fast in Nepal. RNAC, the national airline, has monopoly of domestic flights and runs an extensive network using a fleet of Avros 748, Twin Otters and Pilatus Porters. The airline spider-web spreads from Kathmandu to the west (Dang, Dhangadi, Jumla, Mahendranagar, Nepalganj, Rukumkot, Safi Bazar, Silgari Doti, Surkhet); to the center (Baglung, Bhairawa, Gorkha, Jomosom, Meghauly, Pokhara, Simra); and to the east (Bhadrapur, Biratnagar, Janakpur, Lukla, Lamidanda, Rajbiraj, Rumjatar Taplejung, and Tumlingtar). Details can be obtained from RNAC at their New Road headquarters, tel. 220757.

On certain routes, there are two fares; one fare for foreigners and a lower one for Nepalese and Indian nationals.

An Avro takes visitors on a daily one-hour "Mountain Flights", leaving Kathmandu in the morning to fly along the Himalaya for a view of Mount Everest. At US$94, it is a worthwhile trip.

There is a Rs. 30 airport tax on many domestic flights. Contrary to RNAC's generous international service, in-flight service is minimal.

It is advisable to book ahead, especially to distant destinations where only the smaller aircraft operate. There are cancellation fees of 10 percent if you cancel 24 hours in advance, 33 percent if less than 24 hours in advance, and 100 percent if you fail to show up without informing the airline. If the flight is cancelled due to bad weather or other causes your fare is refunded.

Small planes can occasionally be chartered, but, these are expensive and difficult to book. It is advisable to book through a travel agent. Helicopters can be chartered in addition to emergency rescues from the Royal Nepal Army, though expensive. Alouettes cost US$750 per hour and Pumas US$1700 per hour but check as rates change.

You need to produce a trekking permit at Tribhuvan Airport on departure from Kathmandu to a restricted area. Always take your passport along, as there are occasional police checkpoints on all roads.

DOMESTIC ROAD LINKS

In this mountainous country with deep valleys etched between peaks and ranges, roads are vital for bringing together the various communities. But until Nepal started opening to the outer world in the early 1950s, the kingdom had nothing except village trails and mountain paths. Cross-country trading was generally a tortuous affair measured in weeks and months. Since the '50s, there have been major efforts to construct some roads. Foreign powers have lent a hand – none more so than Nepal's big-brotherly neighbors, India and China, both prompted by obvious strategic considerations. There are presently six main road links:

Tribhuvan Raj Path, linking Kathmandu with Raxaul at the Indian border, 200 kilometers (124 miles) away, was opened in 1956 and built with Indian assistance.

The **"Chinese Road"** or **Arniko Highway** leads to the Tibetan border at Kodari. Some 110 kilometers (68 miles) long, it suffered bad landslides in 1987 and is under reconstruction. Check locally before undertaking a trip. It is normally possible to reach the Tibet border providing you walk across the landslides.

Chinese engineers also helped build the **Prithvi Raj Marg** (1973) covering the 200 kilometers (124 miles) between Kathmandu and Pokhara. There are two recently opened extensions to the Pokhara road: Dumre to Gorkha and Mugling to Narayanghat. In 1970, Indian engineers completed the 188-kilometer (117-mile) extension from Pokhara to Sonauli on the Indian border; this road is called **Siddhartha Raj Marg**.

The most ambitious road is the result of the co-operation of the Soviet Union, the United States, Britain and India. An east-west lowland thoroughfare called **Mahendra Raj Marg**, this 1,000-kilometer (621-mile) route is part of the fabled Pan-Asian Highway linking the Bosphorus with the Far East. Popularly known as the **East-West Highway**, it has been completed east of Bhairawa.

China has completed a 32-kilometer (20 mile) long **ring-road** around Kathmandu, Chinese technicians have also installed an efficient trolley-bus service between Kathmandu and Bhaktapur.

The newest highway 110-kilometer (69-mile) long stretching from **Lamosangu to Jiri** east of Kathmandu was begun in 1975 with Swiss technical assistance and was completed and inaugurated in September 1985. During the rainy season, whole portions of existing roads are damaged and must be repaired. Inquire locally before setting off on a long-distance road trip.

PUBLIC TRANSPORT

All roads are plied by local bus services, with express coaches on the main routes. A bus ride in Nepal is a bumpy, noisy, smelly affair that can nevertheless be fun. Some of these antediluvian beasts are mere sheet-metal boxes on wheels, but they eventually arrive at their destinations, even if passengers have to occasionally alight on the steepest climbs. No matter what, they are a cheap, convenient way of going about inside and outside of Kathmandu Valley. They allow for a long, close look at the local folk inside the bus, if not always at the scenery outside.

BUSES

There are minibuses on the same routes as the buses and coaches. They are less crowded, a bit faster, and more expensive.

Please book one day ahead. The main bus station in Kathmandu is on one side of the Tundhikhel parade ground, opposite Kanti Path. Minibuses start from near the post office; those bound for Pokhara leave from Madras Coffee House (near the Bhimsen Tower). In Pokhara, the bus terminal is close to the post office.

SCOOTERS

Within Kathmandu the three wheel public scooters can carry up to six passengers, always plying the same route and starting from Rani Pokhari. Also available are the black and yellow metered scooters which can be privately hired but perhaps more appropriate are the bicycle rickshaws.

RICKSHAWS

These gaudily painted slow moving honking rickshaws are part of the Kathmandu city scene. They are large tricycles with two seats in the back covered by a hood; a man pedals up front. Whatever the driver may demand, a ride in town should not cost more than Rs. 20, on average; Rs. 5.00 per kilometer. Make sure the driver understands where you are going and that the price is settled before you start. Remember, rickshaws should not cost more than taxis!

By the way, for your own safety, please do not try to swap places with the driver. Keeping control of the vehicle on Kathmandu's narrow streets is quite a feat. If you must, just keep in mind that a broken wheel costs around Rs. 150.00.

TAXIS

Taxis are available to go most places in the Kathmandu Valley. They have black registration plates with white numbers; private cars have white numbers on red plates. Make sure their meters are working and, due to the rising gasoline costs, be prepared to pay a 10 percent surcharge. A short ride within the city will cost between Rs. 12-20. If you want to hire a taxi for half a day or a day trip within the Valley, negotiate a price before starting; you should not pay more than Rs. 400 per day, gasoline included.

PRIVATE TRANSPORT

Much more reliable are private cars hired from any travel agency. They usually cost between US$40 and US$50 for the whole day but they are more comfortable and less likely to break down. The driver will wait until you have done your sightseeing and drivers normally speak at least a little English. A tip at the trip's conclusion will be welcome, but is not mandatory and should not be more than Rs. 50. A car can hold three or four people; a metered taxi usually cannot hold more than two.

CAR RENTAL

Avis is represented in Nepal by Yeti Travels, near the Annapurna Hotel; Hertz by Gorkha Travels, also on Durbar Marg.

BICYCLES

Bicycling is one of the best ways of exploring the town and valley. Many shops in the old part of Kathmandu and near the main hotels have Indian and Chinese bicycles for hire at Rs. 10 for the whole day. There's no deposit; your hotel address is enough. Make sure that the bike's bell rings. This is the most important part of the vehicle – you will need it to weave your way through the throngs. Next in importance come the brakes. Lights are supposedly compulsory after sunset, but few bicycles have lights. The law is enforced, but a flashlight will usually be sufficient.

Near tourist spots, children will compete to be recognized as official caretaker of your bicycle, for a few coins and maybe a free ride on the sly. Elsewhere it is quite safe to leave your bike unattended (but locked) while you visit a temple or go for a walk.

MOTORBIKES

It is possible to hire Japanese motorbikes by the hour (Rs. 50) or the day (Rs. 500) from a garage. But these noisy, polluting nuisances are hardly suitable for the quiet stillness of the valley and its few roads and mountain tracks.

More rewarding are the escorted Himalayan Mountain Bike trips exploring within and beyond the Valley. Call in at their Thamel office to check out this imaginative and fun way to explore Nepal or call c/o the Kathmandu Guest House, tel: 413632, 418733. P.O. Box 2769.

WALKING

Be prepared to do a lot of walking. Taxis and bicycles can only take you to limited distances. Apart from a few well-trodden spots, most of the interesting sites have to be reached on foot. Nepalese do not count distance by miles or kilometers, but by the number of walking hours involved for the duration of the journey.

There's no need to compete with their often brisk pace. A leisurely stroll amid the rice and mustard fields, across villages, up, down and around, is certainly the best way to "absorb" the valley, its people, their culture and way of life.

Do not hesitate to venture off the tourist track. You can expect to be safe wherever you wander. Moreover, you will find the people to be even more friendly than you choose to think. Then you will have the pleasure of discovering this beautiful land and its people for yourself.

WHERE TO STAY

HOTELS & LODGES

Kathmandu has, in the last decade, seen a mushrooming of world class hotels. During the spring and fall seasons, the better hotels work at near full capacity; being booked well in advance. There are, however, plenty of less glamorous but decent hotels to suit everyone's fancies and finances.

Most hotels offer a choice between three packages: bed and breakfast (CP); bed, breakfast and one other meal (MAP); or room and full board (AP). Rates listed however, are for room only (EP), unless otherwise indicated. Add 10 percent to these quotes for service charge and 12-15 percent for government tax, depending on star rating as indicated in the following list of hotels.

Besides these officially recognized hotels, there are a number of small lodges between US$5 and $10 a night depending on facilities; toilets and showers are generally communal and heating is extra. These small hostelries are located in the old part of Kathmandu and in the Thamel District.

KATHMANDU

Abbreviations – (S): Single, (D): Double. Rates quoted are in US$.

FIVE-STAR

Annapurna
(150 rooms)
Tel: 221711, 223602,
Tlx: 2205,
Cable: ANNAPURNA.
150 rooms. $80 (S), $90 (D), 4 suites.
Central. Has swimming, tennis facilities.
Durbar Marg.

Everest
(155 rooms)
Tel: 224960, 220389,
Tlx: 2260,
Fax: 977-1-226088,
Cable: MALARI.
155 rooms. $100 (S), $110 (D), 6 suites.
On airport road. Fine mountain views. Naya Baneswar.

Soaltee Oberoi
(300 rooms)
Tel: 272550-5,
Tlx: 2203,
Fax: 977-1-272205,
Cable: SOALTEE.
300 rooms. $95 (S), $110 (D), 10 suites, 7 regal suites.
15 minutes from city center, casino, swimming, tennis, restaurants. Tahachal.

Yak & Yeti
(110 rooms)
Tel: 411436, 228803,

Tlx: 2237,
Fax: 977-1-227782,
Cable: YAKNYETI.
110 rooms. $95 (S), $105 (D), 5 suites.
Central, swimming, tennis, shopping. Durbar
Marg.

FOUR-STAR

Himalaya
(100 rooms)
Tel: 523900/8,
Tlx: 2566,
Cable: FLO-RA.
100 rooms. $70 (S), $85 (D), 3 suites.
Opened in January 87. Kupondole.

Kathmandu
(120 rooms)
Tel: 410786, 413082,
Tlx: 2256,
Cable: HOKAT.
120 rooms. $74 (S), $91 (D).
Opposite Royal Guest House. Maharajgunj.

Malla
(75 rooms)
Tel: 410320, 410966, 410968,
Tlx: 2238,
Fax: 977-1-418382,
Cable: MALLOTEL.
75 rooms. $56 (S), $80 (D).
Near the Royal Palace. Lekhnath Marg.

Shanker
(135 rooms)
Tel: 412973, 410151,
Tlx: 2230,
Cable: SHANKER.
135 rooms. $65 (S), $80 (D), 10 suites.
Former Rana Palace. Huge gardens.
Lazimpat.

Sherpa
(80 rooms)
Tel: 222585, 228898
Tlx: 2223
Fax: 222026
US$75 (single) US$85 (double)
Durbar Marg, roof-terrace.

THREE-STAR

Crystal
(50 rooms)

Tel: 223397, 223611, 223636,
Cable: CRYSTAL.
50 rooms. $35 (S), $45 (D).
Central. Roof terrace with the best view of
town.

Narayani
(88 rooms)
Tel: 521711/2, 521408,
Tlx: 2262,
Fax: 977-1-521291,
Cable: HONA.
88 rooms. $50 (S), $57 (D).
In Patan. Good pool and garden.

TWO-STAR

Ambassador
(35 rooms)
Tel: 410432, 414432,
Tlx: 2321,
Fax: 977-1-415432,
Cable: BASS.
35 rooms. $19 (S), $22 (D).
Lazimpat. Friendly atmosphere and conven-
ient. Same ownership as Kathmandu Guest
House.

Nook
(24 rooms)
Tel: 213627, 216247,
Cable: NOOK.
24 rooms. $13 (S), $20 (D).
Good location, recently renovated.

Woodlands
(125 rooms)
Tel: 222683, 220123,
Tlx: 2282,
Cable: WOODLANDS.
125 rooms. $44 (S), $55 (D), 2 suites.
Near town center. Durbar Marg.

ONE-STAR

Blue Diamond
(29 rooms)
Tel: 213392, 216320,
Cable: DIAMOND.
29 rooms. $7 (S), $9 (D).
Thamel Tole. Quiet.

Kathmandu Guest House
(80 rooms)
Tel: 413632, 418733,

Cable: KATHOUSE
80 rooms. $14 (S), $17 (D).
Favorite with world travelers. Nice garden. Excellent value. Found right in the heart of Thamel.

Star
(60 rooms)
Tel: 411004, 412100,
Cable: HOSTAR.
60 rooms. $6 (S), $8 (D).
Thamel.

Tibet Guest House
(37 rooms)
Tel: 214383, 215893,
Cable: TIBGUEST.
37 rooms. $13.50 (S), $14.75 (D). Chhetrapati, near Thamel. Quiet, clean. Tibetan-run.

OTHERS

Dwarika's Kathmandu Village
(19 rooms)
Tel: 414770, 412328,
Tlx: 2239,
Cable: KATHMANDAP.
19 rooms. $57 (S), $74 (D).
Traditional bungalows with carvings and antiques. Great charm though it is not central. Battisputal.

Shangrila
(60 rooms)
Tel: 412999, 410108,
Tlx: 2276,
Fax: 977-1-414184,
Cable: SHANGRILA.
60 rooms. $65 (S), $80 (D), 6 suites.
Fine gardens, friendly service, Lazimpat.

Summit
(47 rooms)
Tel: 521894, 524694,
Tlx: 2342,
Fax: 977-1-523737,
Cable: SUMMIT. 47 rooms. $35 (S), $49 (D).
Charming with good mountain view and traditional style rooms. Kupondole Heights.

Vajra
(40 rooms)
Tel: 271545, 272719,

Tlx: 2309,
Fax: 977-1-271695.
40 rooms. $23 (S), $25 (D).
More a cultural experience than a hotel. Tibetan painted roof-top bar, October Gallery.

DHULIKHEL

Dhulikhel Mountain Resort
P.O. Box 3203, Kathmandu,
Tel: 220031, 216930,
Tlx: 2415,
Cable: RESORT.
$42 (S), $44 (D).
More accessible (34 km or one hour drive east of Kathmandu) but with a flavor of the mountains. Perched high on a bluff past the village of Dhulikhel and commands spectacular views of the Himalaya. Recommended for sunrise breakfast or sunset dinners or a day trip for lunch; accommodation is in quaint chalet style cottages.

Himalayan Horizon Sun-N-Snow Hotel
P.O. Box 1583, Kathmandu,
Tel: 225092
$30 (S), $40 (D). Just this side of Dhulikhel, the accommodation is in 12 modest rooms in a sort of Nepali style building.

In addition to the tea houses found in every village on trekking routes, there are some lodges usually located near the airstrips.

More comfortable accommodation can be found at Lukla and Phaplu as well as in the Annapurna Conservation Area.

FOOD DIGEST

WHAT TO EAT

Despite centuries of isolation and a variety of vegetables and fruits, Nepal has failed to develop a distinctive style of cooking.

An exception is Newari cooking, which can be elaborate and spicy; but this is found only in private homes. Nepalese dishes are at best variations on Indian regional cuisines.

In most parts of Nepal, including the Kathmandu Valley, rice is the staple food. It is usually eaten boiled, supplemented with *dhal* (lentil soup), vegetables cooked with a few spices (notably ginger, garlic and chiles), and – in times of festivity – plenty of meat.

There is a predilection for enormous radishes. Hill people eat *tsampa* – raw grain, ground and mixed with milk, tea or water or eaten dry – as a complement to, or substitute for rice. *Chapatis* diversify the diet. Some castes eat pork. Goat, chicken and buffalo meat – or in the mountains, yak meat – is available to all, but beef is forbidden in this Hindu kingdom.

The Nepalis enjoy eating sweets and spicy snacks such as *jelebis* and *laddus*. These come in a variety of shapes and wrappings, not to mention ingredients and tastes. Fruit from the lowlands can also be found in Kathmandu.

Transportation costs have pushed prices up, such that fruit is often sold by the unit or even by the quarter-unit for a few rupees.

Buffalo milk is turned into clarified butter (*ghee*) or delicious curd sold in round earthenware pots. Curd is a good buy, but be sure to scrape off the top layer. Dairy products are rare elsewhere in Asia, but fresh milk, butter and cheese are plentiful in Kathmandu. The main dairy is at Balaju. Excellent cheese is available at the Nepal Dairy at Mahabouda behind Bir Hospital.

Fresh bread can be found in food shops, and doughnuts are sold in the streets. The Annapurna and Nanglo cake shops (both in Durbar Marg) are good, but the best are the Yak & Yeti and Shangrila bakeries.

Certain areas of Nepal have developed regional dishes. The introduction of a potato crop in Sherpa country has revolutionized eating habits there.

Sherpas now survive on potatoes, eating them baked or boiled, dipped in salt or chilies. More elaborately, they enjoy *gurr* – raw potatoes peeled, pounded with spices, grilled like large pancakes on a hot flat stone, then eaten with fresh cheese.

Tibetan cooking, including *Thukba* (thick soup) and *momos* (fried or boiled stuffed raviolis) – is widespread in the mountains and is also available in Kathmandu.

WHERE TO EAT

Restaurants have vastly improved in the last few years. Prices are low by Western standards. Indian, Chinese, Tibetan and even Japanese cuisine is found, as well as a variety of Western menus. The large international hotels have three or four restaurants each, some of them excellent.

Outside of Kathmandu, it is often difficult to find appealing food in the Valley, even for a snack.

Travelers on day outings should carry their own food: snacks from bakeries or one of the Thamel delicatessens, and some fresh fruit will do for a midday picnic before repairing to the more substantial menus of Kathmandu.

Base Camp
Hotel Himalaya
Tel: 521887.
Very pleasant coffee shop in cool white marble lobby with nice views and it serves good food.

Bhancha Ghar
(Nepali Kitchen)
Kamaladi
Tel: 225172.
Traditional Nepalese food served in charming renovated old Newari house. Evening displays of handicraft-making at the entrance are fun but the prices are not. Try the bar on the top floor.

Far Pavilion
Hotel Everest
Tel: 224960.
An elegant Indian dining experience on the top floor next to Ropes for barbecues and the Bugles and Tigers Bar for a drink before. Unrivaled views.

Himthai
Chhetrapati
Tel: 419334.
Delicious Thai cuisine in very congenial garden surroundings.

Ghar-e-Kebab
Durbar Marg
Tel: 221711.
Serves wonderful tandoori and Indian cuisine in comfortable surroundings, accompa-

nied by the quaint but exotic strains of Indian classical music. The restaurant gives excellent value but in view of this, it is advisable that you book your table early as this is one of the most popular restaurants in town.

Gurkha Grill
Hotel Soaltee Oberoi
Tel: 272555.
Most sophisticated restaurant in Kathmandu offering imaginative continental cuisine. Try the spectacular shrimp cocktail or interesting flambes. Dinner will cost about Rs. 500 for two excluding their extensive wine list. Excellent service. Dance to a live band. Open for dinner only. Recommended to book early.

Kushi Fuji
Durbar Marg.
This Japanese restaurant can be found above Tiger Tops' office. There is an open counter with good food for about Rs. 150 per person.

Les Yeux
Thamel.
Wide variety of cuisine with fun rooftop overlooking the action.

Mountain City Chinese Restaurant
Hotel Malla
Tel : 410320.
Delicious Szechuan cuisine is prepared by Chinese cook from Chengdu.

Mike's Breakfast
Seto Durbar off Durbar Marg.
Charming Rana cottage in delightful jungly garden, favorite hangout of trekkers and Peace Corps volunteers. Mike's offers huge breakfasts, limitless coffee, generous lunches and good music. Good value and good fun.

Nanglo Pub and Snack Bar
Durbar Marg.
Cheap Western food including sandwiches are served for lunch on the courtyard or on the roof.

Nirulas
Durbar Marg
Local hangout offering pizzas and delicious icecream.

Rumdoodle
Thamel.
Named after a climbing spoof, this fun bar and restaurant caters to mountaineers and trekkers with hearty appetites.

Sun Kosi
Durbar Marg.
Next to the Tiger Tops office. An excellent selection of traditional Nepalese and Tibetan food is offered in pleasant surroundings. Service can be slow.

Sanghamitra
Thamel.
Run by Boris' son Mischa, offering vegetarian food in pleasant garden surroundings. Try the Tofu Strogonoff.

Spam's Spot
Thamel.
Is the closest thing to an English pub in Kathmandu. Try draught beer and the "Turd Burgers". Amusing menu.

Wong's Kitchen
Lazimpat.
Offers good Chinese cuisine in unpretentious surroundings at rather unpretentious prices.

DRINKING NOTES

The national drink, *chiya* (tea brewed together with milk, sugar and sometimes spices), is served in glasses, scalding hot. Up in the mountains, it is salted with yak butter and churned, Tibetan-style.

Another popular mountain drink is *chhang*, a powerful sort of beer made from fermented barley, maize, rye or millet. *Arak* (potato alcohol) as well as *rakshi* (wheat or rice alcohol) are also consumed in great quantities among the locals.

Coca-cola is bottled in the Kathmandu Valley and Pepsi, Sprite, Fanta Orange and soda are also available. Restaurants serve good Nepalese beer, Golden Eagle, Iceberg, Leo, Star and Tuborg, as well as imported brews, while the classiest establishments in Kathmandu suggest bottles of imported wine at prohibitive prices.

Good quality rum, vodka and gin are produced locally. If you are a whisky drinker, though, be warned against the local variety.

NIGHTLIFE

CULTURE SHOWS

By 10 p.m. Kathmandu is nearly asleep. The only life centers around some temples, Thamel and the big hotels. There are no nightclubs and no massage parlours.

You can dance at the Soaltee Oberoi, the Everest's Galaxy, and at the Damaru Discotheque in Woodlands Hotel in Durbar Marg, tel. 220123. Other than here, the only action late in the evening is to be found in Thamel.

Some hotels have folk dances and musical shows in their restaurants. The best is staged by the Everest Cultural Society, at Lal Durbar near the Yak and Yeti hotel. Folk dances are presented at 7 p.m. daily and, if specially ordered by your travel agent, an authentic Nepalese dinner can be arranged.

Another leading cultural dance group staging classical and folk dance together with songs and music is the New Himalchuli Cultural Group, which performs daily from 6.30 p.m. to 7.30 p.m. (November – February), 7.30 p.m. to 8.00 p.m. (March – October). For more information, you can write to:

New Himalchuli Cultural Group. P.O. Box 3409, Lazimpat, Kathmandu, Nepal. Tel: 4-11825.

For excellent Indian classical music, go to the Char-e-Kebab restaurant in the Annapurna Hotel in Durbar Marg.

But the best show of all is in Bhaktapur, spectacular local dancing amidst ancient squares and courtyards lit by countless oil lamps. This must be specially arranged in advance, and then for groups only; ask your travel agent for details.

MOVIES

Kathmandu has a few movie houses featuring mainly Indian tear-jerkers; Western visitors may enjoy the reactions of the audience more than the action on the screen. For Western films, see the programs of the European and American cultural centers. Video is flourishing among more privileged Nepalis, with video tapes now widely available for rent.

GAMBLING

There is a casino at the Soaltee Oberoi Hotel, where Indians lose small fortunes on baccarat, chemin-de-fer, roulette and other games. The chit value is counted in Indian rupees or foreign exchange; no Nepalis are permitted entry. Casino Nepal is one of the few international casinos between Malaysia and the Suez. If you decide to come, the casino will provide a free taxi ride back to your hotel.

SHOPPING

WHAT TO BUY

Kathmandu is a treasure trove for the unwary. Children sell *khukris*, belts, coins. Traders appear wherever tourists stray. Merchants wait on temple steps. Junk, guaranteed fake antiques, souvenirs are everywhere. Peer into the shops, take your pick or take your leave; try the next boutique or the next mart. There are good buys to be found here, too.

CLOTHING

- Clothes are certainly good value, from lopsided *topis* (caps) to knitted mittens and woolen socks; from Tibetan dresses that button at the side to men's cotton shirts tied diagonally with ribbons across the chest. *Topis* come in two types: somber black ones and multicolored variations. They are like ties, a must for all Nepalis visiting the administration, but with a difference – their asymmetric shape is said to be a replica of Mount Kailash, the most sacred mountain for Buddhists and Hindus.

- Pieces of Nepalese cloth, red, black and orange, checkered with dots, that women wrap around their shoulders. Shawls are made with the same cotton cloth, but are covered on both sides with thin muslin that gives pastel overtones to the cloth.
- Wool and para wool blankets are a typical product of Nepal; made of the finest goat wool called *pashmina*, they are extremely soft, warm and strong.
- "Tibetan" multicolored wool jackets, shoulder bags and boots of geometrical designs. Most are made in India, and jackets sell for about Rs. 200.

FOLK ART OBJECTS

- Various Nepalese folk objects. Among them are the national knife, the *khukris*, worn at the belt and sometimes highly adorned; and the *saranghi*, a small four-stringed viola cut from a single piece of wood and played with a horse-hair bow by the *gaine* (begging minstrels).
- There are all kinds of copper or brass pots, jugs and jars, sold by their weight (but rather heavy to take home).
- Tibetan tea bowls made of wood and lined with silver are also popular.
- Embossed prayer wheels of all sizes are easily available.
- Hand-made paper beautifully tie-dyed by the women of Bhaktapur or woodblock printed in traditional designs.
- Paper-maché dance masks and terra-cotta elephants used as flower pots are made by the hundreds in Thimi, which is a village near Bhaktapur.
- Copper or bronze statuettes of the Buddha and of various Hindu deities, none of them too old are produced semi-industrially, together with filigreed brass animals or ashtrays inlaid with small pieces of colored stones, and dreadful copies of erotic sculptures that always excite tourists.
- Numerous Tibetan trinkets can be found primarily around Bodhnath but also in

Patan and Kathmandu. They include everything from human skulls and leg bones to *thangkas* (painted scrolls). There is silver-plated jewelry inlaid with coral and turquoise (earrings, necklaces, amulets, belt buckles, plaited silver belts and daggers), as well as bronze mandalas, charm boxes, pieces of furniture, musical instruments – gongs, oboes and *damarus* (small drums).

- Carpets, the hand made production of which is flourishing with substantial exports specially made for Europe and the U.S., are excellent value. The ones in the shops, hand made in private homes and factories, are in traditional Tibetan designs in either bright colours or more subtle "vegetable dyes", though all are in fact chemical colours. The old Tibetan carpets, with intricate motifs and beautiful colours, are still available at substantially higher prices.
- Bamboo flutes are also a good buy and make cheap gifts. You will find them in the main streets of old Kathmandu. Look for a couple of vendors who play while toting a tree of flutes on their shoulders. *Hookahs* (water pipes) are tempting, but you might have trouble getting them past suspicious customs officials.
- Beautiful marriage umbrellas in a variety of designs and colors can be bought in Bhaktapur, but these are for decoration and are not waterproof.

ANTIQUES

Unless otherwise certified by specialists, consider "antique" pieces to have been made the week before you see them in the shop, and pay accordingly. Tibetans and Nepalis will not willingly part with their jewels and adornments; it is impolite to pressure them to see their personal heirlooms.

BUYING TIPS

Before going on a buying spree, you should remember a few things;
- Genuine prayer wheels are supposed to hold a roll of parchment or paper bearing a *mantra* (prayer formula).
- An authentic *khukri* should have a small notch at the bottom of the blade to divert blood away from the handle. In the back

the scabbard, there should be two small knives for skinning and sharpening.
- Gold jewelry should show a slight tooth mark when bitten.
- A fine sculpture should have the fingers of its subject's hand separately sculptured, not merely outlined. This qualification leaves out about 99 percent of the modern works to be seen in Kathmandu.

WHERE TO BUY

To get an idea of the variety of things that can be purchased, and of the relative qualities and prices, visits are suggested to:

Jawalakhel, beyond Patan and Thamel in the middle of town are the best places for Tibetan carpets, old and new. You can watch them being made in the Jawalakhel **Tibetan Refugee Center**.

Hastakala (Handicrafts) opposite the entrance to Himalaya Hotel on the way to Patan. All the crafts on sale in this attractive shop are made in Nepal by disadvantaged groups under the auspices of the Nepal Women's Organization, the Mahaguthi and Bhaktapur Craft Printers.

Potala Gallery and **Tibet Ritual Art Gallery,** both on first floors in Durbar Marg, offer the finest quality antiques, Tibetan carpets and rare art objects.

Patan Industrial Estate, to see woodcarving, metalwork and *thangka* painting. See also the **Bhaktapur Crafts Center** in Dattatraya Square.

The main shops in Kathmandu for imported articles are in and around New Road. Shops selling handicrafts to tourists are centered around Durbar Marg and the big hotels but beware the many Indian Kashmiri shops if you are looking for something Nepali. You might find something interesting to buy anywhere in the Valley, however.

Remember, when buying, that old *thangkas* and bronzes are forbidden for export if they are more than 100 years old. Certificates are required to prove their younger age if there is any doubt. Shopkeepers will be happy to help you.

BOOKSHOPS

Kathmandu has many bookshops with a very good selection of books about Nepal, written in several languages. The best ones include

Ratna Pustak Bhandar near the French Cultural Center off Bag Bazaar; **Educational Enterprises** in Kanti Path opposite Bir Hospital; **Pilgrims Book Centre** in Thamel, and **Himalayan Booksellers** in Durbar Marg with other branches in Thamel and Kanti Path.

SPORTS

PARTICIPANT

Sports as a pastime or occupation is an alien concept. It has only recently been promoted into school and the military. Football (soccer) and cricket have become popular while cycling and jogging are attracting some enthusiasts.

Paradoxically, in Nepal, skiing is out of the question, though a few mountaineering expeditions do try it. The steepness of slopes and the exceptionally high snow line (bringing with it attendant altitude problems) make skiing impractical.

However, fishing and swimming, golf, tennis, squash and hockey can be enjoyed even though facilities are limited. There are two golf courses, one at Gokana Safari Park and the new Royal Golf Club course is near the airport. Outsiders can use the tennis courts and swimming pools of the Soaltee Oberoi, Yak & Yeti, Everest and Annapurna hotels, for small entrance fees.

Prudence is needed when bathing in mountain torrents and rivers because of swift, treacherous currents. The larger rivers in the lowlands are safer, but keep an eye out for the occasional crocodile.

Terai rivers and valley lakes are often good fishing grounds. Besides the small fry, the two main catches are *asla*, a kind of snow trout, and the larger *mashèer*, which grows to as much as 80 pounds (36 kilograms). February, March, October and November are the fishing months. Permits are required from the National Parks and Wildlife Conservation Department in Baneswar, just off the airport road. Contact Tiger Tops and West Nepal Adventures in Durbar Marg for information on fishing in the Karnali, Babai and Narayani rivers. Bring your own tackle.

PHOTOGRAPHY

USEFUL TIPS

As the cost of photographic film is expensive in Nepal and can be purchased only in Kathmandu, you are advised to bring enough rolls for your personal use.

With regard to developing your roll of used film, there are photography shops in New Road in Kathmandu which process black-and-white as well as color prints. These shops also supply batteries for your cameras and they can even do simple repairs for your equipment.

But visitors should bear in mind that the range of consumer products and services do not match those in the city centers of the West. Thus it is best to arrive in Nepal self-sufficient with regard to the photographic equipment that you need.

The keen shutterbug should bring along his telephoto and wide angled lenses as these will prove useful to capture the rich variety of wildlife and the awe-inspiring mountain landscape which Nepal is famed for.

When it comes to taking pictures of the Nepalese and their surroundings, tread gingerly. Be sensitive and bear in mind that religion and superstition play an integral part in Nepalese life. So do not simply click away at people, statues, shrines, buildings, trees, boulders, etc. For what may appear to be innocuous may have deep spiritual significance for the locals. Seek permission whenever you are in doubt. It is always best to forego a snapshot rather than risk offending your hosts.

LANGUAGE

NEPALI

There are as many tongues spoken in Nepal as there are races, and almost as many dialects as there are village communities. But just as centuries of intermarriage have left the nation without a pure tribe or race, neither is there any pure language. Throughout history, the main languages have intermingled and influenced one another.

The official language, Nepali, is derived from Pahori, a language of northern India related to Hindi. Nepali and Hindi use the same writing system, called Devagnagari. Nepali has also borrowed heavily from some local dialects as well as from Sanskrit, an ancient scholarly language which has survived (like Latin), as a religious medium. Nepali, Sanskrit and Newari – the language of the Newar people, predominant in the Kathmandu Valley – each has its own distinctive literary traditions. Newari, which uses three different alphabets, has the newer and more abundant literature.

In northern Nepal the Tibetan language – another traditional vehicle for religious teaching – remains widespread both in its pure, classical form and as derived dialects (including Sherpa and Thakali). In southern Nepal, the various people of the Terai speak their own Indo-European dialects. Three times more people speak Maithili, an eastern Terai dialect, than speak Newari, a reflection of the uneven distribution of population in Nepal.

English is widely spoken and understood in official and tourism-related circles. Most taxi drivers and merchants in the Kathmandu valley have a working knowledge of English, as do most Sherpas. Elsewhere, you may find it difficult to make yourself understood, although the younger generation is fast acquiring a smattering of English words. We strongly recommend that you learn a few basic words and expressions. Like elsewhere, you will get big returns on this small investment, in terms of hospitality, friendship and respect.

FURTHER READING

GENERAL

Bernstein, Jeremy. *The Wildest Dreams of Kew: A Profile of Nepal*. New York: Simon and Schuster, 1970. Personal travelogue.

Fleming, Robert and Linda. *Kathmandu Valley*. Tokyo, Kodansha International, 1978.

Frank, Keitmar. *Dreamland Nepal*. New Delhi; S. Chand, 1978. Photographic book.

Gurung, Harka. *Maps of Nepal*. Bangkok: White Orchid, 1983.

Gurung, Harka. *Vignettes of Nepal*. Kathmandu: Sajha Prakashan, 1980. *Nature and Culture*, Kathmandu, 1989.

Haas, Ernst. *Himalayan Pilgrimage*. New York: Viking Press, 1978. Nice photographic book.

Hagen, Toni. *Nepal: The Kingdom in the Himalayas*. Berne: Kummerly and Frey, 1980. Geographical study with many photos and maps. Still one of the best books by one of the first persons to travel widely in the country.

His Majesty's Government of Nepal. *Nepal*. Kathmandu: Ministry of Industry and Commerce, Department of Tourism, 1974. Pictorial survey.

Hoag, Kathrine. *Exploring Mysterious Kathmandu*. Avalok, 1978, City guide.

Matthiessen, Peter. *The Snow Leopard*. London: Chatto and Windus, 1979. Journal of a journey to Dolpo.

Murphy, Dervla. *The Waiting Land: A Spell in Nepal*. London: John Murray, 1967. Travelogue.

Peissel, Michel. *Tiger for Breakfast*. London: Hodder, 1966. The story of Kathmandu's legendary Boris Lissanevitch.

Ragam, V.R. *Pilgrim's Travel Guide: The Himalayan Region*. Gunter: 1963.

Raj, Prakash A. *Kathmandu and the Kingdom of Nepal*. South Yarra, Vic., Australia: Lonely Planet, 1980. A pocket guide.

Rieffel, Robert. *Nepal: Namaste*. Kathmandu: Sahayagi Prakashan, 1978. A thorough guidebook.

Shah, Ridshikesh. *An Introduction to Nepal*. Kathmandu: Ratna Pustaka Bhandar, 1976.

Suyin, Han. *The Mountain is Young*. London: Jonathan Cape, 1958. Novel set in Nepal of the 1950s.

HISTORICAL

Fisher, Margaret W. *The Political History of Nepal*. Berkeley: University of California, Institute of International Studies, 1960.

Hamilton, Francis. *An Account of the Kingdom of Nepal and the Territories Annexed to This Dominion by House of Gurkha*. Edinburgh: Archibold Constable and Co., 1819. Early history of the Himalayan region.

Hodgson, Brain H. *Essays on the Languages, Literature, and Religion of Nepal and Tibet* (together with further papers on the geography, ethnology, and commerce of those countries). London: Trubner and Co., 1974. Reprinted by Bibliotheca Himalayica, New Delhi.

Hooker, Sir Joseph Dalton. *Himalayan Journals*. London: Ward, Lock, Bowden and Co., 1891.

Kirkpatrick, Col. F. *An Account of the Kingdom of Nepal*. London: 1800. Reprinted by Bibliotheca Himalayica, New Delhi, 1969.

Landon, Percival. *Nepal*. Two volumes. London: Constable, 1928. Reprinted by Bibliotheca Himalayica, New Delhi. Popular historical account survives as the best overall early summary.

Oldfield, Henry Ambrose. *Views of Nepal, 1851-1864*. Kathmandu: Ratna Pustak Bhandar, 1975. Book filled with sketches and paintings.

Oldfield, Henry Ambrose. *Sketches from Nepal. Historical and Descriptive* (with anecdotes of the court life and wild sports of the country during the time of Maharaja Jang Bahadur, G.C.B., to which is added an essay on Nepalese Buddhism and illustrations of religious monuments, architecture, and scenery from the author's own drawings). Two vols., London: W.H. Allen, 1880. Reprinted by Bibliotheca Himalayica, New Delhi.

Rana, Pudma Jung Bahadur. *Life of Maharaja Sir Jung Bahadur of Nepal*. Allahabad, India: Pioneer Press: 1909. Biography and description of 19th century palace life.

Regmi, D.R. *Ancient Nepal*. Third Edition. Calcutta: Firma K.L. Mukopadhyaya, 1969. Detailed historiography to 740 from Nepalese religious viewpoint.

Regmi, D.R. *Medieval Nepal*. Three volumes. Calcutta: Firma K.L. Mukhopadhyaya, 1965. Definitive historiography covering period 740 to 1768, plus source material.

Regmi, D.R. *Modern Nepal: Rise and Growth in the Eighteenth Century*. Calcutta: Firma K.L. Mukhopadhyaya, 1961.

Stiller, Ludwig F. *The Rise of the House of Gorkha*. New Delhi: Manjustri, 1973.

Wright, Daniel, editor. *Vamsavali: History of Nepal* with an introductory sketch of the country and people of Nepal. Translated from the Parbatiya by Munshi Shew Shunker Singh and Pandit Shri Gunanand. Cambridge: University Press, 1877. Second edition, Calcutta: Susil Gupta, 1958. Thorough and reliable early history.

PEOPLE, ART & CULTURE

Anderson, Mary M. *Festivals of Nepal*. London: George Allen and Unwin, 1971.

Aran, Lydia. *The Art of Nepal*. Kathmandu: Shahayogi Prakashan, 1978. Mostly about the Kathmandu Valley with an accent on religion.

Baidya, Karunakar. *Teach Yourself Nepali*. Kathmandu: Ratna Pustak Bhandar, 1982.

Bista, Dor Bahadur. *People of Nepal*. Kathmandu: Ratna Pustak Bhandar, 1974.

Brown, Percy, *Picturesque Nepal*. London: Adam and Charles Black, 1912.

Deep, Dhruba Krishna. *The Nepal Festivals*. Kathmandu: Ratna Pustak Bhandar, 1982.

Fisher, James F. *Trans-Himalayan Traders: Economy, Society and Culture in Northwest Nepal*. Berkeley: University of California 1986. An anthropological study of the people of Dolpo.

Furer-Haimendorf, Christoph von. *The Inter-Relation of Castle and Ethnic Groups in Nepal*. London: University of London, 1957.

Furer-Haimendorf, Christoph von. *The Sherpas of Nepal; Buddhist Highlanders*. Berkeley and Los Angeles: University of California Press, 1964. Intensive study of Sherpa society.

Gajurel, C.L. and Vaidya, K.K. *Traditional Arts and Crafts of Nepal*. New Delhi: S. Chand, 1984.

Haaland, Ane. *Bhaktapur: A Town Changing*. Bhaktapur Development Project, 1982.

Hosken, Fran P. *The Kathmandu Valley Towns: A Record of Life and Change in Nepal*. New York: Weatherhill, 1974. Pictorial survey.

Indra. *Joys of Nepalese Cooking*. New Delhi: 1982.

Jerstad, Luther G. *Mani-Rimdu: Sherpa Dance Drama*. Calcutta: International Book House, 1969.

Jest, Corneille. *Monuments of Northern Nepal*. Paris: UNESCO, 1981.

Kansakar, N.H. *Nepali Kitchens*. Kathmandu: 1978.

Korn, Wolfgang. *The Traditional Architecture of the Kathmandu Valley*. Kathmandu: Ratna Pustak Bhandar, 1977. Limited edition with many diagrams.

Kramrisch, Stella. *The Art of Nepal*. New York: 1964.

Kuloy, Hallvard Kare. *Tibetan Rugs*. Bangkok: White Orchid Press, 1982. Nicely illustrated paperback with scanty information.

Lall, Kesar. *Lore and Legend of Nepal*. Kathmandu: Ratna Pustak Bhandar, 1976.

Lall, Kesar. *Nepalese Customs and Manners*. Kathmandu: Ratna Pustak Bhandar, 1976.

Macdonald, A.W., and Anne Vergati Stahl. *Newar Art*. New Delhi: Vikas, 1979.

McDougal, Charles. *The Kulunge Rai: A Study in Kinship and Marriages Exchange*. Kathmandu: Ratna Pustak Bhandar, 1979.

Messerschmidt, Donald A. *The Gurungs of Nepal*. Warminister: Aris & Phillips, 1976. A standard work of this large group of people.

Nepali, Gopal Singh. *The Newars*. Bombay: United Asia Publications, 1965. Subtitled: "An Ethno-Sociological Study of a Himalayan Community".

Pal, Pratapaditya. Nepal: *Where the Gods*

283

Are Young. Asia House Exhibition, 1975.

Prusha, Carl. *Kathmandu Valley: The Preservation of Physical Environment and Cultural Heritage. A Protective Inventory.* Two volumes. Vienna: Anton Schroll, 1975. Prepared by His Majesty's Government of Nepal in collaboration with UNESCO and the United Nations.

Rubel, Mary. *The Gods of Nepal.* Kathmandu: Bhimratna Harsharatna, 1971.

Sanday, John. *Monuments of the Kathmandu Valley.* Paris: UNESCO, 1979.

Singh, Madanjeet. *Himalayan Arts.* London: UNESCO, 1968.

Snellgrove, David L. *Buddhist Himalaya.* Oxford: Bruno Cassirer, 1957. Excellent survey.

Vaidya, Karunaka. *Folk Tales of Nepal.* Kathmandu: Ratna Pustak Bhandar, 1980.

NATURAL HISTORY

Eckholm, Erik P. *Losing Ground.* New York: W.W. Norton, 1976. Nepal in the context of deforestation and world food prospects.

Fleming, R.L. Sr., R.L. Fleming Jr. and L.S. Bangdel. *Birds of Nepal.* Kathmandu: Avalok, 1979. Definitive work with good illustrations.

Gurung, K.K. *Heart of the Jungle: the Wildlife of Chitwan, Nepal.* London: Andre Deutsch and Tiger Tops, 1983. In–depth survey of the fauna of Royal Chitwan National Park with lovely drawings by the author.

Hillard, Darla. *Vanishing Tracks: Four Years Among the Snow Leopards of Nepal.* New York: Arbor House, 1989. A charming study of life in the western Himalaya with zoologist Rodney Jackson.

Inskipp, Carol and Tim. *A Guide to the Birds of Nepal.* Dover, New Hampshire: Tanager Books, 1985.

Inskipp, Carol. *A Birdwatcher's Guide to Nepal.* England: Bird Watchers Guides, 1988.

Ives, Jack D & Messerli, Bruno. *The Himalayan Dilemma, Reconciling Development and Conservation.* London: Routledge, 1989. Important examination of today's problems.

Manandhar, N.P. *Medicinal Plants of Nepal Himalaya.* Kathmandu: Ratna Pustak Bhandar, 1980.

McDougal, Charles. *The Face of the Tiger.* London: Rivington Books and Andre Deutsch, 1977. The classic work on the Bengal tiger, by the director of Tiger Tops.

Mierow, D., and T.B. Shrestha. *Wild Animals of Nepal.* Kathmandu: 1974.

Mierow, D., and T.B. Shrestha. *Himalayan Flowers and Trees.* Kathmandu: Sahayogi Prakashan, 1978. Good handbook.

Polunin, Oleg and Stainton, Adam. *Concise Flowers of the Himalaya.* New Delhi: Oxford University Press, 1987. A much-needed standard work.

Smith, Colin. *Butterflies of Nepal (Central Himalaya).* Bangkok: Teopress, 1989.

Stainton, J.D.A. *Forests of Nepal.* London: Murray, 1972. Standard work on the flora of Nepal.

Storrs, Adrian & Jimmy. *Discovering Trees in Nepal and the Himalayas.* Kathmandu: Shahayogi Press, 1984.

Storrs, Adrian & Jimmy. *Enjoy Trees: A simple guide to some of the shrubs found in Nepal.* Kathmandu: Shahayogi Press, 1987.

Tuting, Ludmilla and Dixit, Kunda. *BIKAS-BINAS/Development-Destruction? The Change of Life and Environment of the Himalaya.* Munich: Geobuch, 1986.

Valli, Eric and Summers, Diane. *Honey Hunters of Nepal.* USA: Harry N. Abrams, 1988.

MOUNTAIN TREKKING

Armington, Stan. *Trekking in the Himalayas.* South Yarra. Vic., Australia: Lonely Planet, 1979. Survey and guide to trekking.

Bezruschka, Stephen. *A Guide to Trekking in Nepal.* Seattle: The Mountaineers, 1981. One of the best books on the subject.

Bezruschka. Stephen. *The Pocket Doctor: Your Ticket to Good Health While Travelling.* Seattle: The Mountaineers 1988. Useful pocket book, never to travel without.

Bonington, Chris. *Annapurna South Face.* London: Cassell, 1971.

Bonington, Chris. *Everest South West Face.* London: Hodder and Stoughton, 1973.

Bonington, Chris. *Everest the Hard Way.* London: Hodder and Stoughton, 1979.

Brook, Elaine and Donnelly, Julie. *The Windhorse.* London: Jonathon Cape, 1986. A blind English girl is taken trekking in Nepal.

Coburn, Broughton. *Nepali Aama: Portrait of a Nepalese Hill Woman.* Santa Barbara, California: Ross Erikson, 1982.

Downs, Hugh. *Rhythms of a Himalayan Village*. New York: Harper & Row, 1980.

Fantin, Mario. *Mani Rimdu Nepal*. Singapore: Toppan, 1976

Fantin, Mario. *Sherpa Himalaya Nepal*, Bologne, Italy: Arti Grafiche, 1978.

Hackett, Peter. *Mountain Sickness*. American Alpine Club.

Herzog, Maurice. *Annapurna: First Conquest of an 8,000-Meter Peak (26,493 Feet)*. New York: E.P. Dutton, 1953.

Hillary, Edmund. *High Adventure*. New York: E.P. Dutton, 1955.

Hillary, Edmund. *School House in the Clouds*. Garden City, New York: Doubleday, 1964. Account of the 1963 climbing expedition as well as the assistance rendered to Sherpa communities.

Hillary, Edmund and Doig, Desmond. *High in the Thin Cold Air: The Story of the Himalayan Expedition Led by Sir Edmund Hillary*. Garden City, New York: Doubleday, 1962.

Hillary, Edmund and Lowe, George. *East of Everest: An Account of the New Zealand Alpine Club Himalayan Expedition to the Barun Valley in 1954*. New York: E.P. Dutton, 1956.

Hornbein, Thomas F. *Everest, the West Ridge*, San Francisco: Sierra Club, 1965.

Houston, Charles S. *Going Higher: The Story of Man and Altitude*. Boston: Little Brown 1987.

Hunt, John. *The Ascent of Everest*. London: Hodder and Stoughton, 1953. Also *The Conquest of Everest*. New York: E.P. Dutton, 1954.

Hunt, John. *The Conquest of Himalayas*. New York: E.P. Dutton, 1954.

Hunt, John. *Our Everest Adventure: The Pictorial History from Kathmandu to the Summit*. New York: E.P. Dutton, 1954.

Iozawa, Tomoya. *Trekking in the Himalayas*. Tokyo: Yama-Kei, 1980. Excellent maps.

Izzard, Ralph. *The Abominable Snowman Adventure*. London: Hodder and Stoughton, 1955. Also Garden City, New York: Doubleday, 1955. Account of a solo journey from Kathmandu to Everest, chasing the Hunt expedition.

Izzard, Ralph. *An Innocent on Everest*. New York: E.P. Dutton, 1954. Laso London: Hodder and Stoughton, 1955. Account of a solo journey from Kathmandu to Everest, chasing the Hunt expedition.

Jeffries, Margaret and Clarbrough, Margaret. *Sagarmatha, Mother of the Universe: The Story of Mount Everest National Park*. Auckland: Cobb/Horwood, 1986. Most useful guide to the Khumbu.

Jones, Mike, *Canoeing Down Everest*. New Delhi: Vikas, 1979.

Kazami, Takehide. *The Himalayas*. Tokyo: Kodansha International, 1973.

McCallum, John D. *Everest Diary;* (based on the personal diary of Lute Jerstad, one of the first five Americans to conquer Mount Everest). New York: Fallet, 1966.

Messner, Reinhold. *Everest: Expedition to the Ultimate*. London: Kaye and Ward, 1979.

Nakano, Toru. *Trekking in Nepal*. Union City, California: Heian International Inc., 1985. Translated from Japanese.

Nicholson, Nigel. *The Himalayas*. New York: Time-Life Books, 1978. Part of the "World's Wild Places" series.

O'Connor, Bill. *The Trekking Peaks of Nepal*. Seattle: Cloudcap Press, 1989 and England: Crowood Press. Excellent detailed guide with useful maps.

Peissel, Michel. *Mustang, the Forbidden Kingdom: Exploring a Lost Himalayan Land*. New York: E.P. Dutton, 1967. Trekking travelogue.

Rowell, Galen. *Many People Come, Looking, Looking*. Seattle: The Mountaineers, 1980. Personal trekking travelogue with good photographs.

Schaller, George B. *Stones of Silence*. London: Andre Deutsch, 1980. Report of a naturalist's survey in Dolpo.

Shirakawa, Yoshikazu. *Himalayas*. Tokyo: Shogakukan, 1976. Also New York: Harry N. Abrams, 1977. Beautiful photographic book.

Steele, Peter. *Medical Handbook for Mountaineers*. London: Constable, 1988.

Swift, Hugh. *Trekking in Nepal, West Tibet and Bhutan*. San Francisco: Sierra Club, 1989. Good general route information.

Tenzing Norgay and James Ramsey Ullman. *Man of Everest: The Autobiography of Tenzing*. London: George G. Harrap, 1955. Also *Tiger of the Snows*. New York: G.P. Putnam's Sons, 1955.

Tilman, W. *Nepal Himalaya*. Cambridge: Cambridge University Press. 1952. Mountaineer's reports of attacks on high peaks.

Tucci, Giusepee. *Journey to Mustag.* Translated from Italian by Diana Fussel. Kathmandu: Ratna Pustak Bhandar, 1982.

Ullman, James Ramsey. *Americans on Everest: The Official Account Led by Norman G. Dyhrenfurth.* New York: J.B. Lippincott, 1964.

Ullman, James Ramsey. *Kingdom of Adventure: Everest.* New York: E.P. Dutton, 1947.

Unsworth, Walt. *Everest.* London: Allen Lane, 1981. Best history written of world's highest peak.

Waddell, L.A. *Among the Himalayas.* Westminister England: Archibold Constable and Co., 1899. Concerns one mountaineer's travelogue.

Wilkerson, James. *A Medicine for Mountaineering.* Seattle: The Mountaineers, 1985.

USEFUL ADDRESSES

Australia, Bhat Bhatani	411578
Bangladesh, Naxal	414943
Burma, Pulchok	521788
China, Baluwatar	411740
	412589
Egypt, Pulchok	521844
France, Lazimpat	412332
Germany (East), Dilli Bazaar	214801
Germany (West), Kantipath	221730
India, Lainchaur	410900
	411699
Israel, Lazimpat	411811
Italy, Baluwatar	412743
Japan, Pani Pokhari	414083
Korea (North), Patan	521084
Korea (South), Tahachal	211172
Pakistan, Pani Pokhari	411421
Thailand, Thapathali	211361
U.S.S.R., Baluwatar	412155
United Kingdom, Lainchaur	411789
	410583
U.S.A., Pani Pokhari	411179
	411601

Australia
Consulate:
Suite 23, 2nd Floor
18-20 Bank Place
Melbourne, Victoria 3000
Tel: 03 602 1271.
P.O. Box 1097
Toowong 4066, Brisbane
Tel: 07 378 0124.
4th Floor, Airways House
195 Adelaide Terrace
Perth, Western Australia 6004
Tel: 09 221 1207.

Bangladesh
Embassy:
United Nations Road
Road No 2, Baridhara
Diplomatic Enclave, Dhaka
Tel: 601890, 602091, 601790.

Belgium
Consulate:
149 Lamorinierstraat
B-2018 Antwerpen
Tel: 03 230 8800.

Burma (Union of Myanmar)
Embassy:
16 Natmauk Yeiktha
P.O. Box 84, Rangoon
Tel: 50633.

Canada
Consulate:
310 Dupont Street
Toronto, Ontario M5 RIV9
Tel: 416 968 7252.

China
Embassy:
No. 1, Sanlitun Xiliujie , Beijing
Tel: 5321795.
Consulate:
Norbulingka Road 13
Lhasa, Tibet Autonomous Region
Tel: 22880.

Denmark
Consulate:
2 Teglgardsstr
DK-1452 Copenhagen K
Tel: 01 143175.

Egypt
Embassy:
9 Tiba Street
Dokki, Cairo
Tel: 704447, 3603426.

Finland
Consulate:
Korkeavuorenkatu 22
00130 Helsinki
Tel: 385 0 6186213.

France
Embassy
45 bis rue des Acacias
75017 Paris
Tel: 462224867
Consulates:
7 bis Allee des Soupirs
31000 Toulouse
Tel: 61 329122.
105 rue Jeanne d'Arc
Rouen
Tel: 35 98 62 14.

Germany
Embassy
Im-Hag 15
D-5300 Bonn 2
Tel: 0228 343097, 343099
Consulates:
Flinschstrasse 63
P.O. Box 600880
6000 Frankfurt am Main 60
Tel: 069 40871.
Landsberger Strasse 191
D-8000 Munchen 21
Tel: 089 570 4406
Handwerstr 5-7
D-7000 Stuttgart 80 (Vaihingen)
Tel: 0711 7864614.
Uhlandstr 171/172
1000 Berlin 15
Tel: 030 8814049, 8814040.

Greece
Consulate
8 Herodotou Str
GR -106 75 Athens
Tel: 01 7214116

Hong Kong
Liaison office:
HQ Brigade of Gurkhas
The Prince of Wales Building

HMS Tamar
British Forces Post Office 1
Tel: 852 8633255.

India
Embassy:
Barakhamba Road
New Delhi 110001
Tel: 3329969, 3327361, 3328191.
Consulate:
19 Woodlands, Sterndale Road
Alipore, Calcutta 700027
Tel: 452024, 459027, 454293.

Italy
Consulate:
Piazzale Medaglie d'Oro 20
00136 Rome
Tel: 348176, 342055.

Japan
Embassy:
14-9 Todoroki 7-chome
Setagaya-Ku, Tokyo 158
Tel: 03 705 558, 705 559.

Korea
Consulate:
541 Namdaemoonnro
Jung-Gu, Seoul 100
Tel: 778 3183, 22 9992.

Lebanon
Consulate:
c/o President of Lebanese Red Cross
Rue Spears, Beirut
Tel: 386690.

Mexico
Consulate:
No. 24 Jardines de Sam Mateo
Naucalpan, Estado de Mexico.

Netherlands
Prinsengracht 687 (Gelderland Building)
1017 JV Amsterdam
Tel: 020 241580.

Norway
Consulate:
Haakon Viis Gt 5
P.O. Box 1384 VIKA
0116 Oslo
Tel: 02 414743.

Pakistan
Embassy:
House No 506, Street No 84
Attaturk Avenue, Ramna G-6/4 , Islamabad
Tel: 823642, 823754.
Consulate:
419 4th Floor, Qamar House
M.A. Jinnah Road, Karachi 2
Tel: 200979, 201113.

Philippines
Consulate:
1136-1138 United Nations Avenue
Paco, 2803 Manila
Tel: 589393, 588855.

Saudi Arabia
Embassy:
Khazan St near Prince Musaed Palace
P.O. Box 94384
Riyadh 11693
Tel: 4024758, 4036433, 4039482.

Spain
Consulate:
Mallorca 194 Pral 2A
08036 Barcelona
Tel: 343 3231323.

Sri Lanka
5th Floor, Vision House
52 Galle Road, Colombo 4
Tel: 583536, 502139.

Sweden
Consulate:
Eriksbergsgatanis
S-114 30 Stockholm.

Switzerland
Consulate:
Asylstrasse 81
8030 Zurich
Tel: 01 475993.

Thailand
Embassy:
189 Sukhamvit 71 Road
Bangkok 10110
Tel: 391 7240, 390 2280.

Turkey
Consulate:
Y.K.B. Ishani Valikonagi Cad. 4/4
Nisantas, Istanbul

U.S.S.R
Embassy:
2nd Neopalimovshy Perulok 14/7
Moscow
Tel: 2447356, 2419311.

U.K.
Embassy:
12A Kensington Palace Gardens
London W8 4QU
Tel: 071 229 1594, 071 229 6231.

United Nations
Permanent Mission:
820 Second Avenue, Suite 202
New York, New York 10017, U.S.A.
1 rue Frederic Amiel
1203 Geneva, Switzerland

U.S.A.
Embassy:
2131 Leroy Place N.W.
Washington D.C. 20008
Tel: 202 667 4550, 202 667 4551,
202 667 4552
Consulates:
1550 Lake Shore Drive
Chicago, Illinois 60610
Heidelberg College
Tiffin, Ohio 44883
Tel: 419 448 2202.
909 Montgomery Street, Suite 400
San Francisco, California 94133
Tel: 415 434 1111
16250 Dallas Parkway, Suite 110
Dallas, Texas 75248
Tel: 214 931 1212.
212 15th Street N.E.
Atlanta Georgia 30309
Tel: 404 892 8152.

INTERNATIONAL ORGANISATIONS

Several international organisations have
offices in Nepal and these include:

French Cultural Center, Bag Bazaar	224326
British Council, Kantipath	221305
Goethe Institute, Sundhara	220528
Indian Cultural Center & Library RNAC Building	211497
International Monetary Fund	411977
United Nations Agencies, Pulchok	523200

U.S.A.I.D. Mission, Kalimati	270144
	272271
U.S. Information Service,	223893
New Road	221250
U.S.S.R. Cultural Center,	
Ramshahpath	216248
World Bank, Kantipath	226792

AIRLINES

Alitalia, Durbar Marg	220215
Air Canada, Durbar Marg	223871
Aeroflot, Soviet Airlines,	
Kantipath	212397
Air France, Durbar Marg	223339
Air India, Kantipath	212335
Air Lanka, Kantipath	212831
Bangladesh Biman, Durbar Marg	222544
British Airways, Durbar Marg	222266
Burma Airways Corporation,	
Durbar Marg	224839
Cathay Pacific, Kantipath	226765
Dragon Air, Durbar Marg	227064
Druk Air, Durbar Marg	225166
Indian Airlines, Durbar Marg	411997
Japan Airlines, Durbar Marg	412138
KLM Royal Dutch Airlines,	
Durbar Marg	224896
Korean Air, Kantipath	212080
Lufthansa, Durbar Marg	223052
Northwest Airlines, Kantipath	226139
Pakistan International,	
Durbar Marg	223102
Pan American World Airways,	225292
Durbar Marg	228824
Qantas Airlines, Kantipath	213772
Royal Nepal Airlines, Kantipath	220757
Saudi Airlines, Kantipath	222787
Singapore Airlines, Durbar Marg	220759
Swiss Air, Durbar Marg	222452
Thai International, Durbar Marg	225084
Trans World Airlines, Kantipath	226704

TRAVEL AGENCIES

Adventure Travel Nepal,	223328
Durbar Marg	221729
Annapurna Travel & Tours,	
Durbar Marg	223940
Everest Travel Service,	
Gangapath	221216
Gorkha Travels, Durbar Marg	224896
Himalayan Travels & Tours,	
Durbar Marg	223045
Kathmandu Travels & Tours,	

Gangapath	222985
Malla Travels, Malla Hotel	410635
Marco Polo, Kamal Pokhari	414192
Nepal Travel Agency,	
Ramshahpath	413188
Natraj Tours & Travels,	
Durbar Marg	222014
Shankar Travel & Tours,	
Lazimpat	422465
Sherpa Travel Service	222489
Tiger Tops, Durbar Marg	226173
Trans Himalayan Tours,	
Durbar Marg	224854
Universal Travel & Tours,	
Kantipath	214192
World Travels, Durbar Marg	226939
Yeti Travels, Durbar Marg	221234

ART/PHOTO CREDITS

GLOSSARY

A

gam—A family, patron or secret deity enshrined in a special building. No one can enter who is not an initiate.

akha—A traditional place where religious dancing is taught.

Ananda—The Buddha's chief disciple.

Ananta—A huge snake whose coils created Vishnu's bed.

Annapurna—The goddess of abundance; one aspect of Devi.

arak—A spirit fermented from potatoes or grain.

Asadh—The third month of the Nepalese year (June-July).

Ashta Matrika—The eight mother goddesses said to attend on Shiva or Skanda.

Ashta Nag—Eight serpent deities who guard the cardinal directions and (if worshipped) keep evil spirits away.

Ashwin—The sixth month of the Nepalese year (September-October).

asla—A freshwater mountain trout.

Avalokiteshwara—A *bodhisattva* regarded as the god of mercy in Mahayana Buddhist tradition, and as the compassionate Machhendranath in Nepal.

avatar—An incarnation of a deity on earth.

B

bahal—A two-storey Buddhist monastery enclosing a courtyard.

bahil—A Buddhist monastery, smaller and simpler than a bahal.

Baisakh—The first month of the Nepalese year (April-May).

Bajracharya—A Newar caste of Buddhist priests.

Bajra Jogini—A Tantric goddess.

Balarama—The brother of Krishna.

Balkumari—A consort of Bhairav.

Bhadra—The fifth month of the Nepalese year (August-September).

Bhadrakali—A Tantric goddess and consort of Bhairav.

Bhagavad-Gita—The most important Hindu religious scripture, in which the god Krishna spells out the importance of duty. It is contained in the *Mahabharata*.

Bhairav—The god Shiva in his most terrifying form.

bharad—A reverential title.

Bhimsen—A deity worshipped for his strength and courage.

bhot—High, arid valleys in the Tibetan border region.

bodhi (also *bo*)—The pipal tree under which Gautama Buddha achieved enlightenment, and any tree so worshipped.

bodhisattva—In Mahayana tradition, a person who has attained the enlightened level of Buddhahood, but chose to remain on earth to teach until others are enlightened.

Bon—The pre-Buddhist religion of Tibet, incorporating animism and sorcery.

Bonpo—A follower of the Bon faith.

Brahma—In Hindu mythology, the god of creation.

Brahman—The highest of Hindu castes, originally that of priests.

Brahminism—Ancient Indian religion, predecessor of modern Hinduism and Buddhism.

C

Chaitra—The 12th and last month of the Nepalese year (March-April).

chaitya—A small stupa, sometimes containing a Buddhist relic, but usually holding *mantras* or holy scriptures.

chakra—A round weapon, one of the four objects held by Vishnu.

chapa—A small house annexed to a temple, in which feasts are held and rituals performed.

chapati—A type of bread made from wheat flour.

chhang—A potent mountain beer of fermented grain, usually barley but sometimes maize, rye or millet.

Chhetri—The Hindu warrior caste, second in status only to brahmans.

chura—Beaten rice.

chitrakar—A Newar caste of artists.

chiya—Nepalese tea, brewed together with milk, sugar and spices.

chorten—A small Buddhist shrine in mountain regions.

chowk—A courtyard or quadrangle

crore—A unit of counting equal to 10 million.

dabur—An urban roadside square, used for religous dancing during festivals and as a market place at other times.

Dalai Lama—The reincarnate high priest of Tibetan Buddhism and political leader of Tibetans around the world.

damai—A caste of tailors who form makeshift bands to play religious music for weddings and other occasions.

damiyen—A traditional stringed instrument, similar to a ukulele.

Dattatraya— A syncretistic deity variously worshipped as an incarnation of Vishnu, a teacher of Shiva, or a cousin of the Buddha.

Devi (or Maha Devi)—"The great goddess." Shiva's *shakti* in her many forms.

dhal—A lentil "soup".

dhami—A soothsayer and sorcerer; also, the priest of a temple, especially a priest claiming occult powers.

Dharma—Buddhist doctrine. Literally, "the path".

dharmasala—A public rest house for travelers and pilgrims.

dharni—A weight measure equal to three *sers,* or about three kilograms.

dhoti—A loose loincloth.

dhyana—Meditation.

dighur—A system whereby a group of people pools money to annually support one of its members in a chosen financial venture.

digi—A place of congregation and prayer.

doko—A basket, often carried on the head by means of a strap.

dorje—A ritual scepter or thunderbolt, symbol of the Absolute to Tantric Buddhists. (Also *vajra*)

dun—Valleys of the Inner Terai.

dungidara—A stone water spout.

Durga—Shiva's *shakti* in one of her most awesome forms.

dwarapala—a door guardian.

dwarmul—The main gate of a building.

dyochhen—A house enshrining protective Tantric deities. Used for common worship.

dzopkyo—A hybrid bull, the cross between a yak and a cow.

dzum—a hybrid cow, the cross between a yak and a cow.

dzu-tch—According to Sherpas, a type of yeti that is about eight feet tall and eats cattle.

ek—The number one, a symbol of unity.

Falgun—The 11th month of the Nepalese year (February-March).

gaine—A wandering minstrel.

gajur—An often-ornate, bell-shaped finial crowning a temple.

Ganesh—The elephant-headed son of Shiva and Parvati. He is worshipped as the god of good luck and the remover of obstacles.

Ganga—A Hindu goddess.

Garuda—A mythical eagle, half-human. The vehicle of Vishnu.

Gautama Buddha—The historical Buddha, born in Lumbini in the 6th Century B.C.

Gelugpa—a Tibetan sect.

ghada—A type of club, one of the weapons of Vishnu and a Tantric symbol.

ghanta—A symbolic Tantric bell, the female counterpart of the *vajra.*

ghat—A riverside platform for bathing and cremation.

ghee—Clarified butter.

gompa—Tibetan Buddhist monastery.

gopala—A cowherd.

gopis—Cowherd girls; specifically those who cavorted with Krishna in a famous Hindu legend.

Gorakhnath—Historically, an 11th-Century yogi who founded a Shaivite cult; now popularly regarded as an incarnation of Shiva.

granthakut—A tall, pointed brick and-plaster shrine supported by a one story stone base.

guthi—A communal Newar brotherhood serving the purpose of mutual support for members and their extended families.

guthibar—The members of a guthi: also, a group of families with the same ancestry.

Hanuman—A deified monkey, Hero of the *Ramayana epic,* he is believed to bring success to armies.

hapa—A bamboo rice-measuring device made only in Pyangaon.

Harisiddhi—A fierce Tantric goddess.

harmika—The eyes on a stupa, placed to face the four cardinal directions.

hiti—A water conduit; a bath or tank with water spouts.

hookah—A water pipe through which tobacco or is smoked.

impeyan—Nepal's national bird, a species of pheasant, known in Nepal as *danphe*.

Indra—God of rain; the chief deity of Brahminism.

jadun—A large vessel for drinking water at public places.

Jagannath—Krishna, worshipped as "Lord of the World."

Jamuna—A Hindu goddess who rides a tortoise.

janti—The groom's party at a wedding.

jarun—A raised stone water tank with carved spouts.

jatra—Festival.

Jaya Varahi—Vishnu's *shakti* in his incarnation as a boar.

jelebi—A sweet Nepali snack.

Jesth—The second month of the Nepalese year (May-June).

jhaad—Traditional rice beer.

jhankri—A shaman or sorcerer.

Jhankrism—Traditional animism, incorporating occult practices.

jhya—Carved window.

jogini—A mystical goddess.

juga—leech.

jyapu—Newar farmer caste.

K

kalashi—A pot.

Kali—Shiva's *shakti* in her most terrifying form.

kapok—The silk cotton tree.

karma—The cause-and-effect chain of actions, good and bad, from one life to the next.

Kartik—The seventh month of the Nepalese year (October-November).

khata—A ceremonial scarf presented to high Tibetan Buddhist figures.

khat—An enclosed wooden portable shrine carried during processions.

khola—River or stream valley.

khukri—A traditional knife, long and curved, best known as the weapon of Gurkha soldiers.

Krishna—The eighth incarnation of Vishnu, heavily worshipped for his activities on earth.

kshepu—A snake-eating figure often depicted on temple *toranas*.

kumari—A young virgin regarded as a living goddess in Kathmandu Valley towns.

kunda—A recessed water tank fed by underground springs.

L

la—Mountain pass.

laddu—A sweet Nepali snack.

lakh—A unit of counting equal to 100,000.

lakhe—Masked dancing.

Lakshmi—The goddess of wealth and consort of Vishnu.

lama—A Tibetan Buddhist priest.

lingum (pl.*lingas*)—A symbolic male phallus, generally associated with Shiva.

Lokeshwar—"Lord of the World", a form of Avalokiteshwara to Buddhists and of Shiva to Hindus.

M

Machhendranath—The guardian god of the Kathmandu Valley, guarantor of rain and plenty. The deity is also a popular interpretation of Avalokiteshwara or Lokeshwar and is enshrined as the Rato (Red) Machhendra in Patan and the Seto (White) Machhendra in Kathmandu.

Magha—The 10th month of the Nepalese year (January-February).

Mahabharata—An important Hindu epic.

Mahabharat—The range of hills between the Himalaya and the Terai.

maharishi—Literally, "great teacher".

Mahayana—The form of Buddhism prevalent in East Asia, Tibet and Nepal.

Maitreya—The future Buddha.

makara—A mythical crocodile, often depicted on *toranas*.

mali—A Newar caste of gardeners.

mana—A measure for rice and cereals, milk and sugar, containing a little less than half a liter.

mandala—A sacred diagram envisioned by Tibetan Buddhists as an aid to meditation.

mandap—A roofless Tantric shrine made of brick or wood.

mani—A Tibetan Buddhist prayer inscribed in rock in high mountain areas.

Manjushri—The legendary Buddhist patriarch of the Kathmandu Valley, now often regarded as the god of learning.

mantra—Sacred syllables chanted during meditation by Buddhists.

Marga—The eighth month of the Nepalese year (November-December).

masheer—A large freshwater fish highly prized in Nepal.

math—A Hindu priest's house.

migyu—Tibetan name for the yeti.

mih-tch—According to Sherpas, a hostile, man-sized, ape-like yeti.

momos—Tibetan stuffed pastas, somewhat like ravioli.

mudra—A symbolic hand posture or gesture often employed during religious prayer and meditation.

munja—The sacred thread worn by Brahman and Chhetri males from the time of puberty.

muri—A dry measure equal to about 75 liters.

It contains precisely 20 *paathis* or 160 *manas*.

muthi—A measure equal to "a handful".

N

naga—A legendary or deified serpent.

nak—Female yak.

namaste—A very common word of greeting, often translated as: "I salute all divine qualities in you."

Nandi—A bull, Shiva's vehicle and a symbol of fecundity.

nanglo—A cane tray.

nani—A type of *bahal* containing a large courtyard surrounded by residences, also including a Buddhist shrine.

Narayan—Vishnu represented as the creator of life. A lotus from Narayan's navel issued Brahma.

Narsingh—Vishnu's incarnation as a lion.

nath—Literally, "Place".

nirvana—Extinction of self, the goal of Buddhist meditation.

Nriteshwar—The god of dance.

P

paathi—A dry measure equal to eight *manas*, about 3¾ liters.

padma—The lotus flower.

pahar—The heavily eroded central zone of hills and valleys between the Himalayas and the Mahabharat Lekh.

panchayat—A now defunct government system consisting of elected councils at local, regional and national levels.

Parvati—Shiva's consort, displaying both serene and fearful aspects.

pashmina—A shawl or blanket made of fine goat's wool.

Pashupati—Shiva in his aspect as "Lord of the Beasts". Symbolized by the *lingum*, he is believed to bring fecundity.

pasni—A rice-feeding ceremony conducted for seven-month-old babies, and repeated for old people of 77 years, seven months.

patasi—A sari-like dress, especially popular in Bhaktapur.

path—A small raised platform which provides shelter for travelers on important routes and intersections.

pathi—A liquid measurement, slightly less than one gallon.

patuka—A waistcloth in which to carry small objects and even babies.

pau—A measure for vegetables and fruit, equal to 250 grams.

paubha—Traditional Newari painting, usually religious in motif.

pith—An open shrine dedicated to a Tantric goddess.

pokhari—A large tank.

Poush—The ninth month of the Nepalese year (December-January).

preta—A spirit of the dead.

puja—Ritual offerings to the gods.

pukhu—A pond.

punya—Merit earned through actions and religous devotion.

puri—Town.

R

rakshi—A homemade grain liquor.

Rama—The seventh incarnation of Vishnu. A prince, hero of the *Ramayana* epic.

Ramayana—The most widely known Hindu legend, in which Rama, with the aid of Hanuman and Garuda, rescues his wife, Sita, from the demon king Rawana.

Rawana—the anti-hero of the *Ramayana*.

rikhi doro—A golden thread which Shiva devotees tie around their wrists to ward off evil and disease.

Rimpoche—The reincarnated abbot of a Tibetan Buddhist monastery (*gompa*).

Rudrayani—A Kathmandu Valley nature goddess. Also known as Shekali Mai.

S

sadhu—A Hindu mendicant.

sajha—A cooperative.

sal—A timber tree (*Shorea robusta*) of the lower slopes of Himalayan foothills.

sankha—The conch shell, one of the four symbols held by Vishnu. It is widely used in Hindu temples and shrines during prayer.

sanyasin—A religious ascetic who has renounced his ties to society.

saranghi—A small, four-stringed viola shaped from a single piece of wood and played with a horsehair bow.

Saraswati—Brahma's consort, worshipped in Nepal as the Hindu goddess of learning.

satal—A pilgrim's house.

ser—A unit of weight equal to four *paus,* or about one kilogram.

serow—A wild Himalayan antelope.

shaki (often cap.)—Shiva's consort, literally, power the dynamic element in the male-female relationship, and the female aspect of the Tantric Absolute.

Shaligram—A black ammonite fossil regarded as sacred by Vishnu devotees.

shandula—A mythical bird, a griffin.

shikhara—A brick or stone temple of geometrical shape with a tall central spire.

Shitala Mai—A former ogress who became a protector of children, worshipped at Swayambhunath.

Shiva—The most awesome of Hindu gods. He destroys all things, good as well as evil, allowing new creation to take shape.

shrestha—A Newar caste.

sirdar—A votive mixture made of red dust combined with mustard oil.

sirdar—A guide, usually a Sherpa, who leads trekking groups.

Sita—Rama's wife, heroine of the *Ramayana* epic. She is worshipped in Janakpur, her legendary birthplace.

Skanda—The Hindu god of war.

Srawan—The fourth month of the Nepalese year (July-August).

stupa—A bell-shaped relic chamber.

sudra—Lowest of the Hindu castes, commonly thought to have descended from Brahma's feet.

sundhara—A fountain with a golden spout.

Surjya—The sun god, often identified with Vishnu.

suttee—Former practice of immolating widows on their husbands' funeral pyres.

T-U

tabla—A traditional hand drum.

tahr—A wild Himalayan antelope.

Taleju Bhawani—The Nepalese goddess, originally a South Indian deity; an aspect of Devi.

Tara—Historically a Nepalese princess, now deified by Buddhists and Hindus.

Terai—The Nepalese lowland region.

Thakuri—high Hindu caste.

thangka—A religious scroll painting.

thelma—According to Sherpas, a small, reddish, ape-like yeti.

thukpa—A thick Tibetan soup.

tika—A colorful vermilion powder applied by Hindus to the forehead, between the eyes, as a symbol of the presence of the divine.

tola—A metal measure equal to11.5 grams.

tol—A street.

topi—The formal, traditional Nepali cap.

torana—A decorative carved crest suspended over the door of a sanctum, with the figure of the enshrined deity at its center.

trisul—The trident, chief symbol of the god Shiva.

tsampa—Roasted grain, sometimes eaten dry, usually ground and mixed with milk, tea or water. A traditional mountain food.

tulku—In Tibetan Buddhism, a religious figure regarded as a reincarnation of a great *lama* of the past.

tulsi—A sacred basil plant.

tunal—The carved strut of a temple.

tympanum—A decorative crest beneath the triangular peak of a roof.

Uma—Shiva's consort in one of her many aspects.

Upanishads—Early Brahministic religious texts; speculations on Vedic thought.

V

vaisya—The "middle-class" caste of merchants.

vajra (also *dorje*)—In Tantric Buddhism, a ritual thunderbolt or curved scepter symbolizing the Absolute. It also represents power and male energy.

varahi—A goddess incarnated as a boar.

Veda—The earliest Brahministic religious verses, dating from the second millennium B.C. They define a polytheistic faith.

vedica—A sacrificial altar.

vihara—A Buddhist monastery, encompassing *a bahal* and *a bahil.*

Vikrantha (also Vamana)—Vishnu in his fifth incarnation, as a dwarf.

Vishnu—One of the Hindu trinity, a god who preserves life and the world itself. In Nepal, he is most commonly represented as Narayan.

Y-Z

yab-yum—Tantric erotica, a symbol of unity and oneness.

yeh-tch—The Sherpa name for the yeti; literally, "man of the rocky places".

yeti—A mythical anthropoid of Nepal's highest elevations, often referred to in the West as "The Abominable Snowman".

yoni—A hole in a stone, said to symbolise the female sexual aspect. Usually seen together with a *lingum.*

zamindari—A system of absentee landlordism, officially abolished in 1955 but still perpetuated in some regions.

INDEX

T

U-V

W-Z